CATHOLICISM IN ENGLAND

Books by David Mathew

Surveys

CATHOLICISM IN ENGLAND

THE NAVAL HERITAGE

BRITISH SEAMEN

ETHIOPIA

Specialized Studies

THE REFORMATION AND THE CONTEMPLATIVE LIFE *(with Gervase Mathew)*

THE CELTIC PEOPLES AND RENAISSANCE EUROPE

THE JACOBEAN AGE

THE SOCIAL STRUCTURE IN CAROLINE ENGLAND

THE AGE OF CHARLES I

Biography

ACTON: THE FORMATIVE YEARS

CATHOLICISM IN ENGLAND

THE PORTRAIT OF A MINORITY:
ITS CULTURE AND TRADITION

by

DAVID MATHEW

Third Edition

London 1955
EYRE & SPOTTISWOODE

To
ALFRED NEWMAN GILBEY

First edition 1936
Second, revised edition 1948
Third edition 1955

This book is printed in Great Britain for
Eyre & Spottiswoode (Publishers) Ltd.,
15 Bedford Street, London, W.C.2, by
The Chapel River Press, Andover, Hants.

CONTENTS

v

FOREWORD TO THE THIRD EDITION

WITHOUT CREATING an effect of patch-work it is not possible to alter extensively a book written nineteen years ago. It has long seemed to me that my treatment of the Cisalpines was unfair and I have made some modifications in the section dealing with the Cisalpine spirit. There is also no doubt that the varied nature of the opposition aroused by Bishop Milner is not adequately conveyed and a companion portrait of Bishop Douglass would assist an understanding of the Edmundian contribution. It is an almost impossible task to focus the eighteenth and nineteenth centuries correctly in a survey of this kind. After 1845 the date relating to the secondary figures becomes suddenly immeasurably rich, but our knowledge is increased out of proportion to the role of the Catholic community in relation to the general life of the country.

No attempt is made to assess the work of those who are still living and in consequence Cardinal Griffin's tenure of the see of Westminster falls outside the scope of the present volume. There is a chapter on Cardinal Hinsley's character and influence and a short postscript. The main present trends of Catholic life in England can be said to be the re-distribution of urban population due to the growth of satellite towns and new estates; the marked increase in numbers in the Midlands as the result of migration chiefly from Ireland and from the north; the fact of penetration into each category and group of the middle class. This feature goes side by side with a continual weakening of religious life in specifically working class districts. The Poles settled in England since the war form a valuable element in the general body. In the villages and country districts the tide of ancestral Catholic life is still receding, while new centres are opening in the smaller towns. The Catholic community in England is united, free from controversies and divisions, and in need of a spiritual awakening. We await the Moving of the Waters.

DAVID MATHEW

LONDON, *January*, 1955.

FOREWORD TO THE FIRST EDITION

THIS BOOK is intended as a sketch of the contribution of Catholics to English life, a brief impression of the influence of individuals and Catholic groups upon the history of England. It begins with the separation from Rome under Henry VIII when a consideration of Catholicism must diverge from that of the general history of the country.

The survey illustrates the continuity of an English Catholic tradition, fathered by St. Thomas More, sponsored by Stapleton, accepted with modifications by Augustine Baker, crystallized in the sober prose of Bishop Challoner. This inheritance was closely bound up with the personal tradition of integrity and of loyalty to the past of England. It had descended from More through Campion and Sir Thomas Tresham and the solid Cavalier Catholics of the country party to Challoner and Milner, the determined unenthusiastic Lingard, Waterton the naturalist and Ullathorne who stood for all that old Catholicism and ensured its survival. Yet around this central core individual Catholics took part in every national movement, the diversity of Southwell, Habington, Crashaw, Dryden, Pope. The taste of each century was reflected in the houses, Rushton, Basing, Stonyhurst, the heavy Italianate Palladian of Thorndon and Wardour, Alton that Pugin fantasy, and Carlton Towers and Exton. In the seventeenth century the embroidered literary artifice of Henry Constable and his companions gave way to Sir Kenelm Digby's search through cordials for elixirs, so serious, so unremunerative. The curious evanescent Catholicism of the Court of Charles II, of Lady Castlemaine and Mrs. Pepys, was succeeded by that of the great eighteenth-century squires, aloof by preference, dilettante by necessity, acquiring the Ince and the Towneley marbles. But field sports were also open to their enforced private life and hunting owes to them the origin of the Quorn; while from the Catholicism of the real country stocks came John and Richard Nyren and through them the Hambledon Club in early cricket. Beneath the changing phases and at the core of the tradition was a toughness, unresilient and in great part north country. Even in the nineteenth century the spirit of Ushaw remained dominant in spite of the changes between 1820 and 1850. The successive waves of Irish immigration; the new industrial Catholicism; the quick, sensitive, Oxford converts; the slight French and German elements, all these were formed in time into a new amalgam. The Irish and English streams were to be complementary, while such converts as Manning followed in the Milner tradition of sympathy for Ireland and for Irish magnanimity and self-sacrifice. The rise of Labour quickened some elements to more active life. At the same time the figure who is perhaps most representative of both old and new is Bishop Ullathorne, rooted in the soil, ancestrally Catholic, popular in thought and expression, whole-hearted and determined.

Since the general English tradition was integrally Catholic at the time of Henry VIII's breach with the Papacy it is inevitable that the following half century should have been a period of flux. A special religious type, built up by the Elizabethan recusants, emerges clearly in the reign of James I and from this time there comes a consciousness of a Catholic society no longer conceived as coextensive with the nation but embedded in it. For this reason the first period is dealt with rather summarily and the study develops into greater detail with the close of the sixteenth century.

It is inevitable that a survey of this character should be confined within strict limits and the very different Catholic traditions of Scotland and Wales fall outside its scope. Similarly the history of the Church of England and of the Free Churches is pre-supposed. Thus Newman is only considered in his influence after 1845 and Pusey's work lies altogether beyond the limits of a volume which deals solely with that section of the nation which remained in communion with the Holy See. In another field the technical aspects of the modern Education Acts have not been dealt with, partly because a treatment of them might so soon be out of date. The education question since the middle of the nineteenth century demands a separate and exhaustive discussion.

And here I can make my acknowledgments. It is a pleasure to express my gratitude for the detailed information that I have received from the Bishop of Lamus, the late Bishop of Menevia in regard to Cardinal Vaughan, from Monsignor King, Canon D. J. Quigley, Dr. Flynn, Fr. Philip Hughes and Fr. Gordon Albion. I wish to give my thanks for the hospitality or assistance which I have enjoyed in working out this reconstruction to Lady Agnes Eyston, Lady Galway and Lady Radcliffe, to Lord Arundell of Wardour, Francis Blundell, Alick Dru, Outram Evenett, Maurice Gorham, Shane Leslie, Wilfrid Meynell and Michael Trappes-Lomax, and perhaps most of all to Douglas Woodruff. For advice in regard to the general passages dealing with the Society of Jesus I am indebted to Fr. Martin D'Arcy and for information on its nineteenth-century history to Fr. Joseph Keating and for Stonyhurst detail to Fr. Philip Watts. I have been aided in the understanding of the English Benedictine tradition by Dom Ignatius Rice and Dom Paul Nevill.

I am also deeply grateful to my cousin Theobald Mathew for the constant benefit of his temperate and discerning comment, to Arnold Lunn for his refeshing outlook on our institutions, to Mother Mary Paul, to the community of the Bar Convent at York and to the Principal of the training-college at Mount Pleasant. My brother Gervase has considered and worked out each chapter with me and shares responsibility for any success which may have been attained in combining crowded detail with some consistent presentation of the stream of movement of Catholicism as it has affected English life.

DAVID MATHEW

CARDIFF, *January*, 1934—WOBURN SQUARE, *December*, 1935.

CATHOLICISM IN ENGLAND

THE HENRICAN SCHISM

PRE-REFORMATION ENGLAND had inherited an unitary medieval tradition instinct with Catholicism ; a tradition which was giving way under the Tudor government before the conceptions of a centralized nation state. Difficult as it is to assess the evidence, the English ruling class in these years before the changes seem to have sat lightly to their ancient faith. A sense of security appears to have carried with it a profound lack of interest and a recognition of the permanence of dogmatic fact. The truths of religion had so long been pre-supposed that they rose before the mind as inevitable and enclosing as the sky.

The piety of the royal house was suitable when regard was had to the sacrosanct character of the coronation ; but as one went back in memory there came no greater freshness. Behind the mystical quality of Henry VI's religious faith there stretched the robust and mechanical piety of the early Lancastrians. For elderly men, too, a measure of devotional interest and practice was not unseemly as they sat in their sober fur-trimmed gowns with their faces peering rheumily beneath the caps with the tight ear-flaps. There is much evidence that the younger men about the Court attended Mass ; there is less as to their frequentation of the sacraments. Again the hierarchic character of the social and ecclesiastical life produced a double effect, envy of the positions of influence held by the higher clergy and a certain atmosphere of disrespectful tolerance towards the chaplains who formed an unimpressive feature in a great lord's retinue.

The great monasteries, lying so quiet and calm and unexciting, ruled their extensive lands with masterful charity. They were good neighbours and hospitable, but a rich landowner would at moments be pre-occupied with this barrier to the extension of his property. They were landed corporations, heirless, hardly subject to those ordinary miseries of extravagance and decay which would bring the fields of laymen into the market. A subconscious strain of irritation is seldom absent when one class of proprietors is faced by another as an immutable possessor. The whole organization of the Church, the

5

properties, the benefactions, the hospitals and leper houses, the glebe lands and the tithes were managed with solicitude. Alms passed to the poor and supplies were voted to the king, but the lords and the rich squires had no reason to look with satisfaction on the ecclesiastical machinery grinding away in security and not to their advantage. They were so long accustomed to it and it is rare to find men convinced of the wisdom of benefactions which they have no means of controlling.

Certain monasteries and notably the Carthusian houses had a deserved reputation for austerity and devotion : most perhaps possessed that cheerful well-ordered character which is associated with a filtered and urbane variant of a religious rule : many were probably functioning at a rather low spiritual pressure. Here the question of scandal arises. Difficult as it is to determine the exact state of affairs it is necessary to note that the government of Henry VIII passed abruptly from a condition of polite non-interference to exacerbated opposition. Evidence of monastic immoralities was eagerly received and it is generally agreed that many of the royal servants were unequalled in their brave, copious and groundless assertions of corruption. In the prevalence of a contented rather worldly good order arguments may be found against the probability of many cases of individual sanctity. But it is still more unlikely that open and notorious sin came to disturb the tranquillity of communities where personal reputation and respectability were evidently highly valued. The issue is further obscured by the fact that a certain loose jocosity had played around the subject of religious virtue for generations. Such lapses as become public appear in general to have been quickly repaired. It was not until the Reformation that an ex-priest could fit into the English social scheme.

The state of the monasteries during their last years was, perhaps, less encouraging than is suggested by the Gasquet-tinted sunset. In the country parishes, however, there was in many cases a deep constant attachment between the parishioners and their priest. For the rich man inevitability might suggest boredom, but for the small squire, the farmer and the labourer the inevitable in religion led to God. The Christian ages and the sacramental life were behind them constantly supporting. Calmly and with faith they regarded God's blessing on the seasons : the poverty of their life kept them within their own countryside ; their violence and their immoralities led them to the confessional. Another effect was produced by the unchanging routine of their existence. Religion was permanent, but god-like and remote rose the royal authority.

In the towns discontent turned easily against religion as a result of the economic security of those who were anchored in the religious houses whether as laybrothers or as priests. But in the towns were to be found the cultivated layman and the quick-thinking ardent priest. London, in the strict sense of the city, gave to English Catholicism St. Thomas More and Dean Colet of St. Paul's. And St. John Fisher came from the town life of Beverley.

In all sections of the country the very close, the inextricable association of State and Church was a fact taken for granted. As the prestige of England increased so did the value of political offices and the bishops in the council and the clerical ambassadors naturally forwarded the national policy. It was very difficult to conceive of a divorce between the episcopate and the State. Cardinal Wolsey during the years of his ascendancy had concentrated odium upon his person, but the lords both spiritual and temporal were united in this dislike. There was no great lay peer of unquestioned ascendancy; no prince of the blood royal. Authority and the long accretion of English national prestige centred in the person of the king.

Henry VIII was forty-two years of age at the time of the first troubles with the Papacy. He had been king since the death of Henry VII in 1509 and had an experience of kingship, a sonorous sense of personal dignity and that profound interest in theology which well befitted the isolation of his lofty state. The taste for broad familiarity and horseplay and a consciousness of his weakness in regard to the control of sensual passions seem to have made him the more determined not to impair his royal dignity. As king he was, perhaps, obstinate because so vulnerable and as man he appears to have suffered from those recurrent but lessening scruples which arose in the wake of his very individual line of conduct. No king was more conscious of the chrism or of the sacred inheritance of Christian kingship. Yet he followed courses of action, both in regard to his successive marriages and to his relations with the Holy See, which had no precedent. It is impossible to dogmatize upon this subject, but possibly his self-assertion cloaked his scruples and the intermittent miseries of a complex and doubtful conscience. He certainly cared so very much for Catholic things, the Sacrament of the altar and the holy seasons. Theology appears as his opiate and it was his misfortune that his policy left him surrounded by those who were most careless of such interests. After the breach with Rome his isolation was more complete than formerly, as the King with the interests and dialectic of a late medieval theologian grappled in his secret policies with the cold and untheological mind of Thomas Cromwell.

After these preliminaries it is possible to dismiss the over-written story of the royal divorce with brevity. The question of the validity of the King's marriage was first raised publicly in 1527. He had at that date been married for eighteen years to the Princess Catherine of Aragon, who was the widow of his elder brother Arthur, Prince of Wales. Queen Catherine always asserted that this first child-marriage had in fact never been consummated. In 1504, at the time of the betrothal of Prince Henry to his sister-in-law, a dispensation couched in very wide terms has been obtained from the reigning Pope Julius II and the marriage had taken place in 1509. There had been one surviving child of this union, a daughter, the Lady Mary, born in 1516, and there were no hopes of further issue.

Under these circumstances Henry VIII applied to the Holy See and two cardinal legates were appointed to try the matter. The Legatine Court was set up at the London Blackfriars in 1529 and the Queen appealed away from it to Rome, while her nephew the Emperor Charles V made serious efforts to oppose the suit. In June, 1531, the King, whose friends complained of the alleged partiality of foreign tribunals, separated permanently from the Queen. An attempt was made to obtain favourable opinions from the universities of Europe on the question of the lawfulness of a marriage with a deceased brother's wife and a letter signed by the episcopate and the peers was sent to the Pope asking him to settle the matter in the King's favour.

The death of Archbishop Warham of Canterbury in August, 1532, enabled action to be taken which would resolve the situation. Dr. Cranmer was made archbishop with the Pope's consent, but the appointment was intended to facilitate a breach with Rome. Events now developed rapidly. In January, 1533, the King went through a form of marriage privately with Anne Boleyn whom he had recently created Lady Marquis of Pembroke ; in April this marriage was solemnized publicly ; in May Archbishop Cranmer, sitting in a specially constituted court at Dunstable, declared the first union with

Catherine of Aragon invalid, since it had been carried out in defiance of God's law. Two months later Pope Clement VII declared the second attempted marrige void and laid the King under a sentence of the greater excommunication which took effect in the autumn. In September Queen Anne gave birth to the Lady Elizabeth and an Act of Succession was framed entailing the Crown upon the issue of the Boleyn marriage from which a male heir was hoped. Finally on 23 March, 1534, Pope Clement VII declared that the marriage of Henry VIII and Queen Catherine was valid and the dispensations obtained from the preceding pontiffs sufficient. In England the Act of Succession was passed the same day.

In June, 1534, the Act of Supremacy, the logical conclusion of these events, was placed upon the statute book. " Be it enacted by the authority of the present Parliament," the Act begins, " that the King our Sovereign Lord, his heirs and successors, Kings of this realm, shall be taken, accepted and reputed the only Supreme Head in earth of the Church of England called *Ecclesia Anglicana.*"

It will be at once perceived that this enactment raised far more problems than it solved. At that period foreign policy was liable to react upon the statute law ; a military alliance, a royal betrothal and a declaratory statute were alike the means by which relations with the external world might well be emphasized. The fact that the Act of Supremacy was in the nature of an official declaration of hostilities against the Holy See lends an artificial character to its theological colouring. From the wording of the Act it would appear that the Crown was to be endowed with sacrosanct power. " Our Sovereign Lord, his heirs and successors, Kings of this realm shall have full power and authority," the Act continues, " from time to time to visit, repress, redress, reform, order, correct, restrain, and amend all such errors, heresies, abuses, offences, contempts and enormities whatsoever." This would seem to establish a Tudor theocracy. But how would it come to the English world, to the uninterested, the indifferent, the comatose and the ignorant ? Who should think out a theory of law for them or interpret the mysteries of the King's intention ? They had never been prepared to act against sovereignty. Besides, the actual responsibility for dealing with the Act of Supremacy and for accepting or refusing it was confined to the ruling class. In this matter the action of the bishops was crucial. It is hardly possible to form a very satisfactory estimate of the situation, but the following statement perhaps represents the most accurate approximation to which we can now reach.

The majority of the bishops came from official life and not from the parochial clergy. As a body they had grown to revere statecraft, that hallmark of the new monarchy ; most had been accustomed to place a serious value on the maxims of expediency. Serenely conscious of their prudence, they had something of the discretion of the *fonctionnaire*, valuing the conduct of affairs and aware of the King's variable moods. It was against their long diplomatic training to renounce these qualities and to go alone to political isolation and, perhaps, to martyrdom. At each point of their career they had made combinations which had proved successful and had brought them to their high place. It must have appeared probable that with care and time ecclesiastical affairs would once more return to that calm to which all their lives they had been accustomed. It was manifest folly to provoke the opposition unnecessarily.

The bishops were in many cases jurists of experience and their theology was explicit ; but this motive was insufficient to move them. Shrouded in a respectable decorum, living softly through their middle years on the wise husbandry of emolument, conventional in their cultivated outlook, they could no longer voluntarily accept political disgrace. There were of course certain cases to which such conditions did not apply and in these instances the leaven of the Conciliarist principles of the previous century may have been working. Some diocesans seem to have followed the lead of the archbishops and especially of the new-comer Cranmer. But the real influence was the incessant pressure of the government. The prelates were overawed by the sovereign power and by that majesty of the King who had raised and made them.

And in the wake of the bishops came the great abbots. Among the heads of the rich abbeys, the more astute and the less spiritual considered the matter in the light of their close knowledge of affairs and came to the same decision by the aid of mundane prudence. It was inevitable that the mass of the temporal peers and lay officials should not refuse that submission which had been made by their fathers in God.

Against this drift there stood the Bishop of Rochester and Sir Thomas More. Their refusal to accept the oath of supremacy, their imprisonment and death on Tower Hill in the summer of 1535 are as familiar as any scene in English history. The testimony of their martyrdom placed them at the head of the modern Catholic tradition and their resistance had an unique value for their contemporaries and successors. St. Thomas More, particularly, by his line of defence, his prose style and his personal legend encouraged the families of the ancient faith in their perseverance. The possession of certain relics, the inheritance of a strain of blood and the present strength of his memory aided his co-religionists who were so strongly bound together by common suffering and exclusion. In the periods when their contact with the active national life was most fettered St. Thomas More remained their solitary hero to receive recognition from the average Englishman.

St. John Fisher, however, belonged very definitely to an earlier time. He was remote from politics, profoundly spiritual, interested in a somewhat formal erudition, and seriously concerned with those problems of scriptural interpretation which had long formed the subjects of meditation for the Christian Fathers. He had an archaic style with a humour which could penetrate the naive rhetoric of his time. "Where is now," he wrote, "the immemorable company and puissance of Xerxes and Cesar, where is now the grete victoryes of Alexander and Pompey, where is now the grete rychesse of Cresus and Crassus." This was the high Middle Ages with its universe of knowledge and the sage reflections and the miniatures of history. It was the spirit of the medieval universities to which townsman and countryman would come for knowledge. And the bishop had, too, a deep understanding of the countryside, that Kentish diocese of Rochester which he had ruled for thirty years. He had written of winter and of "the trees whan they be wydred and theyr leues shaken from them and all the moystour shronke into the rote." As a Yorkshireman he could speak the language of the Pilgrims of Grace. But above all he had a care for the poor of Christ. If he was isolated in his own circle, the Pilgrimage of Grace and the Western Rising were to show that he spoke for the inarticulate.

The case of St. Thomas More was rather different. His tone of mind was much less medieval ; he was a layman and therefore more imitable. Quite apart from his immediate family he left a circle of admirers which was to remain at the core of the intellectual Catholic life for half a century. The great folio of his *English Works*, edited by his nephew William Rastell in 1557, is the literary monument of Queen Mary's reign. On all counts it is essential to attempt a detailed impression of his personality on which some of the elements of English Catholicism were modelled.

Until he reached the last few months before his death St. Thomas More was, perhaps, chiefly known as a highly cultivated lawyer of marked talent in his profession who had risen rather rapidly through the stages of an uniformly successful career. By birth a Londoner and a son of a judge of the King's Bench, he had contacts with civic life and politics both aiding him in his advance. He had been Under-Sheriff of London and on the political side Chancellor of the Duchy of Lancaster; Speaker of the House of Commons; a privy councillor. At forty he had become Master of Requests and for two and a half years Lord Chancellor of England. Academic honours came to him: he was High Steward of Cambridge University. In his middle age his income was very considerable, but his capital limited: he was not of a saving disposition and tended to be carefree about money. His married life was reasonably smooth. Lady More was a widow, six years his senior and of a somewhat tart and economical disposition. St. Thomas's natural affections seem to have been concentrated upon his children.

An intercourse with the Court had developed normally and for a period he enjoyed the favour of the King's friendship. This and other political benefits he was able to assess at a sound valuation. His outlook on the courtiers was detached; his relations with the judges and the members of the Bar cordial and he had a good reputation in the City. Himself a gentleman of coat armour he accepted with simplicity the privileges which this fact conveyed. A native integrity had made him certain enemies and he had a clear sense of the doubtful security of his position. On the other hand he had friends in the learned circles throughout Europe and a prestige such as erudition would not carry in a later age. His humour was at its quickest in his own language and in spite of his European interests he was essentially English in the background of his ideas. He had not travelled beyond northern France and the Low Countries and his tastes in food were insular; small ale, coarse well-leavened bread and salt meats. A great curiosity of the mind was rightly attributed to him and an intense interest in men, their actions and motives; a compendious encyclopædic outlook. His recreations included the study of philosophy, the arts and music. Besides being fond of dogs, he was attracted by all strange animals and had formed an aviary in his house at Chelsea.

Until his last years he passed as a definitely but not obtrusively religious man, rather critical of the condition of the clergy and quick in statement. He was of moderate height and build, with dark brown hair and grey eyes lit by controlled humour.

In this connection it is worth noting that an open cheerfulness of the table, so characteristic an ingredient of English life, appealed strongly to him. " For in theyre onely raylynge," he wrote[1] once in reference to the Lutheran controversialists, " standeth all theyr reuell, wyth onely raylynge is all theyre roste mete basted, and all ther pot seasoned, and all theyr pye mete spiced." He had a deep appreciation of originality, a practical charity and he relieved those nearest at hand. In his own family life there was the same balance and a certain astringent quality is often overlooked in this relation which in the nineteenth century has suffered from being sentimentalized. St. Thomas was affectionate in an age of rather glacial relationships ; he was considerate and equable ; he was never yielding. Delightful with his small daughters " bringing back cakes or fruit or pieces of silk to deck them,"[2] he had the quickest perceptions in regard to character and a profound determination. There was about him nothing soft and both the south wind and the east wind were in his humour, for this had sometimes a cutting edge.

He had a profound detachment from his possessions, enjoying them but not adhering to them ; a realization of transience. The insecurity of his position arising from lack of capital compelled him either to be submerged under material circumstance or to rise above it. The same common sense spiritualized is seen in his attitude towards the clergy. He had a lasting respect for the office of the priesthood and kept his own counsel about the man. At the same time he had a cheerful outlook on the idiosyncracies of individuals and a horror of real scandal. Behind his amusement at the disputatious monk " who had rolled himself up in his spikes like a hedgehog "[3] there lay a belief that every man must work. His sympathies with the parochial clergy were strong and his relations with his parish priest admirable. One quotation from among his views on this subject is most expressive. " So dare I boldly say," he begins,[4] " that the spirituality of England, and especially that

---

[1] *The Apologie of Syr Thomas More*, ed. 1921, Early English Texts Society, p. 50.

[2] Thomas Stapleton, *Tres Thomæ*, pt. III, cap. 6, ed. P. E. Hallett, p. 135.

[3] *Epistola ad Dorpium* ; cf. Rev. T. E. Bridgett, *Life and Writings of Blessed Thomas More*, ed. 1913, p. 91.

[4] *Dialogue against Tyndale*, English Works, II, p. 215.

part in which ye find most fault, that is to wit that part which we commonly call the secular clergy, is in learning and honest living well able to match and (saving the comparisons be odious I would say further) far able to overmatch number for number the spirituality of any nation Christian."

He was without prejudice and preserved his independence and detachment in face of the King, an act of sustained courage whose quality the rise of modern dictatorships enables us to appreciate. As a lawyer he had a deep respect for the Canon Law and a desire for its observance. No man was more remote from the type of the ecclesiastical layman and side by side with this quality went a detestation of prudery and a generous mind. On one occasion he praised St. Francis in his writings for his unwillingness to see imaginary evil. " He had, quod I,"[1] wrote St. Thomas, " a good mind and did like a good man that deemed all things to the best."

His prayer and asceticism were constant. " This one thynge recomforted me,"[2] he declared in his last years, " that syth I was of one poynte very faste and sure that such thynges as I wryte are consonaunt unto the comen catholyque fayth and determynacyons of Christes catholyque chyrche." In all questions his force of character and acute strong intelligence acted on the materials submitted to his judgment. He shaped his course according to his permanent beliefs, he maintained his convictions calmly and frankly ; he worshipped God wholeheartedly and with liberty of spirit and for this freedom to follow Catholic truth he gave his life.

The development of his influence was gradual and it was not his contemporaries but the Marian and Elizabethan Catholics who followed St. Thomas More. The effect of his stand and that of the Bishop of Rochester is, however, seen in the refusal of the leaders of the London charterhouse to take the oath of supremacy. In the same summer of 1535 six Carthusians, the prior of the London charterhouse and three of his community and the priors of Axholme and Beauvale were put to death for this refusal.[3] Official England settled into that uneasy period of doctrinal change which was to last for twenty years.

It was in the countryside that discontent with the religious

[1] *Dialogue against Tyndale*, English Works, II, p. 208.
[2] *The Apologie of Syr Thomas More*, p. 2.
[3] B. John Reynolds and B. John Haile were also executed for refusing to accept the Act of Supremacy in the same year and eleven members of the community of the London Charterhouse were executed or starved in prison in 1537 for this offence. Among others who refused were some of the Franciscan Observants.

changes broke out into rebellion. The first stirs in Lincolnshire in 1536, the Pilgrimage of Grace in the same year and the Western Rising in 1549 were in a line of succession which was to end with the rebellion of the northern earls under Elizabeth. They were feudal in tendency and the people looked for the leadership of the gentry and desired it with a grudging loyalty ; quick to suspect the gentlemen ; never trusting them completely ; yet helplessly dependent upon them for effective action. Behind these movements lay the old medieval conception of the King's evil counsellors and the duty of the loyal subjects to free the Crown from such influence. In the north the insurgents hoped in vain for the leadership of the sick Earl of Northumberland. But in general the shadow of the enclosures and the memory of their economic grievances hindered the co-operation between the northern labourers and farmers and any gentleman of means. They had, too, a simple desire for the restoration of religion. No question of an official career or royal favour confused the issue for them and they could see in simplicity that the unity of Christendom was broken. They had their ballads[1] and their symbol, the banner of the Five Wounds of Christ ; they conceived of their work as blessed and themselves the Pilgrims of Grace. These facts, rather than the military detail, are significant.

The actual details of the insurrections are briefly these. The suppression of the lesser monasteries, all religious houses with an income of less than £200, had been decided on shortly after the breach with Rome and now provided the occasion for revolt. In October 1536 there were popular risings at Louth and Horncastle in Lincolnshire. These were supported with enthusiasm by the priests and with lukewarmness by the gentry, and it was at Horncastle that the banner of the Five Wounds, which was later generally adopted, first appeared. The abbots of Barlings and Kirkstead, both subsequently executed, were among the leaders of the people. The chief royal official in Lincolnshire was Lord Hussey of Sleaford, who was seventy years of age, hesitant and pious. Possibly he was unwilling to act against the insurgent priests with whom his wife had open sympathy. He made excuses, temporized and was later

---

[1] The following verses sung during the rising are said to have been composed by the monks of St. Mary's, York.

" Chryst crucifydd,
For thy woundes wyde
Us Commons guyde,
Which pilgrimes be ; "
        Letters and Papers of Henry VIII, 1536, no. 787.

beheaded as an accomplice of the revolt. The insurgents occupied Lincoln and for a period the whole county was in their hands. Their demands, vaguely formulated, included on the religious side the restoration of the monastic houses.

Into Lincolnshire, apparently on his way back to Westminster after the vacation, came Robert Aske, a youngish barrister, a Yorkshireman of good blood, serious minded and rather devout. He was travelling south from Ellerkar where he had joined Sir Ralph Ellerkar for the cub-hunting. The insurgent Catholics welcomed him at Lincoln and he returned to Yorkshire and put himself at the head of a popular rising. The first great gathering was at Weighton Common where the men came marching in by parishes with crosses from the churches carried before them. On October 15 the insurgents entered York and five days later captured Pomfret Castle after a nominal resistance had been put up by Lord Darcy. At Pomfret the Archbishop of York was taken prisoner. Darcy was an old man, a soldier of distinction and an open opponent of the King's policy in the matter of the divorce. Later he joined the Pilgrimage of Grace and the very large measure of support which this movement now obtained makes his action easier to understand. For Hull soon fell into the hands of the Pilgrims and both Durham and Northumberland had risen in their favour. Sir Thomas Percy carried the banner of St. Cuthbert at the head of five thousand men and the total number of Pilgrims in arms seems to have amounted to about thirty thousand. Under these circumstances the northern lords and the rich squires had been swept into the movement, probably not regarding the matter as a rebellion but rather as a protest against the minister Cromwell whom they all hated. The very size of the force and the number and responsibility of its leaders helped to bring it to a standstill. With the insurgents were Lords Scrope, Conyers, Lumley and Latimer and the heads of a heavy proportion of the northern houses. They had far too much to lose. A royal army had reached Doncaster and the Pilgrims encamped beyond the Don. Negotiations were opened and it was to the interest of the rich men on both sides that they should not fail, while Aske's moderation and constitutional temper of mind assisted this result. No action was fought and the Pilgrims were eventually disbanded and later a haphazard stir organized by Sir Francis Bigod, after the preliminary peace, enabled the King to withdraw in effect his promises of pardon. Aske, Lord Darcy and

Sir Thomas Percy were among those executed and there was a harrying of the north.

One of the claims put forward by the Pilgrims of Grace for consideration by the King in the early negotiations before Doncaster very well reflects the northern standpoint on religion. " To have," they demanded, " the supreme head, touching *cura animarum*, to be reserved unto the See of Rome, as before it was accustomed to be, and to have the consecration of the bishops from him, without any first-fruits or pensions to him to be paid out of this realm ; or else a pension reasonable for the outward defence of our faith." The strong Catholicism of the future generations of north-country yeomen lies implicit in this claim.

Just as the Pilgrimage of Grace had been occasioned by the suppression of the monasteries, so also the Western Rising of 1549 arose from the determination of the government to supersede the Latin Mass by the English Prayer Book. The disturbance began when the parishioners of Sampford Courtenay in Devon persuaded their priest to continue to say Mass publicly in defiance of the law " the common people all the country round clapping their hands for joy." Here again there was the same popular suspicion of the rich as is shown in the rising of the men of St. Mary's Clyst on the day of the burning of the barns at Crediton. An old woman had been molested for saying her rosary in public. " Ye must leave beads now," she had[1] told the villagers of St. Mary's, " no more holy bread for ye, nor holy water. It is all gone from us or to go, or the gentlemen will burn your houses over your heads." This seems the significant fact, the people's sense of loss. In comparison with such a factor the detail of each ineffectual rising has little value. In this instance Humphrey Arundell of Lanherne was the leader of a predominantly Cornish force ; the insurgents marched against Exeter, were held up besieging that city and finally defeated at Clyst by a royal army stiffened with foreign mercenaries recently hired for the Scottish wars. In their weeks of victory the insurgents had put forward their demands. Among the fifteen articles two are noteworthy on account of the impression which they convey. " We will have," they had declared, " the sacrament hung over the high altar, and thus to be worshipped as it was wont to be, and they which will not thereunto consent, we will have them die like heretics

---

[1] According to the accounts printed in Holinshed's *Chronicle*. There had also been discontent, amounting in Oxfordshire to rioting, in connection with the introduction of the Prayer Book.

against the holy Catholic faith." And again, " we will have holy bread and holy water every Sunday, palms and ashes at the time accustomed, images to be set up again in every church, and all other ancient ceremonies held heretofore by our Mother Holy Church." The use of the term Holy Mother Church, fifteen years after the separation, has something of the quality of that bitter lament which found poetic expression in *The Wreck of Walsingham*.

THE "CATHOLIC" COUNCILLORS

A source of confusion throughout this period of tangled policies is the frequent reference made to a Catholic party particularly during the last years of Henry VIII. The term is misleading and the phrase Protestant when used of the majority of the lay ministers in the reign of Edward VI (from 1547 till 1553) is probably equally inaccurate if it is intended to convey any religious connotation. The House of Howard, which is often regarded as the mainstay of tradition, was determinedly opposed to that Catholicism of the people which found expression in the Pilgrimage of Grace and the Western Rising.

A fairly detailed description of the third Duke of Norfolk, who held that peerage from 1524 till 1554, will serve to give an impression of the part played by the great Tudor lords in the evolution of modern English Catholicism. The Duke's career can serve as an example of that wide grouping of the high peers who profited under and suffered from the early Tudors. They applied themselves to the fount of power like leeches ; nothing save death could sunder them from the Court.

The Duke of Norfolk's standpoint is the more appropriate as an example, since his attitude on questions of doctrine was, perhaps, as favourable to the old religion as his rank and interests would allow. The summer of 1536, which preceded the Pilgrimage of Grace, found him at his new house at Kenninghall in Norfolk. He was at this time sixty-three years of age ; a short, black man ; spare, with skin the colour of dark parchment, thin lips, a long, high-bridged nose ; eyes not piercing, but very cold. His health was delicate : in middle life he had become rheumatic : his digestion was much impaired. He had survived to great wealth and high office and his experience as an administrator was considerable. He had a knowledge of the East Anglian trading conditions, a satisfaction in hunting suitable to his position and apparently no more interest in letters than a nobleman would require, although he spoke French with some elegance. The great post of Earl Marshal of England had descended to him through the Mowbrays with their strain of royal blood. Ceremonial appealed to him and the splendour of everyday costume, the Burgundian guards of black velvet on a gown of tawny velvet-silk, which the age indulged. He was separated from his wife and deeply attached to Elizabeth Holland, his steward's daughter.

By this time the King had embarked on his third marriage with Jane Seymour, and Anne Boleyn, who was Norfolk's niece, had fallen. As a pilot in political storms the Duke showed marked dexterity and he professed outward attachment during this year to the King's minister Thomas Cromwell. He also made a point of showing himself affable to such of his inferiors as were of no social consequence ; he was pliant with a quick practical mind and a keen scent for danger. The acquisition of property, especially landed property, was pursued with a relentless satisfaction. Perhaps this detail may seem meticulous,[1] but it is intended to assist an appreciation of the part played in the Duke's life by religion.

Three letters written by the Duke to Cromwell during 1536 throw light upon his state of mind. In the first he is seen bending before the storm. " A bruit doth run," he wrote[2] after the execution of his niece Queen Anne, " that I should be in the Tower of London. When I shall deserve to be there Tottenham shall turn French . . . written at Kenynghale lodge at 10 at night with the hand of him that is full, full, full of choler and agony." But within a month he was recovered. The news from the Court was good and there were pickings to be had from the suppression of the monasteries. " For the time of sowing is at hand," he declared[3] cheerfully, " and every other nobleman has already his portion. I trust well for (the priories of) Bungay and Woodbridge." Soon he was back in the full tide of royal favour. " If," he wrote[4] on another occasion to the minister, " I may have the stewardship of all these (monastic) lands so much the better ; if not at least this side Trent. *Sapienti Amico pauca*. When others Speak I must speak too." He inscribed this : " Mr. Secretary, in haste." With renewed assurance he went north in command of the royal army to suppress the Pilgrimage of Grace.

He was a traditionalist and an authoritarian ; but the well-known statement that " it was merry in England before the new learning[5]

---

[1] References to the Duke's health, tastes, methods and interests are scattered through the correspondence collected in the *Letters and Papers, Henry VIII*.

[2] *Letters and Papers, Henry VIII*, XI, n. 233.   [3] ibid., n. 434.   [4] ibid., X, n. 599.

[5] *Letters and Papers*, XVI, n. 101. John Lassells, an informer in the service of Cromwell, reported these words on the authority of one Maxey.

came up " is the second-hand gossip of a spy. Two statements of the Duke's are, however, authentic. On his imprisonment in 1546 he asked for a book of " Sabellicus ; who doth declare most of any book that I have read, how the Bishop of Rome from time to time hath usurped his power against all princes, by their unwise sufferance." Again he put forward his views in 1538. " I think God intends," he wrote[1] to Cromwell, " to look broadwinking . . . on those who follow their old *mumpsimus* and superstitions, and will shortly punish the bp. of Rome and his ungracious cardinals and all who support their damnable proceedings." The Duke was imprisoned throughout the reign of Edward VI and dying in Queen Mary's days ended a Catholic. He was a natural conservative. The character of his private life prevented him from approaching the sacraments for many years. Given the data it seems simplest to suppose that in regard to religious ideas he had a certain measure of indifference.

Such a poised indifference would seem to have been common among the first generation of wealthy Tudor peers, Sussex, Rutland, Arundel, Huntingdon, Southampton and Winchester. They did not take to the New Learning ; they disliked the sectaries and they had no special view about the Catholic tenets. From 1534 till 1549 the Mass was retained in the Henrican system and was the background of their regular and perfunctory worship. This goes far to explain the attitude of the great lords in Queen Mary's reign ; their tired welcome of the restored Catholicism, their civility and indifference and lack of interest. The ruling class in England had performed a task of much complexity. They had swallowed the whole of the monastic landed areas. Now in the mid-century they rested, as untheological and unspeculative as boa-constrictors.

This essential indifference is also found mirrored in those leaders of the aristocratic tradition who inclined to the side of change. Possibly this has some bearing on the aid furnished by Catholics to the Duke of Northumberland. The latter's career provides a variant of the Howard outlook carried some stages further than the Duke of Norfolk was prepared to go.

Sir John Dudley belonged through his mother and stepfather to the close court circles and passed through a negligent and generous manhood to reputation in the wars. A Catholic in name he had

[1] ibid., XIII, i, n. 784.

married, while quite young, Jane Guldeford, an heiress from the
lands on the edge of Romney Marsh, sprung from those Kentish
squires who formed the class next below that in which he moved.
She was a woman of dominant character, strongly Catholic by upbringing and returning in later years to that religion.   Dudley was
nominated an executor of King Henry's will; passed through the
grades of the peerage as Lisle, Warwick and finally Northumberland; destroyed Protector Somerset in 1549 and for four years was
virtually ruler of England.   For some time he had inclined slightly
to the Reformers' side and, once in power, actively supported their
new measures.   Land appealed to him and theirs was the party of
liquidation.   He looked coldly on episcopacy and the possessions
of the Bishop of Durham's Palatinate came gradually within his
reach.   An incentive to support the organizers of destruction was
present whenever the division of the spoils was entrusted to persons
of quality.   Northumberland had always Catholic allies like his
nephew the indignant choleric Stourton and, at one time, the
Arundells.   When the proclamation of Lady Jane Grey had ended
disastrously the Duke professed on the scaffold his regrets for ever
having abandoned the old religion.   In his period of ruthless control
he had shown a magnetic force, a sense of the land, that painful
desire for possession, little notion of procedure and some military
skill.   The procession of the ministers went forward, Cromwell,
Norfolk, Southampton, Somerset and Northumberland.   However
they might disagree, their century had taught them that the first
necessity was an ordered State, docile as a cow contented at its
milking.

Among the great peers there was, however, one section which was
unaffected by the court movements, those who inherited the blood
of the House of York.   The Courtenays and Poles lived with the
magnificence characteristic of an earlier age.   They had retinues of
gentlemen of unimpeachable birth and rudimentary education and
many servants brought up from their outlying properties.   A slowness of mood, an interest in old-fashioned English sports and a close
contact with the ways of the countryside animated the life of their
large cumbrous households.   Here religion was reflected in each
detail and only at the Court itself were the devotional observances
so embedded in the routine of existence.   The Courtenays were of
the period of the monastic foundations and were bound up with an
earlier England inevitably Catholic.

An account of their line of action and their fate indicates the influences of ancient ways of thought. The Household Books[1] of the Countess of Devon throw light on the life at the dower house of Columb John, which she maintained for her son Lord Exeter. Against a background of the comings and goings of the woodmen, the glaziers from Exeter with coloured glass for the new chamber and the wagon-loads of Lenten fish, there was a recurrence of monastic presents and religious expenses. Partridges and cherries, a cock-pheasant for St. Thomas', swans from the Abbot of Ford, venison from the monastery at Buckland drifted to the kitchens marking friendship and the seasons. The charges, which offset them, indicate a sustained devotional activity. The steward would be sent in to Exeter to buy May strawberries and to satisfy the superior of the Blackfriars. There were offerings on feasts, a requiem in June, accustomed Masses on All Souls' Day and a heavy stipend paid to the prior of the Dominicans in London " for a year's singing for Lord William." Friars preached before the Countess at her expense in the elaborately furnished chapels which were attached to the Courtenay houses. Furnished rooms were retained by the family in the nearest Blackfriars for their use in Lent and Advent. Certainly the influence of religion pervaded their lives.

At the time of the Pilgrimage of Grace Lord Exeter was about forty and his cousin, Henry Pole, Lord Montague a few years older. They had received the religious changes with an unwelcoming passivity. Accustomed to dispense favours rather than to seek them, they felt, like those who were beneath the orbit of Court and government, a distaste for the polite cajolery through which monastic land must be obtained. Nevertheless they attended Parliament and even sat on the Commission sent to try St. Thomas More and the Carthusians ; Exeter accepted religious property. A difficulty had arisen through the retirement to Italy of Montague's brother the Dean of Exeter. Reginald Pole was later to play a decisive part in Catholic England ; but during this reign he remained abroad supporting the measures against the excommunicate sovereign and writing against the royal supremacy. Recently he had been created a cardinal. His relatives disavowed him and the government professed to accept their protest.

In the autumn of 1538 Henry Courtenay, Marquis of Exeter was

[1] *Letters and Papers*, IV, i, n. 771.

living at Horsley in comparative retirement, for he had been compelled to resign the constableship of Windsor Castle. He had had little public employment, had bent with the times and was out of humour and resentful. His wife was a very ardent Catholic interested in mystical phenomena, attractive and delicate. Their heir Lord Courtenay was still a child. They preferred Surrey, where there was excellent hawking, to their London house the " Red Rose," which they had not renamed in the modern fashion. The Marquis was not in general interested in books, but was accustomed to study a fine volume with the arms of the Knights of the Garter very beautifully tricked out. Jugglers appealed to him and he liked to watch displays of wrestling and to hear his servants " sing properly in three-man songs." His wife's attendants played skilfully upon the virginals. He maintained serious good relations with his chaplains and among his equals his chief intimate seems to have been Lord Delawarr.

The Countess of Salisbury, the only surviving child of the Duke of Clarence, was now sixty-five, had been a widow for thirty years and was the mother of the Poles. She lived at Warblington in Hampshire with a considerable establishment amid an atmosphere of hearty devotion. Three chaplains were in residence. Her freedom of speech was characteristic of her strong-minded independence. She was prepared to swear by her damnation when it was necessary to enforce a serious point. Her eldest son Lord Montague lived at Buckmere in the Thames valley, something of a soldier, choleric and extravagant. Since the death of his wife, Jane Neville, a vehement Catholic, he had become more careful in his expressions of political opinion. Men avoided him as he was known to be out of favour at Court.

At the end of August 1538 Sir Geoffrey Pole, a younger brother of Lord Montague, was arrested on a charge of holding illicit communication with the Cardinal. Under pressure he gave evidence which put his brother and cousins within reach of the law and a combing of the household at Horsley provided further data from among the one hundred and thirty Courtenay dependants. After allowance has been made in regard to their accuracy these depositions still give an impression of the character of the discontent. Lord Montague was accused of saying that " he trusted to see the abbeys up again one[1] day " and Lord Delawarr had backed up this

---

[1] *Letters and Papers*, XIII, ii, n. 827, examination of John Collins.

statement. " A time will come," he was reported[1] to have said, " that God will punish for this plucking down of abbeys and for reading of these new English books." George Crofts, Chancellor of Chichester Cathedral confessed that he had encouraged such scruples. " When the statute was made for the abolishment of the Bishop of Rome's authority this examinate,"[2] he declared, " once showed the Lord Delaware that it was a mad thing to go about by making of a law to make men believe that in England the contrary whereof was believed in all places of the world." Sir Geoffrey Pole in his fifth examination described how when riding between London and Horsley, the Lord Marquis had said that he had been compelled to leave his constableship of Windsor and take abbey lands instead. " What," Sir Geoffrey[3] had exclaimed, " be you come to this point to take abbey lands now ? " " Yea," said he, " good enough for a time. They must have all again one day."

And then Lady Exeter confessed that she had discussed the question of those rebellions from which her House had kept free. " Madam," Sir Edward Neville had said[4] to her in reference to the Pilgrimage of Grace, " be afeard not of this, nor of the second but beware of the third." She professed to have feared the development of some conspiracy of Lord Abergavenny's family. " Ah ! Mr. Neville," she had replied, " you will never leave off your Welsh prophecies, but one day this will turn to your displeasure." Other matters were alleged. Exeter and Montague were executed, Lady Exeter and Lady Salisbury imprisoned and the latter was beheaded two years later after the failure of Sir John Neville's stir. Although the great families, like the Courtenays, probably no longer retained the power of effective action, their destruction left a vacuum and marked the end of the feudal principle in leadership except in the north country. The men of the Western Rising paid a final tribute to their memory. " We will have," they demanded, " Doctor Moreman and Doctor Crispin, which hold our opinions, to be safely sent unto us and to them we require the King's Majesty to give some certain livings to preach among us our Catholic faith." This Dr. Crispin had been Lord Exeter's principal chaplain. " We think it meet," the insurgents of the west continued, " because the Lord Cardinal Pole is of the King's blood, that he should not only have

---

[1] *Letters and Papers*, XIII, ii, b. 831, w, iii, evidence of Sir Hugh Owen.
[2] ibid., n. 827, examination of Chancellor Crofts.
[3] ibid., n. 804, examination of Sir Geoffrey Pole.
[4] ibid., n. 804, examination of the Marchioness of Exeter.

B

his pardon, but also be sent for from Rome." In the south the memory of the old Catholicism sank down into the legends of the people.

After the attainders, just described, the King's Councillors became more pliant, judicious in their outlook and accommodating. They were ready to obey their sovereign and to destroy, restore or modify the Catholic forms. Queen Mary harsh and sincere and unequivocal was to find herself isolated amidst the soft cogency of their mental processes.

MARIAN CATHOLICISM

THE TWENTY YEARS which separated the breach with Rome from the reconciliation under Queen Mary had witnessed the gradual and almost imperceptible formation of a determined element of active Catholics in political life. These men were at the core of the very large and amorphous Catholic body which was unprepared for sacrifices in matters of personal religious opinion and was in consequence in process of gradual disintegration.

With all the mass of available material it nevertheless seems probable that it will never be possible to obtain any very accurate picture of the processes by which the national tradition was disentangled from the Catholic religious inheritance to which it had been apparently inseparably bound. The quality of reticence, the care for privacy and the frequently casual acceptance of the ancient faith all contributed their influence to render the separation as quiet and unnoticeable as it was effectual.

At the same time the effect of positive Protestantism was by now important. Under one aspect the new religion appeared as opposed to established privilege and thus fostered that sense of freedom which was to be so dominant a *motif* with the English middle class. The idea of advance and of increasing opportunity made a powerful appeal and in the towns there was undoubtedly a feeling for change and for those wide nationalist horizons which had become linked with Protestantism in the minds of the new men. The evangelical leaven, from which Puritanism was to develop, was already working ; while the two decades of rather listless and comatose schismatic Catholicism had led the evangelical enthusiasm into the channels of the new teaching. At Court the preachers had gained a section of serious adherents in that social stratum which lay between the wealth of the Russells, Earls of Bedford and the comparative insignificance of the poorer friends of Cheke and Bacon. Such men had moved from small beginnings to a great world and there found changed politics, a novel social outlook and a new religion.

Besides, in these circles and throughout the wealthier section of the squirearchy and the peers there came to develop that species of almost purely political Protestantism which was to form one basis for the Elizabethan glory. The idea of the great State had percolated and this appealed to the young men impatient of their fathers, eager for politics and desiring a freedom from restraint. The great State in the line of its English development was inevitably Erastian, and the Elizabethan settlement was calculated to appeal to the men of the new age. They were freed from considering religion and could devote themselves to those engrossing projects of a profitable and adventurous patriotism which led them upon their golden voyages.

In addition, the Catholicism of the regime of Queen Mary had to carry a load of indifference very much more serious than that vague and fatigued, but inevitable acceptance of religion which was to be found in some Catholic countries. A stabilizing factor in such cases had always been the sense of the inevitable and the realization that it was no more possible to escape medieval Catholicism than the forces of nature, than death or the sky. An effect of the twenty years' separation from Rome was that men, apart from the faithful believers, had left the world of inescapable certainties and entered that of preferences. Yet this very fact enables us for the first time to see the English Catholic as a type among the different varieties of Englishman. From the reign of Henry VIII, with the testimony of More and Fisher and the others who had died[1] for the old religion and the determination of the Catholic masses, there had now emerged a Catholicism no longer co-extensive with the nation, independent-minded, ready to suffer, perhaps intolerant, vigorous and rooted in the life of the country. It had preserved the old medieval traditions and was to gather those of St. Thomas More and St. Ignatius. Although intellectual, its note was determination. It has always seemed to me that the type of the English Catholic in late Tudor times was the groom who threw Campion into the pond to save him from discovery and arrest.

In these developments in Catholic life Queen Mary's character exercised a profound effect. She was, in the first place, very much a

[1] An indication of the number of those who died explicitly for the Catholic Faith is furnished by a list of those Beatified by Popes Leo XIII and Pius XI or accepted as Venerable Martyrs by the Sacred Congregation of Rites. In addition to SS. John Fisher and Thomas More and the Carthusian *Beati* and B. Margaret Pole, already mentioned, one Augustinian, five Benedictines including the Abbots of Colchester, Glastonbury and Reading, B. John Forest and four other Franciscans, one Bridgettine monk, nine secular priests and five laymen are included in the lists. None of those executed in connection with the Pilgrimage of Grace were considered in this connection.

Tudor and held throughout her reign that unquestioned authority which her father and sister always exercised. A strain of generosity and a long memory for kindness went with a certain lack of imagination and an unresilient mind. She had a consciousness of her duty as a sovereign towards God which was apt to render her unapproachable. On the other hand the influence of her mother's divorce upon her seems to have been exaggerated by the historians who belonged to that period when Queen Catherine's life was seen through veils of sentiment. There is little reason to suppose that the wrongs of women at the hands of unfaithful husbands awakened compassion in the sixteenth century. While her mother lived the Princess Mary had supported her cause which was also her own, but after the death of Queen Catherine and Anne Boleyn she was reconciled with her father and, indeed, accepted the royal supremacy. Queen Mary seems to have had an admiration for King Henry VIII and a certain hardness and masculine quality of mind had led her to value highly those who could claim to have served him loyally. Her choice of ministers tended to fall upon her father's old advisers. The transitory nature of the return to Catholicism was in part the result of the fact that the execution of the Queen's policy in religion was entrusted to ministers whose loyalty was not to a religious faith but solely to the dynasty.

The occasion of the Princess Mary's change from the position of a pawn in the diplomacy of the Catholic powers to the status of a leader was her father's death in 1547. During the six years of her brother's reign her insistence on the retention of the Mass in her household, in spite of the efforts of Edward VI's ministers, made her house a focus of ardent Catholic life. There gathered around her that circle of the rich squires with court connections, a group which was to prove the strongest support for Catholicism in southern England. Bedingfield, Englefield, Gage and Waldegrave are names found first among her household, then in office during her reign, and finally as organizers of the Elizabethan recusants. For the next two centuries a leading family among the Catholic laity was that of the Lords Montague of Cowdray and the source of their fidelity seems to have lain in the attachment of Sir Anthony Browne first Viscount Montague to Queen Mary. He had been her Master of the Horse, his wife Magdalen Dacre her maid of honour. They carried down with them to a later age something of the Marian tenacity.

Actually only a comparatively small number of families had a personal connection with the Queen and the majority of these came from East Anglia and the home counties where she had passed her life. Still the Jerninghams, Dormers, Windsors and Huddlestons with their spreading connections were a sufficient nucleus to reinforce the Queen's friends among the actual court officials. They were trained to serve the Tudors and loyal to them and quite unmoved, also, in their religious allegiance. In the firm order of the manorial hierarchy they were accustomed to receive respect from the priests unmarred by servility. Their authority derived from their inherited possessions and a certain distaste for the new men encouraged the old-established squires in their fidelity to the ancestral faith.

These sometimes hesitant and private Catholic sympathies of the southern squires were replaced by a vigorous support once the north country was reached. Here the Queen's personal influence was not considerable, but the return of the government to Catholicism was warmly welcomed and the restoration of the earldom of Northumberland to Sir Thomas Percy, whose father had been attainted for joining the Pilgrimage of Grace, was very popular. The great families were entrenched and had recently taken little notice of London's politics. The position pivoted about the strength of the Dacres with Lord Dacre as warden of the West Marches and his son Sir Thomas as his deputy, his daughter Countess of Cumberland and his brother-in-law the Earl of Shrewsbury as president of the Council of the North. These lords had served the different forms of government, but a certain Catholic observance seemed inevitably associated with their train of chaplains and their former protection of religion. They took Catholicism for granted and seem to have regarded the reconciliation with Rome as an unexciting and obviously necessary measure. Perhaps the northern lords never fully awoke to the quality of the Tudor rule, the new centralized power and the weight of London.

Into this world where hesitant, merely hereditary, pusillanimous and indifferent Catholics were mingled with a leaven of determined and enthusiastic followers of the old faith the Queen introduced two new factors, a Spanish marriage and an English cardinal. Possibly the misfortunes of this marriage have been exaggerated. It proved childless and Philip II did not stay long in England ; but it involved an adherence to Spanish foreign policy, which was to end in the loss of Calais, and it could not be popular. As one minor result a certain contact took place between the actual court officials and King Philip. So long as peace was preserved between England and Spain, vaguely Spanish sympathies tended to develop among those Catholics who had belonged to Queen Mary's circle. The marriage would seem to have been undoubtedly an error in policy. The return of Cardinal Pole was a more complex question.

This was the same cardinal who had written against Henry VIII and had seen his mother and brother executed by that sovereign. He was now one of the senior members of the Sacred College, but still a deacon ; fifty-three years of age ; a scholar and administrator, more than once considered a probable choice to fill a vacancy in the Papacy ; tall, with steady eyes and a long flowing beard. The see of Canterbury was vacant through Cranmer's degradation and he was called from Rome to fill it and ordained and consecrated. He had been more than twenty years abroad and he returned filled with apostolic zeal and with a warm confidence in his welcome. This was the day of restoration for the Faith, the day which he always knew would come and which had now arrived. At St. Denis he wrote to the Lord Chancellor, Bishop Stephen Gardiner who had weathered many storms. He referred to the " authority which you have in the sight of that virtuous Lady (the Queen), so devoted and ready in the service and honour of the great Shepherd." Later in the same letter he touched again upon this subject praying for " the preservation of that good Saint the Queen, fair as the moon, whom God hath not suffered to be tainted with any spot, either of schism or of heresy, maintaining over her spirit the full splendour of the Sun of Righteousness."[1] This letter reveals the Cardinal in his sincerity and in the sweep of his devotion, filled with that confidence which is associated with the Tridentine Church, but perhaps not very perceptive in regard to the difficulties of the situation.

Bishop Gardiner had written with the caution of a man who had lived among the Henrican pitfalls. He suggested that the Cardinal should write to the Parliament " a letter[2] which should treat, in general only the question of unity in religion, with such moderation that the right of the Pope would be rather suggested than expressed in clear words." This exchange forms an interesting contrast.

Cardinal Pole combined a generosity of spirit with a deep family

[1] *The Letters of Stephen Gardiner*, ed. J. A. Muller, pp. 500–1.
[2] ibid., pp. 464–5.

affection.   He was much attached to his niece Catherine, Countess of Huntingdon and he seems never to have realized the adverse religious influences in her family and that cold Puritanism of her eldest son which was to make him one of the chief enemies of the Elizabethan Catholics.   Thus on St. Catherine's day the Cardinal wrote to Lady Huntingdon hoping that her children and in particular his godson Walter might be " continual[1] under your wing as the little chicken under the hen."   He was in England only four years and he died on the same day as the Queen.   Looking back his attitude of optimism hardly seems justified.

The Queen herself had a virility which accorded well with the old religion.   In her piercing and near-sighted eyes there was a determination which went with her common sense and that satisfaction in display which was rooted in the sense of her regal dignity.   Her own restoration of the Benedictines of Westminster and the Carthusians of Sheen was of a piece with her integrity.   But she was a sick woman through her reign, prematurely aged and weary.   The necessity for preservation and a Tudor doctrine of security led her to sanction the burning of heretics, a gross error.   In fact the maintenance and increase of the fires of Smithfield constituted her most serious disservice to the Catholic cause.   Her reign had something of the hesitations and uncertainties of a rallying-ground, and for two years before her death the momentary security for Catholicism was clouded by the imminence of the Princess Elizabeth's succession.

[1] Letter dated 25 November, 1555, Cal. Hastings MSS., II, pp. 3-4.   Eighteen months later the cardinal wrote again to his niece of "your little flock of children and especial little Walter," ibid., p. 6.

THE ELIZABETHAN SETTLEMENT

AT THE ACCESSION of Queen Elizabeth on 17 November, 1558, England was in full communion with the Holy See. It was only five years since that strong reaction of conservative opinion which had brought Queen Mary to the throne ; but the indifferent courtiers had been soon exacerbated by the presence of a predominant religious motive. The great majority among the wealthy laymen favourable to the new religion had returned during the late reign to a measure of outward Catholic practice. There must have been many among the wealthy official class who were as ready as Sir William Cecil to lay down their rosaries. Evidence exists of a widespread anti-clerical feeling, which had been strengthened by the unpopularity of the late regime. Men felt irked by the serious appreciation shown by the late Queen for the episcopate.

This episcopate was now solidly Catholic, as were the chief ministers and the Queen's household officers ; but the new sovereign had little contact with any of the old religious groupings. In the few years of her sister's reign she had been forced to live catholically, to hear Mass and to frequent the sacraments from time to time ; but for herself she seems to have possessed a profound and probably sceptical indifference on dogmatic questions. This was allied to a distaste for her sister's methods and beliefs and a consciousness of the political unwisdom of her policy in religion. The late Queen's restoration of religious property had induced a state of insecurity in the minds of the many wealthy Englishmen who had fortified their private fortunes from monastic land. The reign and the Spanish marriage had not brought success either in home affairs or in the foreign war ; Calais had been lost and the old ministers discredited. At the same time the new advisers, men like Cecil and Bacon, were radically anti-Catholic and opposed to the old system of ecclesiastical influence in politics, which the late Bishop Gardiner and Bishop Bonner and the Lord Chancellor, Archbishop Heath would represent. Besides in the eyes of the Papal Curia Elizabeth was a bastard. It is not possible to fathom the Queen's ideas. A determination to keep free from Spain is apparent and she seems to have felt that a Catholic framework for her mental life would be intolerable. Whatever the motives, she almost immediately embarked on a very definite course of action.

At Christmas the Queen forbade the elevation of the Host in her presence, at Easter she received Communion under both kinds. On 29 April, the Act of Supremacy was passed declaring the Queen supreme governor of the realm as well in all spiritual or ecclesiastical things or causes as in temporal and asserting that no foreign prince or prelate had any ecclesiastical or spiritual authority within her dominions. An Act of Uniformity of religion was enacted ; a Book of Common Prayer introduced. By 24 June, the Mass was to be abolished, the Catholic altars taken down and the new service book brought into use. The see of Canterbury was vacant, but the episcopate headed by the Archbishop of York and supported by Abbot Feckenham of Westminster was unanimous in opposition to the changes. No prelate accepted the oath of supremacy with the exception of the aged Bishop of Llandaff ; although some doubt hangs over the position of Bishop Stanley of Sodor and Man who survived apparently unmolested until 1570. The other bishops, without exception, were deprived of their sees on account of their continued allegiance to the Papacy. On the other hand the lay peers and the Commons made little protest. The old order was still further weakened by the death in 1560 of the Earl of Shrewsbury, the leader of the strict Catholic opposition. He was old ; magnificent in his way of life ; hardy ; enriched with monastic land ; but capable of giving a lead to the Catholic squires. The sons of the Derbyshire gentry crowded to his household and he gathered up the threads of the northern Midlands.

This loss was the more unfortunate because most of the Catholic peers, who made some decorous gestures of dissatisfaction in the House of Lords, belonged to the class of Crown officials grown conservative in old age, men like Winchester or Rich and Paget, who both passed into unembarrassed retirement. A number of the peers abstained through prudence, some from the north do not seem to have been present at these sessions but voted in a Catholic sense a few years later. Three who were to be leaders in the next generation, Southampton, Stourton and Vaux, were prevented from voting as minors.

Among the squires attachment to the old religion was deeply rooted, since the restoration of Catholicism had provided a rallying-point for ancient loyalties. Away from the permanent distractions of the Court there was a more definite desire for the support of the sacramental life and the continuance of an unchanging order. Yet in this matter there was variation from county to county. From the very beginning of Elizabeth's reign the actively Catholic element among the gentry seems to have been very weak in Devonshire and Wiltshire and, perhaps, also in Cornwall. On the other hand it was particularly strong in Oxfordshire, fairly strong throughout the Midlands and held centres of great importance in East Anglia. Here and in the home counties the administrative, legal and court families of the Marian period carried considerable weight. Through the north there were solid blocks of the country where attachment to the old faith was profound and unanimous. But any description of the whole situation must stress the existence of many wealthy families, especially in the south, who combined a vague and tenuous Catholic preference with a determination not to run counter to the expressed wishes of the Crown either in politics or in religion.

The religious history of the country gentry in the Midlands and East Anglia is really that of the crumbling of inherited beliefs. Those in whom the desire for the sacramental life was strong survived to form the Catholic minority, while the mere preference for tradition gave way before the pressure of the State and the attraction which a dignified Established Church must exercise on a conservative class. The calm atmosphere of Anglicanism, the fact of the possession of the churches and churchyards secured by law, and a certain fostering religious care for the national honour combined to gain a gradually increasing hold on the imagination of the gentry of the shires. A suitable clergy came in time to minister to their needs and the Anglican spirituality developed as the appropriate background to the magnificent and insular national endeavour.

In the meantime this process had been facilitated in southern England by the fact that the greater part of the country priests accepted the religious changes decreed by government. In the towns a great many clergy followed the bishops in their refusal to accept the separation from Rome and the abolition of the Mass. The higher clergy were as a rule vigorous in their defence of Catholicism and in particular the Deans of Winchester, Worcester, Exeter and St. Paul's and the brothers John Harpsfield, Dean of Norwich and Nicholas Harpsfield, Archdeacon of Canterbury. In these circles the influence of St. Thomas More was strong. At

Oxford the Warden of Merton, the Presidents of St. John's, Trinity and Corpus, the Rector of Lincoln and the Master of Balliol were deprived as Papalists. New College had a determined Catholic element and the headmaster of Winchester was ejected for his adherence to the ancient faith. At Cambridge the President of Queen's and the Masters of St. John's, Christ's and Pembroke Hall were likewise expelled. Dr. John Caius, the re-founder and Master of Gonville Hall, was a Catholic in belief although he was not molested in his college. But the most significant figure upon the Catholic side in either university was a young don William Allen, formerly fellow of Oriel and then principal of St. Mary's Hall, who was to be the founder of Douai College and eventually a cardinal.

Still a more vivid realization of the issues was to be expected in the universities than in the villages where both priests and people had felt the influence of the long Henrican schism acting passively and heavily. In the large towns and, of course, in the universities there had been attack and counter-attack and theological dispute, but in the country there had been less discussion and merely the dulling practical effects of separation.

Throughout the north and especially in Lancashire the situation was, however, totally different. Many of the squires and priests had defied the Crown from the beginning of Queen Elizabeth's reign and the case of the vicar of Blackburn and the Ribblesdale priests who refused the oath of supremacy was typical. Here the centralizing influence of government had little pull, and resistance had the support of local landowners. The feudal character of the social structure, the rugged independence and the distrust of London shown in the Pilgrimage of Grace were still in existence and the hard and stubborn self-reliance of the northern Catholics stood out in marked contrast to the milder outlook of the squires in southern England who were always eager to meet the government halfway and to placate opposition.

For nine years, from 1559 till 1568, the position remained roughly unchanged and if by the term practising Catholic only those who resolutely refused any attendance at the Anglican services are understood it is clear how weak the old religion was becoming in the Court circles and in many parts of the country. Even the leader of the Catholic-minded peers, the Earl of Arundel did not scruple in his conformity. At the same time the government concentrated rather on deprivation of rights than other penalties. The majority of the surviving members of the Marian episcopate were imprisoned or confined to the houses of Anglican prelates and there had been a certain number of prosecutions for hearing Mass. For instance during the summer of 1561 Lord Hastings and Sir Edward Walde-grave and Sir Thomas Wharton and their wives were imprisoned in the Tower for this offence. In general the government was inactive. Lord Robert Dudley, now Earl of Leicester, the Queen's favourite had temporized with the Catholics and had not yet become the champion of nascent Puritanism. Sir William Cecil was primarily a politician and Walsingham, who perhaps alone among the Queen's ministers was to show a bitter personal hatred for the old religion, had not yet come to power. A proportion of the great lords were prepared to favour, but not to suffer for Catholicism.

Even in the north, where divisions were more clear-cut, there were shades of practice. Lord Northumberland was firmly Catholic ; Westmoreland, youthful, vehement, but temporizing ; Cumberland sympathetic to the ancient ways but politically an unknown quantity. Besides, Northumberland and Westmoreland had no sons and this was an important factor in dealing with a feudal background. Everywhere Catholicism was losing ground. And then in 1568 the situation was changed when Mary Queen of Scots was driven from her kingdom and sought refuge in England.

In all that followed the influence of vague sympathy with the former religious traditions is discernible. Thus Lord Sussex, the president of the Council of the North, had carried through a re-establishment of Catholicism in official circles in Queen Mary's reign. The peers of King Henry's council soon felt alarm at the long continuance in office of the Queen's new advisers ; they had been used to brisk changes among the ministers ; the domination of Sir William Cecil seemed to stretch forward endlessly. In this matter the traditionalists and those who were purely indifferent in religion were united in discontent, and it was inevitable that the presence of the Queen of Scots on English soil should provide a storm-centre about which every conspiracy, serious, frivolous or imaginary, would be held to gather. Queen Elizabeth was still unmarried, although negotiations for her marriage were to be an element in foreign politics for many years ; her cousin Lady Catherine Grey, who had been her heir under Henry VIII's will, had died in 1568 ; her other cousin the Queen of Scots, as a granddaughter of King

Henry's elder sister, was the probable successor to the throne and a Catholic.

The first disturbance was caused by the events which led to the imprisonment of the Duke of Norfolk in 1569 after the secret proposals for his marriage with the Queen of Scots. The Duke had succeeded his grandfather in 1554 and was now a man of thirty-three, slender and a little ineffective, thrice a widower, proud and immensely rich, but inactive in character and dependent upon his household officers. He was apparently not a Catholic ; Foxe of the *Book of Martyrs* had been his tutor ; he had quarrelled over a lawsuit with the northern Catholic leaders, the Dacres. Still Arundel was his father-in-law and it was hoped that he would eventually in some way free the old religion. It was a vague plan and he was arrested. The proposals connected with the name of the Florentine banker Ridolfi were still vaguer and these nebulous ideas were dispelled with Norfolk's execution in 1572. But with these matters the general Catholic body had little concern, for they were still numbed from their drastic and increasing exclusion from public affairs.

By the tenth clause of the Act of 1559 the acceptance of the oath of supremacy was required of " all temporal judges, justiciaries, or other lay officer or minister," and by the twelfth clause " all and every person or persons who shall be promoted or preferred to any degree of learning in any university within this realm " were brought within its scope. Again by the Act of 1563 this obligation of taking the oath of supremacy was extended to " all schoolmasters and public and private teachers of children " and " to all manner of persons that have taken or hereafter shall take any degree of learning in the Common Laws." At the same time the Act of Uniformity passed at the beginning of the reign had made even the private celebration of Mass a penal offence and had imposed a penalty of twelve pence for each abstention without adequate cause from the new service on a Sunday. The effect of these laws was cumulative and ultimately dispiriting ; the Marian priests were dying out ; there could be no Catholic representation in the Commons and only a body of opposition peers in the Lords. Pressure on the universities was weeding out those inclined to the old faith as the royal commissioners, in the words[1] of Anthony à Wood, " ever and anon summoned those that smelt of Popery or were popishly affected." There had, perhaps,

[1] *Historia*, i, p. 290.

been too much optimistic hope of alleviation among the Catholics based on the possibilities of the Queen's marriage or her choice of favourable advisers. It seems to have been only very gradually that the idea that the Anglican settlement might prove permanent had begun to dawn upon them. Slowly the knowledge of the seminary which Dr. Allen had opened at Douai in 1568 for the training of priests for England spread among them and then in the following year there came the action in the north.

Throughout the northern counties a strong determination to restore the old faith had become more marked during the ten years that the people had been deprived of the public celebration of the Mass. The new religion of the south remained alien to them and it seemed increasingly probable that the northerners would once more rise in revolt under their hereditary leaders, who had been in opposition since the beginning of the reign. In 1560 Northumberland had laid down the wardenship of the Marches ; since then he had waited. He was to prove the last Englishman to awake the sense of feudal loyalty to military purpose. Hospitable, fond of field sports, far removed from all book learning, he had a great hold in his own country. This bearded cheerful man, going a little bald in his middle forties, rather hot tempered and deeply religious and sincere lived in a different world from the *astutia* of the Elizabethans.

In the early negotiations with the Queen of Scots, whose freedom they were anxious to secure, Northumberland and the young Lord Westmoreland were summoned to London. Fearing arrest they raised the standard of St. Cuthbert at Brancepeth on 14 November, 1569, and, summoning their supporters, marched on Durham. High Mass was said again in Durham Cathedral for the first time for ten years. The Earls professed loyalty to Queen Elizabeth and a desire for " the restoring of all ancyent Customs and Libertys, to God's Church and this noble Realme " and sent out a proclamation to the Queen's "trewe and faithful Subts of this old and Catholique Religion." There was very considerable support but little hope of achieving a real military success ; for ahead of them were the royal forces in Yorkshire and the garrisons of the Wardens of the Marches lay in their rear. Nevertheless they marched by Darlington and Ripon as far as Tadcaster on the road to York and then retreated northwards on the rumour of a Scots invasion. On 16 December with the royal army in pursuit the Earls disbanded their forces and took refuge across the Border in Liddesdale. A quick vengeance was taken throughout the northern counties, between six and seven hundred being executed. A few months later Leonard Dacre raised the tenantry of his nephew and ward Lord Dacre and of his dying brother-in-law the Earl of Cumberland. The new revolt was still less effective ; the Dacres were defeated near Naworth on the Gelt and fled into Scotland.

For every rebel in the field there had been many more in passive sympathy. " There be not in all this countrey," a royal official had written at this time, " X gentilmen that do favor and allowe of her Majesties proceedings in the cause of religion ; and the common people be . . . altogether blynded with th'olde papish doctrine." In May 1572 the government managed to secure Northumberland's surrender by the Scots and he was executed at York in the following August. It appears certain that he was offered his life on the condition of abjuring[1] his religion. Westmoreland, Lady Northumberland, the Dacres and others escaped into the Low Countries and played a leading part among the colony of religious exiles for many years.

[1] In 1886 Thomas, seventh Earl of Northumberland was declared *Beatus* by Pope Leo XIII.

THE RECUSANTS

IT was at this stage, in Lent 1570, that Pope Pius V issued the Bull *Regnans in Excelsis* by which Queen Elizabeth was declared excommunicate and her Catholic subjects freed from their allegiance. A great increase of bitterness on the part of the Queen followed inevitably upon this measure. A Catholic layman John Felton fixed a copy of the Bull to the gate of Fulham Palace and was arrested and executed for treason.

The massacre of St. Bartholomew which took place in August 1572 was used with the revived memories of Queen Mary's burnings to fan popular prejudice against the strict Catholics and a constant attempt was made to prove them anti-national. The fact of the communication between the leaders of the Northern Rising and the Spaniards was stressed ; sympathy with the Queen of Scots was held to be bound up with negotiations with foreign powers, whether Spain or the French Guise faction ; the exiles abroad were accused of plotting. Various circumstances combined to make this anti-Catholic propaganda increasingly successful in England. The old priests of Queen Mary's time were dying and under the Elizabethan government their successors could not be trained at home. Nevertheless, although education abroad was inevitable, play was made with the notion of the " seminary " priests, as the clergy trained in the new English colleges in Douai and Rome were called by the government. These movements were the prelude to increased persecution.

At the same time the effect of the Bull cannot be considered except in relation to the previous policy and there seems no doubt that some stand was essential. The fact that this definite action should have taken the form of an attempt to depose the Queen was merely the result of a logical following out of what had been the former curial practice. The change of feeling consequent upon the Pope's action and the return of the new priests from abroad is of assistance in an attempt to trace out the progressive alienation of the English people from the Catholic Church.

Throughout the Queen's long reign from 1559 until 1603 there was a very large element in the nation which was Catholic in sympathy and by tradition but had not the determination to follow the practice of a creed proscribed by law. It was the presence of these vague, yielding half-Catholics, the " Church Papists " as they were sometimes called, which did so much to weaken the position. They were led by a spirit of compromise and drawn away from the faith by every motive of self interest. If the action of the Holy See could exacerbate their nationalist feelings so much the better for them and each decade found them further from Rome.

During the middle section of the reign, between 1570 and 1588, the prospect of war with Spain became a certainty and nationalist sentiment was growing stronger as the organized buccaneering raids on the Spanish Indies proved successful. And this anti-Spanish trend became inevitably anti-Catholic as Philip II was shown predominantly at the Catholic champion. Again there is little doubt that the continued presence of Mary, Queen of Scots as a prisoner on English soil was also definitely prejudicial to the old religion. She could not fail to be a centre of disaffection and her French upbringing and manner and that delicacy of tone and perception which marked her subtle thought and impetuous action were used to emphasize that " foreign " quality which public opinion was being educated to look for in Catholicism. The characteristics of the Queen of Scots would hardly fit those conceptions of efficient nationalist monarchy to which Englishmen had grown accustomed under the high pompous colouring and perhaps over-emphatically masculine temper of the last Tudor. It was one of Queen Elizabeth's assets that she could always appear downright. She was well fitted to develop the Elizabethan legend which was so majestic, so easily apprehended and apparently indestructible. Beside her the Queen of Scots might seem light and King Philip hostile ; and the English have always had a talent for pouring broad ridicule on the national enemy. This new-found insular sense, which was both aggressive and successful, came as a counterpoise to the weakening remembrance of an united Christendom. Overseas in Douai and in the English College at Rome young Englishmen, many of them from Oxford, were training for the priesthood in order to return and work for Catholicism in England. It is doubtful if they realized in the calm of the Low Countries what difficulties the foreign political situation was putting in their way.

It was about this time that the term recusant came into general use to denote those Catholics who steadfastly refused to attend the Anglican worship. These persons were in any case liable to a fine of twelve pence for each act of non-attendance ; but in June 1577 Bishop Aylmer of London suggested to Walsingham that it might be well " to punishe them by rounde fynes, to be imposed for *contemptuose* refusinge the Communion, according to our order & Commandmentes." A number of priests had recently come back from Douai and the increased strictness of the Catholics was already apparent. The Bishop was convinced of the failure of the measures formerly adopted by the government. " For the . . . imprisoninge of them," he wrote,[1] " whiche hath bin used heretofore for their punishment hath not onlie little avayled, but also hath bin a meanes, by sparinge of their howsekeepinge, greatlie to enrich them ; and such as here upon seute haue ben enlarged, and upon hope of amendment sent into their Cuntries, haue drawne great multitudes of their teanantes and frindes into the like maliciose obstinacie." This advice was pondered and accepted. On 15 October letters were sent to the bishops asking them to complete within a week a schedule of the recusants within their jurisdiction together with details of the annual revenues of these offenders. The returns were not sent as rapidly as had been suggested, but in any case they only covered those whose recusancy was matter of common knowledge to the diocesans concerned and dealt almost exclusively with men and women of property. Soon afterwards recusants worth £40 yearly in land or £200 in goods were assessed for a special tax which was intended to maintain one or more " lances or light horse." In 1581 an Act of Parliament imposed on recusants a fine of £20 per lunar month, a crippling figure.

Incomplete as they are these returns[2] of 1577 still provide some impression of the situation and deal with some sixteen hundred names. Several counties, and among them Durham, Northumberland and Suffolk, seem to be unrepresented and the very rich men are in general tactfully omitted from these lists. Thus only one peer is mentioned, the Earl of Southampton, a young extravagant man who was already politically suspect. But a very fair idea is given

[1] Letter, State Papers, Domestic, Eliz., 114, n. 22, printed in Catholic Records Society, Miscellanea, XII, pp. 1–2.

[2] For a discussion of these returns, cf. C.R.S. Miscellanea, XII, pp. 4–9.

of the position of those wealthy squires who had retained an uncompromising adherence to the ancient faith throughout the first half of the reign. Here again the quota of well-known names is small, Sir John Arundell, Sir Thomas Fitzherbert and Sir Henry Bedingfield being, perhaps, the most distinguished. The list includes the Garter king-of-arms, Sir Gilbert Dethick, Mr. Thomas Egerton afterwards Lord Chancellor Ellesmere and " the wife of William Bird, one of the gent. of her maiesties chappell." In later life Byrd the composer was himself a recusant and represented the invigorated Catholicism as opposed to the quiet traditional religious feeling of his master Tallis.

From these first returns it is possible to reconstruct two pictures in some detail, the hold of the old faith in the town and university of Oxford and in the city of York. At Oxford there was in the first place Mr. George Etheridge, the deprived Regius Professor of Greek " who receiueth preystes in serving mens apparel disguysed, besides a great number of the towne and countrey that suspitiouselye resort to his house to heare a masse." Then Mr. William Napper, the farmer of Holiwell, Mr. Comber a brewer in St. Ebbs, the wife of Philips a draper in All Hallows, Mistress Williams at the sign of The Star, Vicars " a Lovanist who lieth in corners," Barnes, Doctor of Physic in St. Mary Magdalen's parish, Mr. Henslowe, a master of arts " once of newe college, and expeld out of that house for poperie, who lieth now at the sign of the Blue Boar in St. Aldates," and one Redshaw a poor day labourer. This is merely a selection, but it gives some impression of the vigour of the Catholic life and the variety.

After referring to persons backward in religion at All Souls, Balliol, Queen's and Exeter Colleges a special note is appended in regard to the halls.

" Newe Inne. Mr. Denne, a Mr. of arte, fitzsimons, Doring, Pluncket, yong Irishe gents, never come to the church. Edmond Hall. One Ruckwood, an old priest, is never sene, neither at praiers, communions, nor sermons : esteemed to be worthe one hundred poundes.

" Hart Hall. Reading the Manciple there cometh not to the church nor receiueth, neither Mr. Rudde an auntient Mr. of arte, neither Mr. Naile, nor manie moe that lie in his lodginge there, whose names are unknowne to me. The Principall, one Mr. Randoll, is verie much suspected ; he will not present anie thing upon his othe.

"Alborne Hall.   Marshall, an old M^r. of arte and a priest, never commeth to the churche, and is thought to saie masses in corners.

"Glocester Hall.   The house is greatly suspected, and yet the principall there presented nothing to me.   One S^r. William Catesbie lieth[1] there."

This list with its suggestions and omissions very well conveys the continuing rooted life of the ancient faith.

In York the old religion was strong and the authorities were able to report a considerable number of prisoners in custody either at Hull or in York Castle.   These included five priests, three school-masters, a number of esquires and gentlemen, Mr. Thomas Vavasour, doctor in physic, Francis Parkinson, yeoman and William Brimley, labourer " wilfull men and nothing worthe," Stephen Branton, blacksmith, William Tesimond, saddler, Thomas Oldcorne, tyler and Oliver Walker, carpenter.   Many of these men died in prison ; the trades were well represented in the preservation of Catholicism. Among the women prisoners in York Castle was the celebrated Mistress Margaret Clitherow, the wife of a butcher in that city. The reasons given by the prisoners for their refusal to come to the Anglican service show the reactions of a proportion of the townsfolk to the changes.   Thus Mrs. Isabell Porter, wife of Peter Porter of Yorke, tailor, " sayeth that she cometh not to church because her conscience will not serve her, for things are not in the church as it hath been aforetime in her forefather's time " and Mrs. Margaret Taylor declared that " she cometh not to the church, because there is not a priest as there ought to be, and also that there is not the Sacrament of the Altar."   Among the women recusants at large were Mrs. Elizabeth Dyneley, whose husband was Lord Mayor of York that year, and the two daughters of Thomas Hewett who were described as " yonge, and wilfull, worth nothinge."   The younger of these was a seamstress and the elder lived with her father at Ouse-bridge End refusing to attend the service " because there is no priest there nor right sacrament."   George Wilkinson, a felt maker and hatter in Castlegate pleaded his conscience saying that he would

[1] State Papers, Domestic, Eliz., 118, n. 37, i, printed in C.R.S., Miscellanea, XII, p. 101.

remain in the faith he was baptized[1] in. Far removed from politics, those whose attachment to Catholicism had been real and not merely formal awaited the coming of the new English priests whom Dr. Allen was training.

[1] These details come from the list in State Papers, Domestic, Eliz., 117, n. 23, i, printed in C.R.S. Miscellanea, XII, pp. 12–36 and annotated from Fr. John Morris's materials and the Surtees Society's publications. A variant of the reasons for non-attendance is given by Isabel, wife of William Bowman, locksmith. Both husband and wife were recusants and she stated that " her conscience will not serve her, because there is not the Sacrament hung up," ibid., p. 28.

THE JESUITS AND SEMINARY PRIESTS

IT was in 1574 that the missionary priests began to cross the Channel on their way back to England. Three years later Cuthbert Mayne, a secular priest living in the house of Francis Tregian of Golden, was arrested and hanged, drawn and quartered at Launceston. John Nelson a priest and Thomas Sherwood a student suffered in the following year and in 1580 Fr. Edmund Campion and Fr. Robert Parsons, the celebrated Jesuits, came over to work on the English mission.

There is little purpose in describing again the life-work of Edmund Campion. The story of his fame at Oxford, his reconciliation to the Church, his journeyings to Douai and Rome, his entry into the Society of Jesus, his noviciate at Prague and his return to his own country is as well known as the episodes of his last eighteen months of preaching and working across England. His private press, the issue of the *Decem Rationes*, the effect produced by *Campion's Brag*, the details of his last sermon at Lyford in Berkshire, his capture, trial and execution are all familiar. Together with Robert Southwell,[1] who worked in England from 1586 till 1592, he is perhaps the most attractive figure among those Jesuits who gave their lives for Catholicism in this country. There was in both men a great candour of spirit and in Southwell a remarkable literary receptivity which in turn influenced his generation. They both came, but Southwell perhaps more markedly, within the full tide of the influence of the Counter-Reformation and passed on to a wide English circle its confidence and bravery of spirit. (In literature the Continental influences on Southwell are in marked contrast to those affecting Chidiock Tichborne, a young Catholic without such experiences.)

The history of the labours of the comparatively small band of Jesuits working in England has been given under various forms in some detail, but the influence of the Society can hardly be finally determined in the absence of a complete and objective study of the

---

[1] An admirable study of Southwell's influence has been published by Professor Pierre Janelle, as has a delightful and balanced biography of Campion by Mr. Evelyn Waugh.

life of Fr. Parsons and the publication of the manuscripts dealing with his transactions. A brief framework of his life is essential to an understanding of his significance. At the time of his landing in England he was a man of thirty-four, a native of Somerset, and a former bursar and dean of Balliol. During his stay in England as a Jesuit he had considerable success and reconciled many to the Church. In 1581 he returned to the Continent and remained abroad until his death in 1610. It is undeniable that he was a man of strong character and determination, wholehearted in his desire to further the cause of the Catholic Church and the Society of Jesus. Soon after he left England finally he visited Spain and for the next twenty years advocated the restoration of Catholicism in England by force of arms. He had serious quarrels with what was known as the Scottish faction among the Catholic exiles and with the body of the secular clergy, and difficulties arose in connection with the colleges in Spain. On the other hand he retained Cardinal Allen's confidence throughout his life. It is, perhaps, worth describing the effect which his personality created.

A description of Parsons in the last years before his death is given in Sir Tobie Mathew's account of his conversion. " My chief reason for this acquaintance," wrote Sir Tobie of his first meeting with Fr. Parsons, " was to keep that cunning dark man (for so I esteemed him at that time) by that appearance of courtesy and respect from doing me any ill office. And next out of a curious desire which I had . . . to know and converse a little, hand to hand, with a person of so much reputation throughout the world for great experience and wisdom." And then he goes on to describe[1] Fr. Parsons' conversation and how " he took occasion from somewhat which was said of Savoy to speak much to me of the hideous rocks and mountains of that country, and with how extreme hazard and pains men were glad to climb, or rather indeed, to creep up by inaccessible ways, to pick out handfuls of earth which they might either plant or sow for the getting of a miserable poor subsistence. And if this (said he) be discreetly done for such a poor kind of life, as this is, how well must it deserve another manner of labour and care, when there is question of acquiring another kind of life, which is to be infinite and eternal." The two paragraphs give an interesting impression and we must wait for a final judgment.

As a whole it may be said that the Jesuits actually working in

---

[1] *Relation of the Conversion of Sir Tobie Mathew*, ed. A. H. Mathew, p. 16.

England were no more concerned than were the other missionary priests with those problems which might result from a foreign invasion. The Bull *Regnans in Excelsis* had had the effect of rallying the Catholics, but the practical question of the possibility of the Queen's deposition hardly presented itself to her subjects. From an early stage an English independence of mind became manifest and the priests thought no more about politics, determined to reconcile to the Church the followers of the weakening Catholic tradition. In spite of the hopes of some of the exiles, both priests and people knew well that in the case of a foreign invasion every Catholic would in fact support the English government without regard to its religious policy. Between 1568 and 1587, when the Queen of Scots was a prisoner in England, the situation was more complex, as it was always possible that some elements among the Catholics might support an insurrection in her favour. The limited nature of the support which might have been obtained for her is, however, revealed in the development of the Babington Plot. This was a conspiracy which aimed at releasing the Queen of Scots by force of arms and developed as a result of the energy of Anthony Babington, a wealthy young Derbyshire squire, ardently but recently Catholic. A group of the younger courtiers were devoted to Babington and followed where he led. Babington's romantic enthusiasm for Queen Mary was early known to the government who naturally fostered this plot as they would any other form of disaffection which they could keep under control. The Elizabethan government had a great talent for probing each possibility of enmity to the State. The official discovery of the plot was made in August 1586 and the conspirators were executed soon afterwards : the death of the Queen of Scots was determined on and she was beheaded at Fotheringay in the following February. Whatever action the Catholics might have taken in her favour, it was clear that they would never assist the Spaniards.

At the same time it is not difficult to understand the line of thought which led the government to take measures of exceptional severity. Every Englishman who was reconciled to the old faith would certainly prefer that the Queen should choose other advisers in religious matters than Lord Burghley (as Cecil had become in 1571) and Sir Francis Walsingham. Again it is probable that the influence of the Spanish party among the exiles upon their co-religionists in England was exaggerated in government circles and this would make the authorities more inclined to adopt a ruthless policy. And Don Bernardino de Mendoza, who was the envoy of Philip II from 1578 until 1584, was incautiously meddlesome.

Two statutes stand out as the basis of the subsequent prosecutions. By the Act of Persuasions (23 Eliz., c. 1), passed in 1581, it was made High Treason for anyone to reconcile or be reconciled to the Romish Religion and four years later the Act against Jesuits, seminary priests and other suchlike disobedient persons (27 Eliz., c. 2) declared that every priest within the Queen's dominions was guilty of High Treason by his presence in England. Under this same Act it was made a felony for anyone to receive or relieve a priest. Although there is a fairly copious literature dealing with the martyred English Catholics, the actual incidence of the prosecutions has not yet been made the subject of a complete and detailed study. The names of three hundred and sixty men and women who died under the penal laws in England were considered at Rome[1] in the various processes relating to martyrdom, and in the great majority of cases the prosecutions had been initiated under these statutes of 1581 and 1585. It is significant that the immediate reaction to these laws and to the fines levied for non-attendance at Anglican worship was not of a political character ; it was a strengthening of the defences to enable the religious life to be carried on.

Although prosecutions were fairly continuous between 1581 and the end of the reign, their incidence in different parts of the country was spasmodic. The search of private houses for the discovery of priests depended to a great extent on the local magistrates, although these latter could always be stirred to action by government agents from London. As a consequence the arrangement of means of concealment became essential during this period of the religious conflict when the long spells of calm were varied by occasional intensive search. Definite hiding-places were constructed ; small masked cupboards for the vestments and chalice and larger spaces, frequently behind masonry, for the concealment of priests. Difficult as it is to piece together the evidence on this subject much confusion

---

[1] Between 1581 and 1588 at least sixty-four priests, eighteen laymen and two lay-women, Margaret Clitherow and Margaret Ward, were put to death for religion. Sixty-one persons who suffered between 1570 and 1588 have been declared *beati* by the Holy See. As early as 1583 Pope Gregory XIII had allowed pictures of the martyr-doms in England to be painted on the walls of the church of the English College in Rome. In regard to the lives of the victims of the Elizabethan persecution much work has been done by Fr. J. H. Pollen, S.J., by Fr. C. A. Newdigate, S.J. and by Dom Bede Camm.

has been caused by the tradition which asserted that every cupboard behind a sliding panel in a Catholic house was a priest's hiding-hole.

The real hiding-places seem first to have been contrived in the manors of Catholics living in the south of England and the Midlands, probably because the strength of the old religion in the north made this method less necessary. In Lancashire, Yorkshire and Northumberland there were in the early days of the persecution so many cottagers on whose fidelity the priests could rely ; but in the south the strain was greater. Many of the more celebrated hiding-places were constructed by Nicholas Owen, a Jesuit laybrother, a small man with a limp who developed a very resourceful invention in the course of the twenty-five years which he spent in assisting the fathers and carrying on this work. He was twice captured and on the second occasion was starved out of one of his own refuges at Hindlip after a search lasting four days. He would reveal nothing and died in the Tower under severe torture.

Some of the earlier hiding-places were behind chimneys, a dangerous arrangement which later led the pursuivants to light the fires in the house which they were searching so that those in concealment would be smoked out of their refuge. In the smaller houses attic and loft spaces were frequently utilized. The use of sliding panels and of any wall space which might ring hollow in a search was obviously inadvisable ; some houses contained both rather amateur refuges and those of more expert construction. Possibly the very best hiding-hole at present extant is that at Sawston near Cambridge where the entrance is concealed in the staircase flooring and the walls have all the thickness of Tudor masonry. Baddesley Clinton is remarkable in that an old sewage tunnel seems to have been employed.

Among the English counties Warwickshire and Worcestershire possess the greatest number of refuges which have so far been discovered ; a fact perhaps accounted for by the presence of a considerable Catholic minority among the gentry without any very solid support from the farmers and labourers. In the west country there were few hiding-places, the examples at Lulworth and in the Waldegraves' manor at Chewton Magna being among the rare specimens. Two areas had a purely adventitious importance ; the Thames valley, across which lay the routes that a priest would take when moving from London to the western Midlands ; and those sections of the counties along the sea-coast which were within reach of unfrequented landing-places and not far from the capital. In London itself there were numerous hiding-places ; but in the houses of the great peers, like Arundel House or Southampton House, it was possible to live privately without fear of arrest except in times of emergency. It is probable that many refuges were contrived in the inns frequented by the Catholics.

In the country parts it is sometimes found that the hiding-places were constructed at the time of the erection of the house as in the case of the Tudor building at West Grinstead originally belonging to the Carylls and now used as the presbytery. Derbyshire is notable for the number of refuges which are to be found in farms as well as in manors, a tribute to the rooted Catholicism of the county where Mr. Garlick, Mr. Ludlam and Mr. Simpson[1] laboured. Some of the places of concealment in the Midlands and the north are obviously of later date than the sixteenth century. So many old houses have been pulled down or reconstructed that it is clear that only a small proportion of the total number of hiding-places have been discovered.[2]

In an age when individuals of rank possessed so much influence it is interesting to attempt to calculate the effect of the work of the missionary priests during their early years in England. There seems little doubt that it was during this period that the Catholics in the Midlands were reanimated ; partly by the work of Edmund Campion and partly by the memory of his death. The leading recusants of the reign had all become strict in the practice of their religion before the year of the Armada ; Lords Vaux, Stourton, Mordaunt and Windsor, Sir John Petre and Sir Thomas Tresham. These men belonged to the generation which had grown to maturity since the Queen's accession, Vaux the eldest of them was born in 1542 and Windsor the youngest in 1559, and now in manhood and early middle age they came back to a firm adherence to Catholicism. As a body they were wealthy and Tresham had a mind of great originality and talent which has left to us the garden house at Lyveden and the triangular lodge at Rushton with their secret monograms " in laud of the Mother of God " and their recondite symbols of the Trinity. The houses of these leaders were to be, with Hindlip and Coughton, among the chief Catholic centres. This group was constantly

---

[1] These three secular priests were executed at Derby for their priesthood in July 1588.

[2] The volume by Mr. Granville Squires is the most recent detailed study of the subject of hiding-places.

reinforcing its ranks by intermarriage and building up with the aid of Throckmortons, Bedingfields and Dormers that secure, steadfast and self-conscious old Catholicism ; very charitable, a little aloof and infinitely conservative. This was to take a couple of generations to develop, while the recusants were becoming sharply distinguished from the bulk of their fellow-countrymen ; but it can be traced back clearly to these early years.

In some quarters the reconciliations of the Campion-Parsons period were less permanent. The unsatisfactory Lord Oxford, whose curious interests and morals were so troublesome to his father-in-law Burghley, seems to have been avowedly a Catholic for some years. And there appears to have been a transient support for the old faith on the part of the first Lord Compton at Compton Winyates. A conversion of some political significance was that of the eighth Earl of Northumberland, who had been for twenty years a strong supporter of the Queen's religion. He was a dissatisfied man and never entirely entrusted by the government since his elder brother's rising ; in 1584 he was arrested at his house at Petworth on a political charge and in the following year was found shot in the Tower of London apparently a case of suicide. But, as far as direct influence was concerned, the most considerable result of the activity of the missionary priests in the circle of the Court was the reconciliation of Philip, Earl of Arundel.

The whole development of Arundel's religious standpoint throws much light on the early Elizabethan position in this matter. He was the eldest son of the fourth Duke of Norfolk and had been born in 1557 and brought up in the Queen's faith. His father's execution diminished, but did not mar his prospects ; he inherited the earldom of Arundel from his maternal grandfather in 1580 ; the Queen received him with favour. He had made a child marriage with Anne Dacres, the eldest of the three co-heiresses of the Dacres of the North. Unlike her husband she had been brought up strictly Catholic, and although after her marriage she had attended the Anglican service, had always refused to receive the Communion. In 1581 the Countess and her sister-in-law Lady Margaret Sackville were reconciled to the Catholic Church. Arundel, himself, had two uncles who adhered to the old faith, Lord Lumley openly and Lord Henry Howard with circumspection. Still he himself conformed without difficulty ; was prominent in tourneys ; received literary dedications ; was suitably extravagant.

Then in September 1584 he was reconciled by Fr. Weston. As it was impossible for him to continue at Court in the then state of the law against Catholics he decided to retire to France declaring in a letter to the Queen that " I resolved to take the benefit of a happye wind to avoide the violence of a bitter storm." In this he was unsuccessful; he was captured and lodged in the Tower where he remained for the next ten years until he died. In 1589 he was condemned to death on the charge of having had Mass said for the success of the Spanish Fleet : the evidence adduced was unconvincing. A description of Arundel at the time of his trial survives. " The Earl," the account[1] runs, " came in to the Hall, being in a wrought velvet gown, furred about with martins, laid about with gold lace and buttoned with gold buttons, a black satin doublet, a pair of velvet hose, and a long high black hat on his head ; a very tall man looking somewhat swarth-coloured." Meanwhile Lady Arundel became one of the strongest supports of the recusants and Fr. Robert Southwell lived for a time in her house. Arundel was devoted to religious exercises, and to the writing of devotional verse. In August 1595 he became seriously ill and it was suggested by his friends that this was the result of poison put by the prison cook into the sauce poured over a roasted teal. He died in the following October in the Tower of London and his will is characteristic. " In nomine patris filii et spiritus Sancti, Amen," it begins, " I, Phillipe, Erle of Arundell, being a member of the trewe, auncient Catholique and Apostolick Church." As far as mundane values were concerned, his was a singularly unsuccessful life.

[1] The materials for a life of Philip, Earl of Arundel have been collected in the publications of the Catholic Record Society, vol. xxi. He was declared *beatus* by Pope Pius XI in 1929.

THE ATTITUDE OF THE LATE ELIZABETHANS

THE LAST THIRTEEN years of the reign of Elizabeth, from about 1590 until the Queen's death in 1603, have a very different character from the rest of the period. The Spanish fleet had been scattered in 1588 and a mood of happy confidence had not unnaturally been induced in the prosperous circles in England. Then the religious issue was more clear cut and much less confused than in the earlier sections of the reign. The executions continued and there is no year between 1581 and 1603 which has not supplied a name or names to the list of English martyrs, and in the year of the Armada there was a more severe harrying of the Catholics than at any other time before or since. Still that majority of the population which was no longer definitely attached to the old faith was becoming used to such severities. To them the actions of Fr. Parsons and the pro-Spanish party abroad may have appeared to warrant the government's action and it is probable that the sympathy which Campion seems to have evoked had vanished after the disastrous fact of the Armada. With all the means of propaganda under their control the government could do much to rouse suspicion of the loyalty of the priests in England who in fact seldom meddled in any way with politics. The coming of the Armada and the avowedly Catholic object of the expedition was probably one of the more severe blows that the cause of the old faith suffered in England. Catholicism had been associated in the mind of the people with Mass and the sacraments in the parish churches and the monasteries jogging along quietly : all that was peaceful and insular was quite unconnected with such an idea as a foreign invasion.

By this time the first purely Elizabethan generation had reached maturity and the men under thirty-five had never had even a childhood's memory of the Catholic life. The legend of the Queen had crystallized ; her marriage projects were far behind her ; she had moved out into a new Spenserian atmosphere. The power of the State was growing and consolidating, the earlier protagonists had vanished, Leicester and Walsingham and the Queen of Scots were dead. Burghley remained and Queen Elizabeth had come to peace and there was something wonderful to her subjects in such survival. This was a generation which glory and riches and easy hazardous conquest had affected somewhat headily. Sir Philip Sidney had supplied the chivalric legend and Sir Walter Raleigh with much experience and Essex with none both sought to interpret the Elizabethan ideal of magnificence. Here there was hardly question of the Christian values and, as far as the Court was concerned, both the vague hereditary Catholicism and the incipient Reforming spirit of the elder generation tended to be liquidated in the scepticism of a period of too great material good fortune. A show of scriptural feeling was no longer fashionable and the older manner had passed away when Sir Humphrey Gilbert went down in the *Squirrel* with his Bible.

In the Court circle this scepticism opened the way towards conversion and this was particularly noticeable among the group which gathered round the Queen's favourite the Earl of Essex. He himself seems to have been light, carefree and Italianate in his sympathies ; his friend Southampton was moving away from Catholicism into the new less Christian trend of thought ; his younger companion Sir Oliver Manners had turned back again towards the Catholic Church. A new convert element was developing among the sophisticated courtiers and this temper of mind finds a clear expression in the work of Henry Constable. It followed inevitably that a proportion of Catholics were involved in that meaningless stir the Essex Rising which cost the Earl his life in 1601.

In the last two years of the reign Catholics practically vanished from the neighbourhood of the Court ; for they would all tend to support Essex in his casual and unplanned rivalry rather than Burghley's son and successor Sir Robert Cecil. At the same time the Puritan feeling was growing, especially in London, and Essex curiously enough was in touch with some of its leaders. To the Puritans the transition from scepticism to Popery appeared obvious and simple and it is probable that these courtier converts helped to increase their hatred of Rome. It was one of the minor causes of the determined Puritan hostility that these Popish courtiers, later supported by two foreign queens, were to remain on the steps of the throne for another century.

There is little doubt that in the country at large the popularity of the Queen was well maintained and a determined anti-Spanish feeling had struck root. This was particularly strong in the western seaports and in the southern counties and London ; in the north it was difficult to conceive of any foreign enemy except the Scots.   In the towns Foxe's *Book of Martyrs* had had great success and the fires of Smithfield and the massacre of St. Bartholomew took their place in the rather sombre imagination of the merchants and tradesmen. The Catholics had now been in opposition for forty years and there appeared no prospect that they would receive a share in the government.   To those who took full advantage of the political situation it seemed fantastic that men should condemn themselves to spend all their lives in the wilderness.   Certainly the succession opened no real hope of the coming to the throne of a Catholic sovereign. When the Queen should die the next heir was King James VI of Scotland whose grandfather was the son of Henry VIII's elder sister.   But other claims were suggested ; Lord Beauchamp represented the Suffolk line on whom the Crown had been settled by King Henry's will ; Lady Arabella Stuart was a first cousin of the King of Scots and might be preferred to him since she had been born in England.   Neither of these latter claimants had any interest from a religious standpoint, although the possibility of Lady Arabella's accession was canvassed among the exiles abroad.   The fantastic idea of the Crown passing to the Infanta Isabella, which had been mooted by the Spaniards and some English exiles at the time of the invasion, had ceased to be considered since her marriage to the Archduke Albert.   Like the rest of the world the Catholics for the most part acquiesced in the idea of the King of Scots' accession which was for some time seen to be inevitable.

As a consequence they were little interested in the political situation.   They had their own internal troubles ; the difficulties which broke out between the secular clergy and the Jesuits over the appointment of Mr. Blackwell as archpriest on the English mission ; the absence of organized leadership ; the case of individual secession. It was in this generation that the squires of the old faith began to manifest that spirit of reserve which was later to be so characteristic a feature of their outlook.   As the reign progressed the coming and going of the missionary priests tended still further to knit the ardent Catholics into a compact body often united by family ties, uninterested in politics, devoted to sport and deeply wedded to the life of the countryside.   Among these stocks a certain pride was to develop which would in time make the idea of their children's marriage to Protestants distasteful to them.   The religious position

c

was gradually clarifying and the households where the husband conformed to the Established Church, while the wife was a recusant, were often in close contact with the strict Catholic families. A desire for the free exercise of the ancient faith united them in a world which was increasingly uninterested in such matters. Besides in these cases where the parents were divided in their external religious allegiance the children were often determinedly Catholic. In the religious history of a country it is usual to find a weak generation from time to time. Such a state of affairs had occurred in England in regard to those Catholics who passed their youth in the early years of Queen Elizabeth's reign. Many individuals had come back to a strict practice, but as a general rule the men born in the south and Midlands between 1553 and 1563 had been brought up in an atmosphere of some confusion. They were now the heads of families, traditionally Catholic, with a tendency to temporize with the government and forming the bulk of the " Church Papists " at the end of the Elizabethan period.

Undoubtedly in the south the Jesuit fathers had a great deal to do with the reviving and strengthening of the religious life. The sons reacted against that indifference and over-caution which their fathers manifested. They were ardent and desired a clear-cut faith ; peril attracted them, as did that vivid spiritual energy which characterized the Counter-Reformation.

It was not so much a direct struggle between opposed religions, for the Puritan section was little touched by the activities of the missionary priests and the strength of the Anglican feeling had not yet found expression in Bishop Andrewes. The conflict was rather between the values of the new Elizabethan world and the Christocentric standards of the old religion. The element of high conscious adventure, which appealed so greatly to this generation, was manifested in the manner in which these alternatives were presented. It is worth giving some brief account of that characteristic figure on the Catholic side, Fr. John Gerard.

In the last days of October 1588 shortly after the ships of the defeated Armada had returned to Spain, Fr. John Gerard a young Jesuit priest of twenty-four landed with his companion Fr. Oldcorne on a solitary part of the Norfolk coast near Bacton and passed the night in a wood by the sea-shore in the soaking rain. Within a few days he was in Norwich and had met a wealthy Catholic, Edward Yelverton and his labours had begun. Gerard was a man of very straightforward and determined character ; remarkably courageous, as his sufferings on the rack were to show ; interested in field sports and hawking ; ready and capable. He came of ancient family from Bryn in Lancashire, had had a desultory education and was little interested in book learning. A description found in the Salisbury MSS. gives a remarkable impression of his personality. " Mr. Gerard," the account runs, " was of stature tall, high shouldered, black haired and of complexion swarth, hawk nosed, high templed and for the most part attired costly and defencibly in buff leather, garnished with gold or silver lace, sattin doublet and velevet hose of all colours with cloaks correspondent, and rapiers and daggers, gilt or silvered." With him there came in that quickness and assurance of the Counter-Reformation, the sense of the old religion suitable to men of birth, the impression of an adventurous loyalty which appeared as the inevitable Christian background for a man of honour. In the circles in which John Gerard moved for the next seventeen years the point of honour was dominant. On this he could bring to bear the actuality of the *Spiritual Exercises.* It was a question as to whether the young men with whom he came in contact would choose the standards of a reinvigorated Catholicism or those of the military courtiers of the period who lived with quick gains and dangers against a background touched with patriotism and lit by a mounting and consciously heroic self-sufficiency. Fr. Gerard's success was very great and it is not surprising that he and some of his companions became the unique guides of those young men to whom they had shown the Christian alternative. Two severe losses were sustained in the middle portion of this period by the capture and execution of Robert Southwell and of another Jesuit Henry Walpole, both of whom were condemned for their priesthood in 1595.

In the north country the situation was very different. There the anti-Spanish feeling was much less strong ; the people had little interest in the mercantile adventures of the west-country men ; the rivalries of the Court were unheeded. The Queen seldom went on progress in these parts and the solidity of the northern character was somewhat unresponsive to her legend. In the north a determined Catholicism had endured throughout the reign and was well served by a strong supply of priests mainly belonging to the secular clergy. Thus in the years between 1588 and 1603 eight secular priests, one Jesuit, and eleven laymen were executed at York for their religion, while seven priests and three laymen suffered at Newcastle and Durham.[1] Here there was a definitely Catholic section of the townspeople as in York and Lancaster. Again in these country parts, where the old faith remained strong there was equal opportunity for Mass and the sacraments and for instruction open to farmer and labourer alike.

This factor raises a point which has never been adequately considered. To what degree was it possible for the poor in the Midlands and the south of England and for the artisans and workers in London to frequent the sacraments and remain in touch with their religion ? It is only possible to put forward a very tentative answer to this question. The position of London was unique as a result of its constant growth and the large floating population. For a Catholic with some connections among the recusants it was probably not too difficult to gain information as to where Masses were being said and there was very likely a tendency for ardent Catholics to gravitate towards employment which was controlled by their coreligionists. There were great households, like that of Lady Arundel, which provided for very numerous dependants and almost required Catholics in the key positions. In other cases a steward who belonged to the old faith could do much ; the recusant tradesmen preferred apprentices who could be trusted not to spy upon their movements ; there were inn-keepers who catered for the numerous Catholic gentry. In general the inn-keepers had an excellent record for common sense and fidelity. The search records indicate the presence of numerous Catholics following this trade in London and give interrogations of their stablemen and ostlers. This was also noticeable in other towns. The two priests and Mr. Belson, who were executed at Oxford in 1589, were taken at the Catherine Wheel, an inn belonging to Balliol College, and with them was hanged Humphrey Pritchard, a Welshman serving at that house, who was charged with relieving them.

At the same time it must have been very difficult for Catholics living in the poor and crowded districts in London to obtain instruction for their children. The members of the foreign colonies settled in London were often bitterly opposed to their religion and they had public feeling as well as the law against them. In their dealings with the small employers of labour they would come up

---

[1] Within the same period there were four priests, including the Dominican protomartyr Fr. Robert Nutter, executed at Lancaster and one at Carlisle.

against that growing Puritanism which had hardly yet impinged upon the consciousness of the Catholic gentry. Living in the courts and alleys of London and surrounded by hostile neighbours it was most difficult for the labourer or wherryman to pass on a knowledge of his religion to his children. Among the lay martyrs in London three have an especial interest; Alexander Blake an ostler hanged in Gray's Inn Lane in 1590 for assisting priests, John Roche an Irish waterman hanged for helping a priest out of Bridewell in 1588 and Richard Martin " a layeman executed only for being in the company of Mr. Robert Morton, Priest, and paying vj^d for his supper."

The question of the survival of Catholicism among the agricultural labourers in the south of England is a simpler matter. Here it depended entirely on the presence of missionary priests in the neighbourhood and this in turn could only be assured as a result of hospitality offered by some landowner or substantial farmer. The extinction of Catholicism among the people in the western counties soon appeared to be imminent as the families which could offer shelter for the clergy diminished in number. Over large areas of Wiltshire, Somerset, Dorset, Devon and Cornwall it became literally impossible for poor men without horses and bound by their work to the soil to come within reach of the sacraments. And this perhaps accounts for the very rapid destruction of the old religious tradition in the west country. In Cornwall the process was rather slower and here the people passed into that post-Catholic state which made them so ready to receive the teaching of the great eighteenth-century preachers. It would be interesting to trace the connection between the gradual starvation of the Catholic tradition and the subsequent readiness of a people for a strong adherence to the Free Churches.

On the other hand in the home counties and in East Anglia and the Midlands it would not in most cases have been difficult for the labourers and their families to remain in contact with their faith. But they were terribly dependent upon the maintenance of Catholic centres and with the turn of the century the burdens of recusancy, the growth of positively Anglican sentiment and the general vague patriotic feeling against the Church tended to sap the allegiance of their children. Very serious efforts were required to keep those countrymen who were not actually tenants of recusant landowners in contact with their hereditary faith. Besides, as the position of the

---

[1] From a memorandum printed in *Documents relating to the English Martyrs*, Catholic Records Society, V, p. 290.

priests became more settled and they appeared as chaplains to the squires' households a tendency developed to take their duties more easily.   By the mid-seventeenth century it needed exceptional zeal to induce the clergy of the Midlands to make long journeys across country to revive the fading Catholic tradition of some family who no longer themselves made any effort to find a Mass.   Thus the reign ended with the adherents of the old religion weakening but tenacious ; a great gulf between the outlook of rich and poor, the latter apparently dimly satisfied and the former aware of each current and its possibilities ; one certainty in the situation, the accession to the throne of the King of Scots.

CATHOLICISM UNDER JAMES I

THE DEATH OF Queen Elizabeth and the ending of the high-strained period of glory had a profound effect upon the English Catholics. The government remained unchanged, Cecil was strengthened in his predominance, but the Crown ceased to be the focus of that belligerent nationalist interest which the great reign had so well sustained. The country slid easily into a decline from the high tension to the more pacific values, the delicate speculative studies, the sport and hunting without thought of foreign wars, the new orientation of architecture and that undignified lavish court life which marked the Jacobean period. It was a time of relaxation after effort. For the first time, since the emergence of that species, the Protestant hero was at a discount. James I had a distaste for naked steel and the well-lined romance of the Indies was out of fashion. Throughout the country there was a distaste for alarms and it was a misfortune for the Catholics that the new quietness tended to exaggerate any disturbance of the peace. In this new age, from which the followers of the old religion hoped so much, the public opinion in England was peculiarly susceptible to the effect of gunpowder.

The long reign had had a numbing and paralysing effect upon the Catholics. The barrier which separated the strict recusants and especially the " Jesuited Papists " from the lax favourers of the old faith had been clear throughout the last twenty years of Erastian sovereignty. The casual unorthodox supporters of the former religious tradition had enjoyed the royal protection and had entered fully into the loyal enthusiasm and the strong nationalist sentiment. If there was one force capable of reconciling the " Church Papists " to the Anglican Settlement it was the star of Elizabeth.

That the new king would declare himself a Catholic was naturally not regarded as probable. He had indeed a secular respect for the Papacy and the great kingdoms still in union with Rome ; but there was that in his Scottish blood, in the weariness of just-successful kingcraft and in the peculiar sense of his own unrecognized talent which prevented him from appreciating the Tridentine spirit. The

63

Ignatian approach in particular was uncongenial to his vain, un-regulated, over-affectionate nature and to his curious lay theology.

The situation was not made easier by the probability that the new Queen, Anne of Denmark had been secretly reconciled to the Catholic Church. The inconclusive evidence[1] does not, however, indicate that the Queen gave any active support to the Catholic cause after she came to England. These sympathies or allegiance only served to stiffen the King in his attitude and between 1603 and her death in 1619 she had no more than a negative political influence. When dying she accepted the ministrations of the Archbishop of Canterbury, but she never consented to receive the Anglican sacrament. At the time of the King's accession the royal children Prince Henry and Prince Charles were aged nine and three respectively. Everything depended on James I.

In one direction particularly there was ground for hope. Vague promises of toleration had been made to the Catholics by the King of Scots before his accession and their friends among the great families would now gain in influence. Cecil could do much. He was to become Earl of Salisbury in 1605 and to hold chief power until he died in 1612 ; but he could not keep the peers and the rich squires away from the King who took a naive delight in meeting English deference with familiarity and in receiving hospitality based on an uncontrolled expenditure. Among the great families a restoration of the Howards might appear likely to assist the old religion.

In the year following his accession King James restored the earldom of Arundel to Philip Howard's son Thomas, a boy of seventeen, ardent, dilettante and brought up as a most strict Catholic. Lord William Howard was active in the Borders and Lord Henry Howard came to power.

Lord Henry, a brother of the fourth Duke of Norfolk, had had a long, hazardous and doubtful life. He was Italianate in his tastes ; interested in the Civil Law ; a great contriver and designer, the builder of Audley End ; deeply concerned with astrology ; an opportunist with a Catholic foundation.[2] He had worked his way

---

[1] The narrative of her conversion as described by Fr. Robert Abercromby, S.J. is published in Bellesheim *History of the Catholic Church in Scotland*, Appendix V, p. 353 sq. A different standpoint is taken in the introduction to Cal. Salisbury MSS., vol. xv, which contains some letters bearing on the Queen's attitude.

[2] As an instance of the vagueness of religious allegiance at this period both Ben Jonson and John Dowland the lutenist were Catholics for about a dozen years in their early middle life.

to influence in the last days of the old Queen, had vaguely suggested toleration of the Catholics to James I and had a curious half-distrustful alliance with Robert Cecil. His letters had impressed King James, who referred to them characteristically as " Asiatic and endless volumes." He was created Earl of Northampton and became Warden of the Cinque Ports and, later, Lord Privy Seal. Other Catholics like Lord Worcester, the Master of the Horse, were also in contact with the new government, but Northampton's influence was dominant.

These were encouraging factors and the adherents of the old religion came out once more to feel the sun. They had hopes, too, from quite a different quarter. Northumberland, who numbered so many of the old faith among his tenants and whose brothers and household officers were Catholics, had interceded for them with the King of Scots. Everywhere the outlook was hopeful. Yet the optimism was induced precisely by that balancing of political elements which was to prove so insecure. There were economic factors which made the return of Catholicism less probable and the influence of seventeenth-century capitalism was hostile. Later in this period there was to be the effect of colonial expansion and all these elements combined with the more obvious interplay of politics. But the subject of this survey is the actual development of Catholicism in England and not the forces which militated against its victory. To the contemporary Catholics it was only the domestic episodes which were apparent.

Very soon there began the obscure developments of the Main and Bye Plots, the latter apparently aiming at a gathering to force toleration for Catholics and both having some vague connection with projects for placing Lady Arabella Stuart on the throne. The chief political effect of these movements was the disgrace of Sir Walter Raleigh. Two priests, Watson and Clarke, were implicated in the Bye Plot and executed. Their pastoral careers had been undistinguished ; they had little personality ; both had a profound antipathy[1] to the Jesuits. These latter and the archpriest took the occasion to demonstrate their loyalty to the new King. No laymen of consequence were concerned except Anthony Copley and Sir Griffin Markham, who belonged to the raffish section of Court converts. It is worth while considering Sir Griffin's career since it

---

[1] *A Jesuitarum turbine libera nos domine*, letter from Clarke to Markham, Cal. Salisbury MSS. xv, p. 223.

is typical of the sixteenth-century swordsmen who, from the time of Babington and Ballard to the Gunpowder Plot episode, had hung about the *purlieus* of the palace, gaming, haunting the lords of the opposition and adventuring in the foreign wars. They were soon to vanish with the coming of the peace with Spain and the King's objection to the duel. By chance many were Catholic, but by nature all were of the opposition. Their religion was an accidental, but a hampering accident to the Catholic cause.

Sir Griffin was thirty-nine years of age and had suffered imprisonment in the Fleet and had been one of Essex's captains in Ireland. He had been accused without much probability of coinage in Gray's Inn and was beset by creditors. He was a cousin of Babington's, an importunate " alliesman " of Cecil, loud, assertive and tolerably scrupulous. In the late reign he had become a Catholic. His aspect was courageous, " a large broad face, black complexion . . . big nose, and one of his hands maimed by a hurt in his arm received by shot of bullet."[1] It was obvious that such a man would ground at last on the temptation to conspiracy and after the Bye Plot he vanished from the scene.

But the Catholics were little affected by these events, since the Church leaders had proved themselves so admirably loyal. In fact the recusants themselves began writing[2] to Cecil hopefully about the new age of freedom. The Edict of Nantes in 1598 had seemed to show that toleration of two religions in one state was not impossible. In this connection much capital has been made out of the disappointment of the Catholics at finding that the King enforced the recusancy laws while he was willing to discuss the difficulties of his Puritan subjects. The Hampton Court Conference in 1604, although it was a gesture towards the Protestants of the left, undoubtedly confirmed King James in his sense of the blessings of Anglican Episcopacy. Still it is probable that the disappointment in the Catholic body has been much exaggerated and no group were more surprised than the careful, determined, insular squires of the old religion when they were overtaken by the misfortune of the Gunpowder Plot.

The atmosphere of the Powder Plot belongs to the sixteenth and not to the seventeenth century. It was the last and so disastrous adventure of the simple-minded gentlemen of the sword and, like

[1] The same note gives details of his brothers. " All are tall of stature, of exceeding swarthy and bad complexion and all have very great noses," Cal. Salisbury MSS., xv. p. 193.
[2] Cf. the letters of Henry Constable and John Stonor, ibid., pp. 131 and 199.

all such attempts, benefited no one save the cool politicians. The idea governing such movements was that of support given to some great lord by an almost feudal retinue of swordsmen of good birth. This was essentially the support of an individual whose influence with the sovereign might lead him to become the chief political adviser of the Crown. The Earls of Leicester and Essex, and the Duke of Norfolk had each exercised an independent influence gained by wealth and reinforced by a personal following, which formed almost a satellite court. But in the new century such leaders were to be replaced by the Howards and Cecils considered collectively, and by the houses of Cavendish and Russell. The Tudor *magnifico* gave way before the corporate influence of the great family which was soon to develop into the Whig ducal house.

The main drift of the episodes of the Gunpowder Plot seems to have been as follows. Robert Catesby, a dependent of Essex and one of the survivors of his rising, broached a matter to Thomas Percy, a cousin and factor of the Earl of Northumberland, to Guy Fawkes, a soldier of fortune from Yorkshire then serving in the Low Countries, and to Thomas Winter, a skilled swordsman about the Court. The circle was later widened to include Winter's elder brother Robert Winter of Huddington, his brother-in-law John Grant, and his distant cousins John and Christopher Wright. Two minor members added to the group were Robert Keyes and Catesby's servant Bates. All were Catholics, several had returned to the practice of that faith, most had been in some way dependent upon Essex and none were politically influential. They were all between forty-five and thirty years of age. Catesby had had experience of wealth and was related to the inner circle of Catholic families ; his prospects were considerable, but his immediate position was encumbered by extravagance. With this exception none of the group could be considered rich, nor were they closely in touch with their leading co-religionists.

From one point of view Thomas Percy held a key position among these men. He was the eldest and, through Northumberland's influence, one of the gentlemen pensioners at Court. For this reason, perhaps, he hired the house in Westminster from which a passage was made and gunpowder placed in the cellars beneath the Houses of Parliament. Percy had returned to Catholicism when about thirty-five and had married a recusant, the sister of John and Christopher Wright who were later his companions. He was a tall man " with a great broad beard," firm eyes, curling moustaches, of soldierly bearing and with experience of life.

At this point in the obscure situation it is necessary to consider the actions and knowledge of the government. Lord Salisbury was admirably provided with those *agents provocateurs* who were for so long considered a necessary adjunct to any government which dealt with the opposition by repressive measures. The majority of the men involved in the plot were well enough known in official circles as " disaffected." According to the confessions of the conspirators the plan developed slowly. Three dates emerge. The practice " was first propounded unto me," declared Fawkes, " about Easter last was twelvemonth (Easter 1604) beyond the seas in the Low Countries of the archduke's obeyance." " Thomas Percy hired a howse at Westminster," he continues, " . . . and there wee begann to make a myne about the XI of December, 1604." An anonymous letter warning Lord Mounteagle against attending the opening of Parliament on November 5 was delivered to his servant at Hoxton on 26 October, 1605 and its contents communicated to the government. Just before midnight on 4 November Guy Fawkes was arrested in the cellars below the Houses of Parliament and thirty-six casks of gunpowder were discovered hidden under a store of firewood.

It seems most improbable that government agents were not aware of the plans in their early stages and very likely that agents cultivated the " practice." Possibly one of the early conspirators was in touch with the government. Catesby, Percy and the Wrights were killed fighting on 9 November and the possibility that one of them was discovered early and offered to keep the government informed in return for a pardon can hardly be excluded. It is perhaps more likely that Percy was influenced by some agent in whom he confided, but whose name he concealed from his companions. It seems against the whole nature of Cecil's efficient administration that it should have been unaware of the " practice " for very long.

But attached to the plan for blowing up the King and the Lords and Commons by gunpowder there were vague suggestions for a rising and the seizure of the person of the King's daughter the Princess Elizabeth and his sons should they survive. Money was needed, other friends were enlisted, and the extended plan brought the Jesuits within reach of the law in this connection.

It appears that in the months before the date fixed for the

" practice " Catesby obtained the aid of three wealthy Catholics, his cousin Francis Tresham of Rushton who had been with him in the Essex Rising, Sir Everard Digby of Gothurst and Ambrose Rookwood of Coldham Hall in Suffolk. The two last-named were young, inexperienced and bound to Catesby by deep personal affection. Rookwood had an unusually fine stud of horses ; Digby contributed heavily to the funds and arranged for a hunting party of his Catholic friends to meet at Dunchurch, near Rugby, to be ready for any emergency following on the fifth of November. It is not suggested that these friends were aware of the fantastic plans. After the arrest of Fawkes Catesby and his companions rode to Dunchurch, where the hunting party dispersed and the conspirators moved towards Wales. They went to Huddington in Worcestershire and then to Holbeach where some of them separated. At this house Catesby was attacked by the sheriff and killed with three of his companions. The others were captured either at Holbeach or elsewhere.

On 19 January, 1606 the government made an important capture which they linked up with the Plot. Fr. Henry Garnet, superior of the Jesuits in England and Fr. Edward Oldcorne and two laybrothers Ralph Ashby and Nicholas Owen were taken in the hiding-places at Hindlip, Mr. Abington's house in Worcestershire, which had long been the headquarters for the work of the Jesuits in the Midlands.

Altogether the names of four Jesuit priests were connected with the plotters. No evidence worth considering implicated the laybrothers. As to the others, Fr. John Gerard, S.J., a priest of great resource and common sense, had a wide assured knowledge of the principals and has never been supposed to have given any approval to the " practice." He left the country wearing the livery of one of the foreign ambassadors and was never embarrassed about the Plot. Fr. Edward Oldcorne, S.J., had worked for some years in Worcestershire and was a man of deeply apostolic spirit. He had great influence among the quiet loyal Catholic squires ; men like the Abingtons of Hindlip, the Talbots of Grafton, the Throckmortons of Coughton. His only offence was to offer shelter to his superior at Hindlip when the hunt was up and he suffered death for this generosity.[1] The case of Fr. Garnet was very difficult. Here we enter on more debatable ground, but it will be generally conceded

---

[1] Fr. Edward Oldcorne and the laybrothers, Nicholas Owen and Ralph Ashby were beatified by Pope Pius XI.

that Lingard is unduly harsh to him. He was only fifty, but harassed by a long period of superiorship. It seems that he was quick and sympathetic in his manner with an inner spiritual tranquillity. His position was affected by his close relationship to Fr. Parsons and was either strengthened or hampered according to the view taken of that priest's activity. It appears that in July 1605 Catesby had consulted a certain Fr. Tesimond under the seal of confession, but had given the latter leave to mention the plot in confession to Fr. Garnet should he so desire and empowered both priests to use their knowledge thus obtained, after the failure or the abandonment of the enterprise, if they should judge this expedient. In addition Fr. Garnet seems to have possessed a certain knowledge of the " practice " *in confuso.*

Deeply troubled in mind and disturbed at the rashness of the young Catholics, like Everard Digby and Ambrose Rookwood, Fr. Garnet seems to have endeavoured to save them. In October he was with Sir Everard at Gothurst ; on 29 October he removed to Coughton ; on 16 December he went to Hindlip. Here he was captured, taken to London, tried and executed for treason. At the trial he was accused of equivocation for which Lingard blames him. The general impression left upon the mind is that he was worried and made unhappy by the development of the disaffection, probably quick in his reactions, possibly imprudent and quite definitely an innocent man.

The case of Fr. Oswald Tesimond, S.J., is obscure and the following suggestion gives a favourable reading of his character. He had only returned to England about 1597 and had for some years taught philosophy in Sicily. He seems to have been a hearty and not clever Jesuit, very jovial and simple. He was of strong political opinions and a friend of Catesby. When the plotters were at Huddington Court during their flight he went to the house to hear their confessions and give them Communion ; the army chaplain standpoint. He was a big noisy man and escaped from England in a pig-boat.

Four of the conspirators had died at Holbeach and the surviving nine were executed, with the exception of Tresham who died in prison. He was commonly supposed to have written the letter to his brother-in-law Mounteagle. Northumberland was arrested, tried for misprision of treason and condemned to imprisonment for life. He suffered as the one man in high politics with whom any of these obscure country gentlemen had a definite connection. The Catholic peers Montague and Mordaunt were fined, although they were clearly ignorant of any design. Opposition from Northumberland was henceforth impossible, anti-Catholic animus developed and hatred of the Jesuits struck root. No one gained save the government whose prestige increased. It will probably always remain impossible to estimate Salisbury's share in the development of the plot. The whole plan was as fantastic as it was barbarous ; but Salisbury was faithful to the great maxims and how Machiavelli would have nurtured it.

Public feeling was inflamed and it was to the advantage of the government to translate this into terms of penal legislation. The character of the new Acts reflects the temper of the age and that cast of thought whose political elements derived from Salisbury and whose theological conceptions were contributed by the King. By an Act for the due execution of the Statutes against Jesuits, seminary priests, etc. (1 *Jac*. 1, c. 4) the existing penal laws had been confirmed in 1603. Now in 1606 came Acts for the better discovering and repressing of Popish Recusants and to prevent and avoid dangers which may grow by Popish Recusants (3 *Jac*. 1, cc. 4 and 5) by which a new oath of allegiance was enforced. Apart from the oath a fine of £10 was to be exacted monthly from all persons keeping servants who absented themselves from church, a measure aimed at the great body of Catholics in service throughout the country. The statute forbidding recusants to go more than five miles from their homes was confirmed and they were now prohibited from practising at the Bar, acting as attorneys or physicians, from executing trusts committed to them as executors of a will or acting as guardians to minors. Of more interest to the King was the new oath which might be offered to all recusants, not being noblemen or noblewomen. Refusal would involve the penalties of præmunire ; acceptance did not carry with it any alleviation. It seems probable that James I really felt that an oath had been framed which would serve to distinguish those Catholics who might have sympathy with conspiracy from the bulk of their co-religionists ; for he had little direct experience of England or of the currents of Catholic feeling in Europe and the deepest concern for high regalian theory. Salisbury must have possessed a more realist outlook, for in the oath, which was in the main unexceptionable, the Catholics were obliged to swear that the doctrine of the Pope's power of deposing princes was

" impious, heretical and damnable." Such phrases as these stuck in the gizzard.

The archpriest Blackwell at first gave out that he considered the oath permissible and then endeavoured to retract this opinion. In September 1606 Pope Paul V issued a Brief condemning the oath, an action which was expected and approved by the great majority of English priests. Blackwell refused to publish the Brief, took the oath and was deposed in 1608. Henry Birkhead, a Douai man who had served on the English mission for many years, succeeded him as archpriest of England and survived until 1614 when his place was taken by Dr. William Harrison, professor of theology at Douai, who worked for the restoration of normal episcopal government and remained the leader of the English Catholics until his death in 1621.

A minority of the laity, not very considerable in numbers, were prepared to accept the oath as it stood. Among these men Lord William Howard was the most influential. They represented that section of opinion which was manifest through the later seventeenth-century controversies and was to crystallize into the Cisalpine frame of mind. From the first they were unenthusiastic towards Rome, feeling that the Vatican had not made the necessary effort to understand the English problem. Their outlook on immediate ecclesiastical affairs was autocratic; they made sacrifices to maintain private chaplains and felt entitled strictly to limit the spheres on which priests should express an opinion. They abhorred " busy men " and, as a whole, cordially disliked the Jesuits. The Ignatian ideal had no appeal for them, but the Papacy was integral to their system of thought.[1]

At the same time the great majority of Catholics who objected to the oath were constantly exploring possibilities of a re-draft which would enable them to prove their loyalty without violating their consciences. The executions of priests began again in 1607 and continued[2] until the end of 1612, when they ceased for reasons of foreign policy. One secular priest was executed in 1618 and

[1] The presence of Marco Antonio de Dominis, Archbishop of Spalato in England between 1616 and 1622 does not seem to have had any effect upon the Catholics. He had quarrelled with the Holy See and was given the deanery of Windsor in 1617. Five years later he returned to Italy.

[2] Excluding those executed in connection with the Gunpowder Plot, seventeen priests, three Benedictines, a Jesuit and thirteen seculars were put to death during this reign and six laymen were hanged for relieving them or " persuading to Popery." Thirteen of these men have been beatified.

there was an outbreak in the spring and summer of 1616 when five executions took place including those of John Thules, a secular priest from Lancashire, and Roger Wrenno, a Chorley weaver who relieved him. With these exceptions the last thirteen years of the reign of James I, from 1612 till 1625, marked a relatively peaceful time for the Catholics. The King would sometimes harass families by removing their heirs to Protestant guardianship and on occasion show an unexpected tolerance.

In the country at large the division between the Catholics and the rest of their fellow-countrymen was widening. A proportion of the squires' families of the old religious tradition returned to a strict practice, but the children of the Elizabethan " Church Papists " who did not take this course were gradually assimilated to the full Anglican position. And the Puritan feeling against Rome was growing strongly with all the vitality of that doctrine which has always possessed a curious detached integrity and an unrivalled power of focusing animus. This horror of Rome, perhaps concentrated on the Jesuits, was also characteristic of wide Anglican circles and it seems indisputable that this sentiment was growing during the first forty years of the century.

In any discussion of Catholicism in England it is essential not to shirk the question of the profound unpopularity of the Jesuits. It is very difficult to explain it completely. The governmental propaganda, the mass of hostile legend, the false charges of equivocation, the efficiency of the Jesuit organization, the perjury of such witnesses as Titus Oates, the effect of Pascal's writings in educated circles, all these are admitted. The complete self-sacrifice of the Jesuits, the intense devotion with which they were regarded by their friends, their personal humility and magnificent corporate solidarity were always remarkable. How is it that they gained an unpopularity in non-Catholic England which the Benedictines, Dominicans and secular clergy have never shared ? In regard to the seventeenth century one small point may, perhaps, serve as an indication. The contemporary records give us for the first time an adequate picture of the entire English priesthood. We can see that while the old crusty testy Benedictine sat in his skull-cap over the fire in the chaplain's room making no bones about his dislikes, and the robust secular clergy quarrelled loudly, honestly and frankly, the Jesuit repressed his irritations. So much seems clear, but the further suggestion now made is purely tentative.

It certainly seems that the work of the greatest and most sympathetic fathers of the Society ought to have dispelled the prejudice. They have had very considerable success aided by the ease of their contacts and the power of wide movement which the resources of the Society gave them during four centuries. From the days of the first landing they have possessed men who were almost national figures. It does not seem that the causes of prejudices can be found in those leaders who possessed such wide charity and imagination. It might be possible to consider the matter along another line.

It will hardly be contested that a high standard of general education was provided for the Jesuit scholastics. But the ideal of a level of cultivated knowledge and the use of wide general information was kept in sight and attained through the channels of a certain uniformity of method. The mould of the training was European and attuned to the modern sixteenth-century world. The men of talent and perception and those of strong character drawn by the Ignatian ideals have always gained by this framework; but the docile and unimaginative characters have sometimes tended to give a stereotyped presentation which easily awakes distrust in their critics.

On the other hand the men of the old orders and the seculars had interests which were as purely spontaneous as their deep and haphazard loyalties. What prudence they had was merely developed common sense. They allowed their political views and prejudices to develop unhindered; they were not centralized, but tended to live with originality in oases of Catholicism. And at a rough guess it may be suggested that this last series of qualities fitted in with the general English body even in penal times.

During the last years of James I two other factors contributed to the unpopularity of Catholics, the King's plans for a Spanish marriage for his son Charles, Prince of Wales and the impression that men who were secret adherents of Catholicism were to be found in the high offices of State. The influence of the Spanish marriage question only lasted from 1613, when the project took shape on Gondomar's arrival in London as ambassador, until 1623 the year of its practical abandonment; but the rumours of concealed Catholicism continued to gather strength until the outbreak of the Civil War.

It is clear that the idea of the prestige of Spain and a marriage alliance with that royal house appealed powerfully to the high regalian outlook which King James sponsored. Several factors, however, made the plan unpopular in England, the manner of its execution, the way in which the Spanish Court demanded specific guarantees in regard to the treatment of English Catholics and the death of Sir Walter Raleigh, who was beheaded at the request of Spain after his attack on San Tomas and the failure of his expedition to the Orinoco. In these matters it was always a question not so much of popular opinion as of that public opinion which was vocal. Regarded in this restricted sense the popularity of the royal family seems to have centred upon Henry, Prince of Wales, who was supposed to sympathize with the Elizabethan and anti-Spanish tradition. He had died unmarried in 1612 and feeling had strengthened against his father's policy. Difficult as it is to assess the ideas of a distant age it appears that it was the apparent derogation of sovereignty involved in submission to Spanish *dictation*, in regard to Raleigh and the recusancy laws, which was at the basis of the opposition.

Again the anti-Spanish feeling led to an atmosphere of suspicion of the government and this was deepened when Sir George Calvert, who was one of the two secretaries of state from 1619 till 1625, resigned his office and declared himself a Catholic. Far from being disgraced he was soon raised to the peerage as Lord Baltimore and became in the next reign the founder of Maryland. Among other converts Sir Walter Aston, the ambassador in Spain, had the most substantial reputation and Lord Rutland the highest rank. But the court converts did not all attain to this respectable character and the Puritans could note with satisfaction that the neophytes included the young Lord de Ros, the heir of the Exeter line of the Cecils, who was involved in a political *cause célèbre*, and the beautiful Countess of Banbury, the heroine of many dubious adventures. And then, just when the Spanish marriage was passing over, the Catholics became involved in the increasing unpopularity which came to be associated with the Duke of Buckingham.

King James had always had favourites, but the Scots to whom he was attached in early manhood and maturity had little contact with Catholicism, although the last and greatest of them Robert Kerr, Earl of Somerset was dependent politically on that curious character Lord Northampton. But Northampton died in 1614 and the head of his family Thomas Howard, Earl of Arundel conformed to the Church of England in the following year so that the weight of the

Howard influence was again lost to Catholicism. In their place came Buckingham.

George Villiers, the new favourite, was a decided Anglican and sacramental in his outlook ; fresh ; ingenuous ; a mere boy ; dominated by the King. He married Lady Catherine Manners, a Catholic, and, urged by King James, insisted that she should accept Anglicanism. Lady Catherine suffered herself to be persuaded, remaining half-Catholic ; a large, fair, easy-going woman, lymphatic, devoted to her husband, on whose death she returned to her own religion. Prince Charles, who had at first been hostile to his father's favourite, became in time deeply attached to him and made him the sole confidant of his inhibited and solitary life. For ten years, until his murder at Portsmouth in 1628, Villiers who had become Earl, Marquess and finally Duke of Buckingham remained virtually the chief minister. And in this intimate family system of government the Catholic Church made inroads by conversion. Two of Buckingham's brothers, Lords Purbeck and Anglesey, and his mother Lady Buckingham became Catholics, not quietly but with noise and emphasis and when he was at the height of his power. Something of the unreal quality of the Court Catholicism at this period can be attributed to Lady Buckingham's influence ; the determined turbulent mother of the Shogun winning fitful exceptions and exemptions from the penal code proscribing a religion which was distasteful both to the sovereign and his minister. The opposition, who regarded Buckingham with hatred, particularly disliked[1] his mother's influence ; but away from the febrile atmosphere of the Court the great mass of the Catholics plodded on quietly bearing their burdens.

[1] An indication of this feeling is apparent in the verses on the Isle de Rhé expedition which are quoted by Rouse. " Could not thy mother's masses nor her crosses, Nor sorceries prevent those fatall losses." *Diary of John Rouse*, p. 20.

THE STUART BACKGROUND

IT IS PROBABLE that the most contented and peaceful period which the harassed Catholics were to enjoy between the outbreak of the Elizabethan repression and the last years of the eighteenth century was that space of a generation lasting from the middle of the reign of James I to the outbreak of the Civil War in 1642. Actually the eighteenth century was more placid and less burdened, but it was a dispirited autumnal peace. Under Charles I, in spite of exactions and hostility, there was a strong Catholic corporate life marked by the establishment and maintenance of religious houses of men and women abroad and colleges for ecclesiastical and secular studies.

To take a single instance of this development. The Flemish community of the Augustinian Canonesses Regular at St. Ursula's at Louvain had been governed from 1569 till 1612 by an English Prioress, Margaret Clement whose mother had been the ward and adopted daughter of St. Thomas More. In 1606 there were twenty-two English religious in this community and an English house, St. Monica's at Louvain was founded three years later. Houses of Augustinian Canonesses were founded at Bruges in 1629 and at Neuilly in 1633 ; the Canonesses of the Holy Sepulchre were established at Liège in 1642. A traveller in the first year of Charles I would find English houses of Poor Clares at Gravelines, Franciscans and Benedictines at Brussels and Carmelites at Antwerp.[1] There was no doubt of the vigour of the life, the generous support from England and the abundance of vocations. These later were found mainly among the daughters of the country gentry, who had the money for the journey and were sufficiently literate for the choir. There was a come-and-go of prosperous visitors in the convent parlours and a certain number of conversions. Travel to the Low Countries was a simple matter and, since the conclusion of peace, there were no longer unpatriotic implications in visits to the territory of the Archdukes. Thus, according to the Chronicle of St. Monica's, " Sir William Roper and his wife came into these parts (Louvain), that he might escape taking the oath and also be reconciled, for he

---

[1] All these religious houses are now represented by communities settled in England.

had gone to church." On the spiritual side this Catholic life in the Low Countries has left us the writings of Dame Gertrude More, who was one of the first religious to enter the new English Benedictine house at Cambrai on its foundation in 1623; while Douai and Cambrai were the scenes of a great part of the teachings and writings of Fr. Augustine Baker.

At the same time the religious life of the Catholics was not without its material vicissitudes and its bitter mounting controversy, and the way in which they managed to maintain such hearty animosity against a background of repression is very remarkable. As a body they have never been inclined to mince their words or to curb the free expression of opinion and, even in the lowered vitality of the eighteenth century, they achieved the most vigorous differences. No one could deny that the controversies were most regrettable, but they were very characteristic. A special difficulty attaches to the consideration of this subject in a general survey, for no considerable and detailed study of the controversies yet exists. In general the differences can be said to turn upon the question of church government. Until his death in 1594 Cardinal Allen had been the virtual leader of the English Catholics with the designation in 1581 of Prefect of the Mission. The ancient hierarchy had become extinct in 1585; the rule of the archpriests without an episcopal character lasted from 1598 until 1621; the appointment of Dr. William Bishop as vicar apostolic of England was made in 1623. This rule of vicars apostolic endured until 1851, but the situation was further complicated by the fact that between 1631, when Bishop Smith was compelled to go abroad, and 1685 when Bishop Leyburn was appointed there was no vicar apostolic in England.[1] During this period much influence was exercised by the Chapter which had been founded by Dr. Bishop in 1623 during the year of his brief episcopate. Originally he had divided England into seven vicariates, each under a vicar general, and nineteen archdeaconries with their appropriate officials. He added ten more priests to these twenty-six and in this way formed the Chapter.

The authority to institute and the wisdom of carrying out these arrangements was constantly in dispute. On the occasion of nearly every new development from the time of the nomination of the archpriest there was acrimonious conflict, recriminations, appeals

---

[1] Some illuminating data on this period has been published in the *Clergy Review*, by Fr. Philip Hughes.

and pamphleteering. Later accusations of Gallicanism were brought forward which were parried by charges of disloyalty ; nor was the situation eased by the appearance of Thomas Blacklow, a theologian of Gallican tendencies and considerable productivity. The Catholic life of the period suffered from all the difficulties inherent in a break-down of effective leadership ; a breakdown continued over half a century in an atmosphere of well-ventilated grievance. Inevitably the Jesuits and seculars tended to divide the sympathies of the laity. It was perhaps a fair statement of the case to say that the Jesuits received from that section of the laity to whom they ministered an unqualified support, and a deep respect for their powers of leader-ship in a country without an episcopate. There was little neutrality where they were concerned. There are writings of the secular clergy which are very bitter in their tone where the Society of Jesus is in question, still it seems improbable that this attitude was reflected among those wide clerical circles which were so fortunately un-interested in the acid of literary debate. The serious secular priests went forward working generously and wary of their rights.

One result of the lack of organization was a number of disedifying scenes in London, since the machinery was lacking for keeping the less-energetic clergy well employed. But a primary effect was the increase in importance of the isolated Catholic unit, the squire's house and its chaplain. It was a time of consolidation when country families which had tended to conform were ranging themselves definitely upon the Catholic side. The Tichbornes provide an excellent example of this tendency. In other cases the return was transient as at Stanton Harcourt where the family, which had been " Church Papist " under Elizabeth, came back to Catholicism for a generation before settling down into that Church-and-State religion with which it was to be so long associated in the public mind. South of Trent the doubt which had surrounded the religious affiliations of so many wealthy families cleared away and revealed a socially homogeneous Catholic body among the squires. The old faith was well represented among the holders of Stuart baronetcies, a revealing factor and, as far as post-Reformation times are con-cerned, there were many houses for whom the seventeenth century was to be their Catholic period.

In regard to the total number of Catholics it is impossible to make an estimate until the meaning of the term is defined more closely ; but it is worth referring to the figures given in a dispatch of

Gondomar's[1] who suggests that there were 300,000 recusants and 600,000 Catholics attending Protestant worship. Whatever may be said of his second figure, the first for the recusants is interesting. The solid character of great areas of Catholicism in the north was a permanent factor.[2]

[1] These figures are reproduced by Dr. Albion in *Charles I and the Court of Rome* where a careful study based upon the Barberini archives is made of the missions of Con and Panzani, which lie rather outside the scope of the present survey.

[2] At this point mention should be made of the work of Mary Ward. " In England itself," writes Mother Mary Paul, Provincial S.H.C.J., " one name bridges the gulf between the dissolution (of the monasteries) and the return of the exiles three centuries later. Mary Ward, born in 1585 of a northern recusant family, came overseas like many another to try her vocation in a Flanders convent, but with seemingly tragic unsuccess. Yet she was to be the first of many Foundresses to realize the possibilities of the Jesuit Rule adapted to the needs of women, and the work that might be done by a Congregation—unenclosed and centrally governed—sent out to challenge the world on its own tilting-ground. A striking and gallant figure in her " phantastical yellow ruff " she perilously crossed and re-crossed the narrow seas, mixed in social life, visited prisons, taught in town and village, established schools—short-lived because of their dangerous illegality—and gathered subjects to be trained in her houses abroad for the work of the English mission. Two early foundations of her Institute survived in England, one in Hammersmith and the other in York. Since its foundation in 1677 the Bar Convent, York, ' the pride, delight and rendezvous of the Catholics of the North,' has maintained its honourable tradition and in our own day has put forth fresh branches."

CATHOLICISM UNDER CHARLES I

WHEN CHARLES I came to the throne on 27 March, 1625 he was twenty-five years of age and betrothed to the Princess Henrietta Maria, the youngest sister of Louis XIII of France. He had at one time favoured the proposed marriage with the Spanish Infanta and had gone to Madrid with Buckingham to prosecute his suit. The journey had been a failure, the Prince of Wales had returned home opposed to Spain and somewhat resentful of Catholicism. He had now embarked on another Catholic alliance. In this case also assurances of toleration of English Catholics had been required by the French King and these ran counter to the promise given by the King in Parliament that the recusancy laws should not be relaxed. In addition the new Queen was permitted by the marriage treaty to bring over a great French household including an almoner, the Bishop of Mende and twenty-seven priests. If this last provision seems altogether excessive the reason is, perhaps, to be found in the rarity of mixed marriages in the royal houses ; the technique of negotiating marriages between Catholics and Protestants in the royal circle had yet to be acquired.

In June 1625 the Queen, who had been married by proxy in Paris, landed at Dover and a period of difficulty set in. The promises of toleration could not be kept, the French household caused embarrassment and was eventually in great part dismissed. Even so the Queen was allowed to retain twelve Catholic chaplains according to an agreement negotiated by the French ambassador Bassompierre. Her relations with the King, which were at first stormy, became very close after Buckingham's murder in 1628 and two years later she received eight Cupuchin priests from France who henceforward supplied her Masses.

King Charles' point of view was clear. The sacramental Anglicanism in which he had been brought up satisfied him completely ; but the assurance of his religious standpoint assisted him to show a cool and dignified forbearance towards the adherents of the old religion. A certain moral fastidiousness, which his father lacked, perhaps led him to refrain from interfering in the concerns of gentlemen. The custom of taking minors of rank from their Catholic guardians and handing them over to the Archbishop of Canterbury now ceased. At the same time the King was anxious that his personal attendants should frequent the Anglican Communion and he showed favour to lapsed Catholics like the young Lord Caernarvon. Beyond this he did not go. It is not surprising that the recusants should have proved themselves grateful.

Again, with the removal of Buckingham, the aggressive foreign policy in favour of the Calvinists in France, which the Duke had supported in the last two years of his life, collapsed very quickly. With the death of his friend King Charles' reticence deepened and he remained without an intimate friendship. No man ever replaced Buckingham and it was one of the difficulties of the situation that Charles I found it hard to give his complete trust without affection. At the same time the officially friendly terms on which the King remained with foreign powers did not fail to benefit the recusants[1] and in general throughout the seventeenth century they had more ease when the country was at peace.

In this second period of the reign the Queen's influence increased and the King grew devoted to her and curiously dependent on her judgment. The Van Dyck portraits enable us so easily to picture Henrietta Maria, slight and very graceful with her delicate features, the dark vivacious eyes, the chestnut hair. Her petulance and gaiety are clearly shown in the early paintings. She was quick-thinking and imprudent, indiscreet in her confidences, devoted to the play, childish at times yet half-sophisticated, always preferring London to the country. It is no wonder that she was never popular in England. Her religion was sincere, in some ways perhaps a little superficial ; her outlook and thought wholly French, and for the first eight years of her reign her spoken English was very poor. She was comprehensible and, in fact, attractive to the court gallants, but infinitely remote from the Catholic squires in the country. And, if remote from the Catholics, she had still less in common with the Protestant country gentry of the shires.

The Queen with her private chapel in St. James' was the focus around which new liberties and a mitigated court favour for the old religion could develop. She was a rallying-point for the influences

---

[1] There were only two executions between 1625 and 1641, those of B. Edmund Arrowsmith and B. Richard Hirst carried out at the instigation of Parliament.

making for toleration; but she was in no way responsible for the slight but very genuine movement towards Catholicism which this freedom encouraged.

Inevitably converts appeared in her own immediate circle, the most notable being the diplomat Walter Montagu and the Queen's friend Lady Denbigh, who was Buckingham's sister and was to be Crashaw's patron. In the course of time Catholic chapels were built in Somerset House and St. James' and in the one country palace which she cared for, Woodstock. To balance this there attached to the foreign " popish " Queen a great burden of un-popularity, which was to break out all the more forcibly later as a result of fourteen years' suppression. Faced by this intensifi-cation of hostility it was an error on the part of Charles I to permit the exploratory missions of Con and Panzani, who were sent from Rome and accredited to the Queen. For it was just the compara-tive outward success of the Catholic cause during these years which brought its dangers. Slight as was the movement towards the Church, which was encouraged by the King's passivity and the Queen's zeal, its influence was most marked in those circles which the country gentry, the peers and merchants of the opposition already regarded with grave suspicion. A consideration of some of the more distinguished converts will serve to emphasize this point.

Lord Weston of Neyland, who had become Lord Treasurer in 1628, was practically the chief minister for the seven years after Buckingham's assassination and received such marks of favour, the Garter and the earldom of Portland, as the King was prepared to bestow in the years following the loss of his friend. He was a heavy man; prudent in financial matters; extravagant in an ungenial fashion; married to a Catholic. It was a misfortune for the Church that he was long regarded as a masked Catholic and confirmed this opinion by being reconciled by a priest in his last illness. The case of Lord Cottington was rather similar, that of a man of cosmopolitan experience and cultivated tastes, subtle and exact in thought, deeply attracted by Catholicism. He had, indeed, been received into the Church in Spain, but had not persisted in so rash a line of action and was at this time an Anglican with nostalgic Roman leanings. He, too, was to die a Catholic. Finally Sir Francis Windebank, who was one of the secretaries of state from 1632 till 1640, although a definite Anglican of Laudian principles seems to have shared these sympathies. In his case this religious attitude was inspired by a hope for that reunion of the Churches which his friends hardly regarded as a question of actuality. Such a position in a way appeared even more detestable to Puritan opinion and like the others it was the prelude to a deathbed conversion. The actions of three ministers may not appear to have any great significance ; but this was the flame within the smoke of legend regarding a government turning to Popery.

Such substantial men were naturally quite uninfluenced by the Queen and her *entourage* ; they were alien to her frivolous circle ; Portland was hostile to her. At the same time these Romeward sympathies of the ministers were not the result of any interest in this subject on the part of Charles I but rather of his apathy. He enjoyed surface theological discussion and supported Archbishop Laud's churchmanship ; for the rest he was reticent and uninterested. The Catholicism of the court circle and of his wife's friends repelled him by its exotic quality, which was particularly notable in the last years before the Civil Wars. As the opposition to the Queen began to consolidate she made less efforts to conciliate, became more foreign. In spite of the excellent English conversation of her middle years, few queen-consorts have re-absorbed so completely the atmosphere of their native country. There was a quickness of apprehension about her convert friends like Mrs. Porter, a French background to the religion of the Stuarts d'Aubigny and a general atmosphere of swift conversions and secret popish marriages which served to disturb profoundly the Protestant mind.

The Catholicism of the Court was, however, hardly less remote from that of the settled families of the old religion throughout the country. The way in which the Catholic tradition survived without leadership is indeed one of the more remarkable facts of seventeenth-century life. For two generations there was no recognized ecclesiastical leader ; the Court was a source of protection, but hardly of confidence or inspiration ; there was in a sense no single outstanding layman. It was a curiously and even ominously peaceful time into which such adherents of the old faith as Inigo Jones and the playwright Philip Massinger and Sir John Beaumont, the poet, had survived. Into this England came Sir Anthony Van Dyck from his devout home in Antwerp and with his strong Catholic associations and here his religious outlook took on the utilitarian character of his later years. A certain mannered fashion of approach cut off the Court from the nation and this is suggested in the writings of William Habington, especially the *Queene of Arragon*. The light, quick, allusive quality of Queen Henrietta's court is again reflected by the same writer.

> " So rich with jewels hung, that night
> Doth like an Ethiop bride appear."

Ethiop brides were the very last thing in which the Catholic gentlemen could be expected to display an interest and one can almost see them turning to the fireside seat and the ale.

Still protection ensured peace and the years 1638–9 seem to have been the peak period of a prosperity and established quiet which the Catholics would not experience again until two centuries later. It was a time of security very different from the abrupt swing of the pendulum in the reign of James II. Sharing in the good returns which the landed gentry then received the recusants were able to offset in some measure the heavy damage of the fines. Secessions among the wealthier classes ceased ; the strain under which the Catholic body laboured had lifted.

In Monmouthshire Catholicism now found open support in the Marquess of Worcester and the administration dependent upon Raglan Castle, while in Hampshire the come-and-go of Lord Winchester's chaplains made a centre for the old religion in the Caroline grandeur of Basing House. This peace among so many calming effects enabled Fr. Augustine Baker, now again in England, to compose his works of spirituality against a settled background. Priests representing such different schools as the Welsh courtier Sir Tobie Mathew and the Benedictine Dom Leander à Sancto Martino had both prospered in the reign. The great Jesuit college at St. Omer had nearly two hundred lay pupils, the secular college at Douai was going well, as was the smaller Benedictine foundation. As far as vocations to the religious state and to the priesthood are concerned the houses and colleges abroad were for the most part full and in a good condition. The means of their continuance, that steady supply of recruits and regularly paid donations came out to them unfailingly from the Catholic farms and manor houses. In the south of England the old tradition might continue to weaken, but this was hardly perceptible so gradual was the withdrawal. At the same time even the opposition against the King did not at first seem specifically anti-Catholic, since the questions turned on the economic grievance, Ship Money, the political actions of Strafford and Archbishop Laud's ecclesiastical policy. But, after 1641, when the coming struggle had been defined there was to be no further peace.

THE CIVIL WARS

ON 22 AUGUST, 1642, King Charles I raised his standard at Nottingham and the Civil War against the adherents of the Parliament in London had begun. The immediate effect was to make the Catholics and their loyalty conspicuous; the ultimate result was a further movement towards the disintegration of English Catholicism. There was never the least doubt as to the side upon which the men of the old faith would be found; they were inevitably detached from the actions of a House of Commons from which they were debarred; both sections of the opposition to the royal policy were equally hostile to them. Neither the moderate Parliamentarians, nor the later stronger party with which Cromwell was identified had any really friendly contacts with the Catholic community. The significance of the Court diminished and the King appeared as a symbol around whom the forces of tradition rallied with the Catholics as among the most generous and faithful, but, inevitably in the seventeenth century, the least rewarded of his followers.

Even before the opening of the struggle the executions had recommenced under the pressure of the Puritan party in the Long Parliament. But there was, however, a notable contrast between the eleven priests who suffered in 1641-2[1] and the young eager Elizabethans who were condemned in the sixteenth-century persecutions. The Caroline martyrs were for the most part experienced missioners with a lifetime of pastoral work in England behind them. Some, like Dom Alban Roe and the secular priest, John Lockwood, were well past seventy; even those in middle age, like Dom Ambrose Barlow, had completed nearly a quarter of a century on the English Mission. They had lived quietly and laboriously without concealment. None had any direct contact with the Court; some had suffered terms of imprisonment; all were well known to the authorities who had suddenly descended upon them. Jesuits,

[1] Among those put to death in 1641-2 the following were beatified by Pope Pius XI in 1929, the Benedictines Dom Ambrose Barlow and Alban Roe, the Jesuit Fr. Thomas Holland and the secular priests William Ward, Thomas Reynolds, John Lockwood, Edward Catherick and Hugh Green.

priests and seminarists had been banished under penalty of death
by a royal proclamation forced through by the Parliament in 1640.
There was no charge of political activity and the eleven suffered in
each case for their priesthood.

Curiously enough the number of executions for religion decreased
during the progress of the war, two priests suffering death in each
year from 1643 to 1645 and four dying in 1646.[1] This is explained
to some extent by the fact that no such prosecutions took place in
the area controlled by the King after he had broken with the Parliamentarian leaders. At the same time the danger of an intensive
search by the Puritan authorities, the fact that the Catholic gentry
and yeomen were concentrated in the royalist armies and the small
number of Catholics in the eastern counties led to a certain temporary concentration of priests within the zone of the King's influence. Throughout the struggle London was the one centre,
where a large number of the old faith were grouped, which was
always in the hands of the Parliament. In this connection mention
should be made of Robert Apreece of Washingley, a small landowner
in Huntingdonshire who was shot by the Puritan troopers as a
Catholic. Among all those opposed to them the Puritans were
convinced that the Papists alone fully deserved the name
" Malignant."

During the first eighteen months of the war, the period between
the battles of Edgehill and Marston Moor, it certainly appeared that
the royalists and with them all the King's Catholic subjects might
triumph. The defence of Wardour Castle by Lady Blanche Arundell
and William Blundell's campaigning indicate how deeply this
struggle stirred the quiet life of the recusant squires throughout the
country. Their richer co-religionists poured out their fortunes, the
lesser men were found in every garrison and Catholics, for once,
rose to high command as in the cases of Aston, Gage, Bellasis,
Widdrington and Langdale. These leaders were all come from the
hereditary Catholic families, some of recusant stock, others from
that section in which the old religious tradition had revived with the
long peace. They were zealous, over-courageous sometimes, fertile
in suggestion. Thus Glamorgan proposed to send for Irish aid.
None of these men, with the exception of Langdale, were in the

---

[1] The *beati* of 1929 included the following victims of the prosecutions of 1643–6,
the Benedictine Philip Powel, the Jesuits Fr. Ralph Corby and Fr. Henry Morse and
the secular priest John Duckett.

strict sense courtiers and his contacts were not with the Queen's circle.

Lord Glamorgan, the eldest son of the Marquess of Worcester, was a country peer, remote from the Court, the heir to Raglan, with a scientific and literary bent, deeply attached to the Jesuits. As a man of science, the potential inventor of the steam engine, he stood outside all categories. His meteor presence in the royalist conflict serves to emphasize the way in which every Catholic in England was drawn into the active service of the Cavaliers. Still there remained an impassable gulf between the country gentlemen turned soldiers and the cultivated and frivolous courtiers of their faith.

The time of tranquillity for the old religion was ended by the outbreak of the war, but the Court at Oxford, the King's head-quarters from 1643 till 1646, reflected as in a broken mirror the interrupted life of that royal circle whose slightly affected and careful dignity has been preserved by Van Dyck's brush. The Queen at Merton was still the centre of a ring of courtiers, herself more anxious, considerably more religious, but no less indiscreet. Clarendon has recorded that there were many Catholics in Oxford at that time, including two successive governors of the city. The Parliamentarian armies lay to the eastward; but to the south in Hampshire, as a last symbol of that passing order, stood the royalist stronghold, Basing House.

After the King's defeat at Naseby Oxford became untenable and the politico-religious system of Charles I was doomed. Not long before Basing House had been stormed and Lord Winchester taken. The Puritan troopers breaking in found ten priests sheltering and a richly furnished chapel and in the gallery the motto *Aimez Loyauté* cut with diamonds on the window-panes. The conjunction at that time and place would seem almost inevitable. It marked in a sense, as far as the Catholics were concerned, the end of an epoch.

The King went into captivity and to his death; the Queen crossed to France and directed the royalist exiles from her apartments in the Louvre. Around her gathered the more devoted survivors of the defeated cause, men for the most part politically inexperienced, some extravagant, others lacking in balance, nearly all disillusioned. The bizarre tone, which marked this gathering, was apparent in the actions of the Queen's Chancellor Sir Kenelm Digby, son of Sir Everard Digby of the Gunpowder Plot. As a Catholic he was an enthusiast and seldom quite orthodox; vehement in his love affairs;

D

addicted to alchemy ; a great fighter, quick-brained at intrigue ; altogether a character by far too volatile for English life.

Among these exiles a movement towards the Church was manifest and affected both the military men and the literary-clerical coterie. From the first section two men stand out from the other converts ; Lord Goring, a cavalry leader and an intimate friend of the Queen, who ended his life in Spain as a Dominican and the picturesque adventurer Bellomont. The other group of new Catholics had greater significance.

It appears to be a fact that the Laudian ideal was singularly impervious to the assaults of Rome. It was profoundly Anglican, ordered, sacramentalist and national : it went well with a patriotic motive, with the love of the countryside and that care for the material fabric of the parish churches and the associations of the Prayer Book. Bishop Andrewes with his sober Anglican devotion had inspired them. In view of this situation it is a tenable hypothesis that the converts from Laudian Anglicanism during the conflict had not moved, as is sometimes suggested, by an inevitable progression along the path to Rome, but were drawn by the idea of order which they held to be existing in Rome alone after the destruction of the King. This explanation would serve to account for the brief period over which the conversions actually took place.

The most considerable figure among those who submitted to the Catholic Church was Godfrey Goodman, Bishop of Gloucester, an aged prelate who had lived through the earlier period as an advanced sacramental High Churchman. Other clergy of standing included Dr. Thomas Bayly of Wells and that Dean of Leighlin known to the literature of spirituality as Serenus Cressy. Laymen who had been Catholics earlier, like Sir William D'Avenant the laureate, moved on the fringes of the royalist circle centred[1] on Paris. A few passed forward to Italy. Thus Richard Crashaw, the poet, had forsaken the Cambridge Laudian background of Peterhouse for a minor canonry at Loreto. Remembering Bayly in Cardinal Ottoboni's household and Crashaw with Cardinal Pallotta it would seem as if every post-Reformation age had brought its tribute to the Curia. But such influences could not be lasting ; the converts were impoverished proscribed exiles and Serenus Cressy was the one fairly prominent

---

[1] The Journal of Sir John Finch for 1651 indicates these Parisian contrasts. " I was acquainted," he wrote, " with Sir K. D(igby) who lodged in the Colledg of Bon Cœur. He lived in Paris like an anchorite in a long gray coat accompanied with a great English masty and his beard down to the middle," Cal. Finch MSS., p. 64.

figure to survive through the Commonwealth. The fantastic Lord Bellomont died in India in a sandstorm on the road to Delhi going as a royalist envoy to the Great Moghul; but all this new Catholicism of the vanished Court was in fact poured out upon the sand.

.   .   .   .   .   .

After the close identification of English Catholicism with the royal cause it is not surprising that the period of Cromwell's rule in England was marked by severity. Perhaps the Catholic body had put too much ardour into politics ; certainly they were exhausted and had few outstanding leaders. The spur of martyrdom hardly existed,[1] but the Catholics suffered doubly as royalists and recusants. They had no layman of character who could influence the victorious side in their favour, for the Puritan leaders were for the most part wholly Protestant in their connections and generally without even a vague Catholic friendship.[2] Cromwell was notably innocent of even the remotest friendly contact and although the Protector's youngest daughter Mary married a lapsed Catholic, Lord Fauconberg, it was a necessary preliminary that he should purge himself by the profession of a sedulous attachment to the Protestant religion.

[1] Two *beati* belong to this period, one of whom John Southworth is very familiar to modern Catholics through the preservation of his relics in Westminster Cathedral.

[2] Nevertheless they were not inactive. " I know," declared Mr. Butler on 29 May, 1657, " where they (the Papists) have increased one hundred in a year in one or two parishes . . . . Will you suffer the limbs of Anti-Christ to grow rich within your bowels." *Parliamentary Diary of Thomas Burton*, ii, p. 153.

THE CATHOLIC SQUIREARCHY

THE RESTORATION IN 1660 brought unalloyed relief to the Catholics, since for the moment the nature of the compromise to which Charles II had submitted was not apparent, nor the strength of the anti-Catholic feeling. It was merely obvious that their side was victorious and few had greater claims on the King than the Marquesses of Winchester and Worcester; but throughout the penal times no sovereign would give the final reward of a dukedom to a Catholic. Nevertheless even secure re-establishment would have seemed a great benefit and the influence of the Catholic landed interest might still appear strong. The privileged position of the peerage was never more firmly buttressed than in the century which followed the Restoration. Even if the House of Commons was closed to recusants, they could still frequent the Court and peers could take their seats in Parliament.

Meanwhile, if there were few rewards, there was a certain amount of restitution. In North America Maryland was restored to its Catholic lord proprietor, Baltimore, and the dukedom of Norfolk was given back to the Howards. This family had now regained its place of leadership; but personal accidents had impaired the Howard influence in politics. The fifth Duke of Norfolk, who had been restored in 1661 and survived till 1677, was insane and the leadership of his family passed to Evelyn's patron, Lord Henry Howard; honest; rather stupid; rough mannered. It was a severe misfortune in an era of personal government that the Catholic leader should on these three points be the antithesis of the sovereign whose confidence and intimacy he never gained. In the background were Lord Henry's uncle, Lord Stafford and his brother Philip Howard the Dominican and their cousin Lord Berkshire, an elderly convert Cavalier.

In the Midlands the squires of the old faith looked on Lord Shrewsbury as their leader; a young man; weak; married unhappily; a generous devout nonentity; killed in a duel in 1678 by Buckingham, his wife's lover. Absence of leadership: this defect in the organization of the recusants appears time and again in the seventeenth and eighteenth centuries. Possibly as one consequence of this disadvantage the Catholics are seen as curiously remote from contact with the government. For instance, neither Shrewsbury, nor Stafford could help them to test the feeling in the Commons or the changing trend of the King's policy.

Thus in the situation under the Stuart rule two very curious factors are discernible. On the one hand the general Catholic body lived without any contact with the court circle, although unthinkingly and pathetically loyal to the sovereign. On the other hand this royal entourage, separated as it was from the recusant squires, was itself amenable to Catholic influences of another order ; an influence often foreign in its emphasis, exotic in expression, seldom if ever rooted in English feeling. In so brief a sketch this point can only be made tentatively and with hesitation. The general argument runs as follows. During the period from 1625 till 1688 there were two movements connected with Catholicism in England, that in the community at large and that in the special circle of the Court. This chapter deals with the former section. Considered as a whole the Catholic body was primarily agricultural in its pursuits, depending chiefly upon a still substantial landed interest which was centred upon isolated manors in the southern counties and upon strong groups of squires and lesser gentry and freeholders scattered across the faithful north. Certain urban elements were closely bound up with them. Some Catholics were to be found in commerce, principally in the wool and cloth trades ; while there was a proportion among the wine merchants, a class to a great extent supported by and sometimes recruited from the landed gentry. Conveyancers and men of business of the old faith were found in London and the greater towns. The political complexion of nearly all these men was royalist ; then after the Restoration high Cavalier ; finally high Tory. As the history of the Blundells of Crosby emphasizes, the more prosperous element became in time united by a criss-cross of marriage ties. Debarred from membership of the Commons and from the offices of justice of the peace and sheriff, they played their full part in social gatherings and in sport. Some, educated at Douai or St. Omer, had acquired a mental background very different from that of their friends who had gone up to Cambridge or Oxford ; but the great majority, even among the gentry, stayed in England and were obliged through lack of means to content themselves with that rustic education which they shared with their less prosperous Protestant neighbours.

Still such matters were of small importance in comparison with the one great disadvantage from which the Catholics suffered. The exaction of the fines was intermittent, but the unemployment was continual. The military rank of the Civil Wars was the sole recognition that the recusants could receive. They had no further apportunity for service. This, undoubtedly, was their greatest permanent difficulty ; the deadening of initiative, the complete inaction forced upon their sons. It was a gradual atrophy. There was still some employment for the fortunate under Charles II, but it would soon end completely. At the moment, however, this miserable outcome was not yet in sight. Dignities, but not posts, were still bestowed and these titular distinctions served to mask the situation.

At the same time differences of this kind did not affect the homogeneity of the Catholic group. Thus a number of the greater squires held baronetcies imposed on the wealthy landlords by the early Stuarts and a few of the richest recusants were peers, like Dunbar at Burton Constable, Aston at Tixall, Brudenell at Dene. But during these Restoration years all the prosperous Catholics were being welded into one consistent society, markedly rural in its tone. To keep a chaplain was a common experience, to possess a town house in London was very rare.

No description would be in any way adequate which did not refer to the religious organization. The Orders, in particular the Jesuits, the Dominicans and the Benedictines, had now staked out their claims and their system of government was fully developed. The administration of the Jesuit Province was notable for a competent smoothness in working and in certain families a strong hereditary attachment to the Society had been formed. The seventeenth-century writings of Benedictine spirituality were now in vogue and Father Cressy's version of Augustine Baker's *Sancta Sophia* had been printed. The regulars and seculars together supplied the needs of the countrysides and the priests' position would often approximate to that of domestic resident chaplains. In these cases the duties of tutorship fell on them, while among the rich families they had a definite place in the household tacitly acknowledged even by Protestants.

It was perhaps due to the chaplains' persuasions that these squires would so often marry within their own religious communion and when arranged marriages were common this detail presented small difficulty. In the south the poorer recusants who could not go far afield for a bride found it difficult to follow their masters' example, but in the north the presence of a considerable proportion of Catholics among the yeomen farmers and their labourers made purely Catholic marriages frequent. It is not hard to imagine that these factors made the general situation seem safe and, in fact, bound to improve. As far as the squires and their tenants were concerned it may have appeared that a state of equilibrium had been achieved with the Restoration. Such a belief was perfectly possible to those who did not realize the strength of anti-papal sentiment and the fatal character of the King.

One fact is noteworthy in regard to the leading Catholics ; they belonged to the elder band of Cavaliers. For thirty years the recusant opinion was reflected by men whose active public service had been closed on the final defeat of Charles I. It was this genera-tion which guided their community in the Restoration period, suffered in the persecution of the Popish Plot and survived under James II to be the neglected Elder Statesmen. Such affinities as they possessed with the government linked them to the old staid official Anglicanism represented by Clarendon, who was chief minister from 1660 till 1667, and to the older re-established Cavaliers. The King had a Catholic tendency with which they had no contact. The survivors of his mother's Court, the polished witty French-minded priests, like the Abbé Montagu or Lord Charles Stuart d' Aubigny (who would have been a cardinal had he lived), had little save a common faith to link them to the slow-moving English squires. In these early years only one lay recusant had been within the King's close circle, John Digby second Earl of Bristol, who had been a secretary of state in exile. This man combined with great talent and ill-controlled imagination that touch of the fantastic which marked the Digbys. During the Commonwealth he had become a Catholic in Brussels, holding to religion, as to all else, with a difference ; quick in thought, punctilious in conduct, enigmatic. There is some colour for the suggestion that he subsequently repented of his Catholicism, but was held back by his pride from a second change. He certainly acted at times against his co-religionists ; he was impatient and they distrustful.

These preliminaries will serve to introduce the question of the religious attitude of Charles II. Save for his death as a professed

Catholic, all that concerns the King's beliefs is an enigma ; probably incapable of solution.   Baptized by Archbishop Laud, he had been brought up as an Anglican, a position which was presumably re-inforced by his father's attachment to the Church of England and by his dying admonitions.   Two years later in the escape from Worcester, after his attempt to recover his father's throne had failed, Charles II's life was saved by Catholic royalists.   The King's gratitude was enduring and was especially marked in the case of Fr. John Huddleston, a Benedictine who had helped to conceal him. On the other hand in the years of exile, between 1651 and 1660, Charles II was undoubtedly opposed to Queen Henrietta's crude attempts to force her younger sons to accept Catholicism and he was permanently alienated by the pietism with which her religion was presented.   It is, however, suggested that it was during this period that the King found his own very different way towards the Church. The date and extent of any such change of attitude remains con-jectural.   Certainly he was already a confirmed sensualist, an im-portant factor.   It is possible that, since he did not intend to live as a practising Catholic, he may have put the whole subject from him. He was not studious, his interests were scientific, his zest was for horse-racing, his quick mind unusually coarse.   In politics his instincts were reliable and sharpened by cynicism.   He could see that open Catholicism seemed incompatible with secure English sovereignty.   A strong common sense made him popular in England and may have helped him to postpone a solution.   His own astuteness gave him pleasure, perhaps a legacy of his Medicean blood.   Determined not to alienate the heavy Cavalier opinion it is remarkable how much he managed to conceal from such chief ministers as Clarendon and Danby.   The desire to conciliate this Church-and-State opinion is probably responsible for his uncon-ditional assent to the measures of anti-Catholic legislation.   Where another man might have opposed, Charles II would try to circum-vent ; but it was characteristic of him that he did not try very hard. Thus he never managed to carry out the promise of toleration contained in the Declaration of Breda, which was made on the eve of his return to England, and the tentative move of the first Declara-tion of Indulgence in favour of religious dissidents had small result. On the other hand the Parliament and his ministers imposed on him the Five Mile and Conventicle Acts, which hindered the movement of recusants and forbade private assemblies for worship.   In these early years such Catholic preferences as the King had acquired were hardly perceptible. Throughout his reign public opinion never conceived that His Majesty's own sympathies might be Catholic: attention was concentrated upon the adherents of the old religion by whom in time he came to be surrounded.

THE RESTORATION CATHOLICS

CATHOLICISM IN ENGLAND had long suffered from its enemies, and it was now to suffer from its friends. It is impossible to grasp some of the reasons for the hardening of Anglican opinion, for the mass credulity of the Popish Plot and for the later bitterness towards the Church without considering the actions of Charles II. That sovereign was already past thirty at his accession and his public attitude towards religion was remarkably consistent, a strong dignified attachment to the Anglican Church on account of which he had resisted his mother's attempts to induce him to turn Catholic. Yet all the time an inner circle was aware of the King's attraction towards Catholic doctrine. This may have accounted for the fact that some of his intimates of disreputable character had, perhaps imprudently, accepted Catholicism. But, if the nation at large manifested an almost hectic attachment to the sovereign, there was no readiness to concede approval to his dissolute friends. The nominal but in some cases ostentatious Catholicism of such royal favourites as the Duchesses of Cleveland, Portsmouth and Mazarin seemed hardly a recommendation ; nor did the conversion of the keeper of the royal closet, Chiffinch, nor that of the companion of the King's pleasures young Harry Jermyn. The dramatist Wycherley only emphasized very clearly the raffish character of some Catholics at the Restoration Court.

At the same time the foreign Catholic influence had not diminished ; while the talk of the new coffee-houses magnified every instance and was retailed in remote counties by the homecoming Protestant squire. The Queen-Mother, Henrietta had come over to England before settling finally at Colombe in her own country. Her interests were now concentrated on religion and in particular on the establishment of the Capuchins, who served her palace chapel, as a missionary element in the English capital. Then in 1662 Charles II had himself married the Catholic Princess of Portugal. Catherine of Braganza, as the Infanta was generally known, had a grant of religious privileges similar to those accorded to her mother-in-law. In this case, however, many circumstances combined to render her influence on the fortunes of English Catholicism very slight. She never evoked the hostility which Queen Henrietta had aroused, nor any devotion. On the political side the marriage, which brought an immense dowry and the possession of Tangier and Bombay, was almost popular. As far as the personal equation was concerned, the development of the new Queen's influence was nullified by a slowness in learning English, an ignorance of French, a complete innocence of politics in which she had not been trained and a certain archaic and perhaps faintly ludicrous personal dignity, heightened by the wide Portuguese dresses and the black curl trained across her forehead above her wide too-childlike eyes. She was old for a marriageable princess and her physical attractions soon vanished; her short stature was emphasized by the stoutness which developed early; her complexion became sallow. In all ways she was very southern; for her race had no admixture of blood save Portuguese and Spanish. Finally she was barren and she failed to hold the King. It was from another direction that the real influence of Catholicism on the King's policy was to come.

In a sense the Stuarts were never to free themselves from the effects of the marriage of Charles I and Henrietta Maria. Quite apart from religion the French strain in Charles II made his outlook very different to that even of his closest English advisers. His wit, his attitude to Parliament, his approach to moral questions, his sympathetic understanding of King Louis XIV; all these facts bear out this point. The personality of the *Grand Monarque* acted by attraction upon the Stuarts and by repulsion upon the English governing class, for the seventeenth-century squires were nothing if not insular. They feared the French Alliance and regarded the French polity uncomprehendingly but with alarm. And in time this detestation of the Bourbon absolutism was coloured by a righteously moral and religious feeling which became more intense after 1685, when the Edict of Nantes was revoked by King Louis and the secure position accorded to the Huguenots by Henry IV was destroyed. It was widely and in many circles genuinely believed that a Catholic sovereign in England would in time persecute Protestants.

There were clear signs of that identification of the French with the Catholic interest which had coloured the public mind since Henrietta Maria had first landed in England. Those who were familiar with the inner movements of foreign policy attributed significance to the role of King Charles' younger·sister, the Duchess of Orleans who was torrentially vivacious, witty, French in her whole outlook, ardently and sophisticatedly Catholic.   For the last years before her death in 1670 she certainly seems to have possessed an intermittent but unapproachable sway over her brother.   Again, the Duchess of Richmond, *La Belle Stuart* with whom the King was infatuated so deeply, while quite unremarkable intellectually, was profoundly French in her rather flowery Catholicism and in her whole mental background. Meanwhile the secret Treaty of Dover between Charles II and Louis XIV, with its clauses for financial aid and for King Charles' declaration as a Catholic, was carried through by Arlington and Clifford, ministers of very different character but both secret in their preference for the old faith. Nevertheless neither these half-concealed policies, nor the Queen's presence were responsible for the outbreak against Catholics. By far the most important event of the reign, from this point of view, was the reception into the Catholic Church of the heir-presumptive to the throne, the King's brother, the Duke of York.

BACKGROUND TO THE POPISH PLOT

IT was characteristic of the ill judgment of the prince, who was afterwards to ascend the throne as James II, that he should centre upon himself so much hostility in connection with his change of religious allegiance. A stiff man, humourless, hard to persuade, the Duke of York was thirty-seven before disquieting rumours of his Catholic tendencies were spread abroad. He had been born in 1633 and had held the office of Lord High Admiral since the Restoration. In 1665 he had won the victory of Solebay, and as a naval commander showed courage untempered by imagination. His administration indicated tenacity, loyalty to his subordinates and a certain lack of foresight. In 1660 he had married Anne Hyde, the daughter of Lord Chancellor Clarendon, and had two surviving children, the princesses Mary and Anne who were subsequently to reign as queens. The Duchess was stout, lethargic and extravagant, with a direct simplicity of outlook which was attractive to her husband. She became a Catholic secretly in the summer of 1670 and this conversion was made public a few months later when she was anointed by a Franciscan on her deathbed in March 1671. Few doubted that this change of faith had the Duke's sympathy and when the question of a second marriage arose he insisted that his bride should be a Catholic. Negotiations were set on foot for a marriage with the Archduchess Claudia Felicitas through the medium of an Anglicized Italian soldier of fortune, Sir Bernard Gascoigne, formerly Guasconi, who was at that time English envoy in Vienna. This project failed to materialize and a search was made for eligible princesses. Finally, in 1673, the Duke was married by proxy to the Princess Mary Beatrice of Modena. The rumour of these plans and of their completion percolated through the English country houses and the embittered feelings of the anti-Catholic squires were reflected in the protests in the Commons when the " popish marriage " was presented to them as a *fait accompli*.

It seems that the secrecy which so often accompanied the profession of Catholicism throughout this period did much to inflame suspicion and hostility. The Test Act, which was introduced with the purpose of debarring all those who would not receive the Anglican Sacrament from holding office, had the effect of clarifying the situation. A similar enactment affecting the right of peers to take their seats in the House of Lords was passed in 1678 and spelled the end of the crypto-Catholics. Those doubtful sympathizers with Rome henceforward vanish from English life. At the same time in regard to converts the temptation to conceal a change of faith so disadvantageous to worldly prospects had hitherto been reinforced by the desire of the Protestant relatives to avoid all reference to a peculiarly fatal, although not undignified form of aberration. Thus the eleventh and last Earl of Northumberland of the Percy line seems to have been deeply attracted by Catholicism and to have left for Rome in 1670 with the intention of making his submission to the Holy See. He died unexpectedly at Turin in the course of his journey. The mystery surrounding this episode resembles that which was associated with other cases at this period and does something to explain the doubts rising to suspicion where the actions of Catholics were concerned. At the same time it is probable that the strength of the old religion was exaggerated in the public mind until after the passing of the Test Act and its extension to the Lords. Yet this second measure revealed that there were still twenty-one peers of full age who were ready to be deprived of their seats as Catholic recusants ; while two other lords, Abergavenny and Clifford, were minors. Still it was seen that the Marquesses of Winchester and Worcester had abandoned their fathers' faith ; a defection most important in regard to the Somersets, since the loss of this family deprived the Catholics in Monmouthshire of their protectors. Meanwhile the rich young men were growing up in the atmosphere of the Restoration Court, which in any case tended to sap their religious observance, and now found the avenue to promotion finally barred. Youths of elegant promise joined the Anglican Communion and the most notable losses were those of Lord Arundel, who was to succeed as Duke of Norfolk in 1684, and the boy Earl of Shrewsbury ; the latter changing his opinions after elaborate arguments had been laid before him with great respect by Dr. Tillotson. Apart from Lord Henry Howard, who had become Duke of Norfolk in 1677 and died in 1684, the Catholics were without any leaders among the highest ranks of the peerage. This fact explains why the lords singled out for attack during the Popish Plot were men of such small political significance.

It was clear that as a Catholic the Duke of York was moving against the tide. That deep and rooted dislike for Catholicism, working to a pitch of hatred among those affected by the old Puritan and Cromwellian leaven, centred upon his person and he was a man to attract political hatred, capable of repelling but never of conciliating an enemy. The links with France and the new attitude in that country towards religion only tended to increase the bitterness. The spirit which was to produce the Revocation of the Edict of Nantes was already stirring and that expulsion of French Protestants would soon result in the establishment in England of colonies all of whose members had suffered gravely from an officially Catholic government. It mattered little in England that Louis XIV was himself in conflict with the Papacy and that the French ministers and to some extent the episcopate also were affected by a Gallican outlook; for it has seldom been customary for the English to make the effort required for the mastery of a detailed foreign political situation. All that they knew was that the *Grand Monarque* and his religion appeared profoundly distasteful. It has been a misfortune for the Catholic Church in England that the two champions Philip II and Louis XIV could be caricatured with such facility: the simple lines of their representations, as later in the case of the Emperor William II, delivered them over as victims to the broad humour of a nation so richly endowed with the comic spirit.

In all the actions of the Duke of York a form of clumsiness of spirit is apparent, that sense of the unaccountability of his actions to any human tribunal which was turned by this characteristic to his destruction. With such a brother as Charles II it was fatal for the Duke that he should be lacking both in taste and in the sense of the ridiculous. He gathered about him a considerable and sincere loyalty, which was a natural response to his innate sense of justice, but he entirely failed to win an equal friendship. He was honourable, but it was a disaster at this moment to be so pedantically honourable, struggling forward heavy footed with his honest burdened conscience.

Opposed to him were politicians who gathered with great skill all the varied discontents of those who were disappointed by, or opposed to, the rigid forms of the restored kingship. Those who blamed the Duke of York's later actions did not consider the shocks which the opposition lords and their leader, Shaftesbury, had caused to him. After his conversion the Duke had trusted the Jesuit fathers, discussing his intimate affairs with them and seeking their spiritual guidance in his struggle with those sensual impulses which, until he was nearly forty, he had made little effort to conquer. Then in the course of the anti-Catholic campaign these fathers were to be arrested and killed. Such wounds as these his faithful mind would not forget. Again, while opposition made others distrustful, this seems to have lent to the Duke a kind of dignified eagerness for support, which he always seems to have felt as due to his royalty. Surrounded by the rapid mocking minds of the Restoration Court he appears never entirely to have lost the belief, so marked in his own reign, that in the last resort their subjects would revere and be faithful to the Royal Stuarts.

It was on 13 August, 1678, that Charles II was stopped in Windsor Park and warned of what was to develop into the Popish Plot. Information was laid by Dr. Titus Oates, a clergyman who had first met with Catholics as chaplain to the Protestants in the Duke of Norfolk's household and had recently spent several months as a church student at the English College at Valladolid. After his expulsion he had reverted to the Church of England and was now financed and supported by the Opposition lords. The revelations which he made found for a time sincere acceptance among great sections of the nation and the whole episode is one of the more remarkable passages in English history. Further publication of family archives may come to our assistance in regard to this uncharted region.

Oates's career had been violent, unfortunate but not notorious. His expulsions and prosecutions had taken place without *réclame*. He could never possibly have succeeded in the days of newspaper publicity. As for his appearance the great purple moonlike face and the long chin above the short bow-legged body were not in themselves an asset. The loud and pious voice would at a later period have excited unfavourable prejudice ; but there was a determination in the figure of this poor, strong, bible-reading man which for the moment persuaded men to credulity. And there is this to be remembered that were his accusations against the Catholics well founded they would fully have justified all their antagonism.

It was only in September that Oates was summoned before the Council and began, with the unskilful support of various colleagues, the building up of his remarkable depositions. Two circumstances then gained credence for him. He had had the prudence to attack

Edward Coleman, secretary to the Duchess of York, an indiscreet convert layman, light-headed and busy. Oates accused him of being an agent of the General of the Jesuits and of receiving a commission from him as principal secretary of state and of arranging the details of a bribe of £10,000 to be given to the murderer of the King. So far, so mad ; but on a search being made compromising papers were discovered, a correspondence dating from 1674–1676 with certain French Jesuits and the Nuncio in Brussels. These letters implicate no one except Coleman and a phrase suggests that Père la Chaise, the French King's confessor, did not trust him ; there was nothing of significance written between 1676–8. The correspondence gives the impression of windy and vague projects and an incautious desire on Coleman's part for " the utter ruin of the Protestant Party." Not directly treasonable, it was certainly damaging. Nevertheless these statements would not have thrown opinion into its transient state of sincere alarm ; this was accomplished by the disappearance and death of Sir Edmond Berry Godfrey.

Sir Edmond, a Protestant magistrate of melancholy disposition, had received some of Oates' depositions. On 3 October he disappeared and his body was found three days later run through by his own sword in a ditch on Primrose Hill. The body bore marks of strangulation and he was said to have taken no food during the two days previous to his death. The mystery has never been solved, but popular opinion decided that he had been murdered by Jesuits. There are difficulties in the way of the possibility of suicide and it has sometimes been held that he was killed in a private quarrel. A complication was introduced by the fact that he had been on friendly terms with Coleman who mingled too freely with every party. A recent very ingenious view suggests that Oates' partisans may have been shadowing him as an associate of Coleman's and that he committed suicide by hanging. If this was indeed the case it was very quick-witted of Oates' associates to cut the body down and run it through with Godfrey's sword.

In the middle of the ensuing ferment Parliament reassembled on 21 October, hot against Rome. The penal laws were enforced strictly and priests were arrested all over the country. Meanwhile Oates was ready with his further stories and it was clearly decided who should be struck at, some thought having been expended upon this question. The informers declared that the General of the Jesuits had granted commissions to Lords Arundell of Wardour, Belasyse,

Petre, Powis and Stafford, that a military force was to land at Bridlington and that murder plots had been contrived for the removal of the King and the leading Anglican peers of both parties. It was also asserted that all those who refused to accept Catholicism would be " utterly extinguished."

The Lords named were at once committed to the Tower, but the list of men chosen for attack is interesting. Care was taken to avoid reference either to the few Catholics who were intimate companions of the King or to those who possessed strong personal support. Both Stafford and Belasyse had private enemies among the peers, Arundell had been employed in France and Powis lived retired on his Welsh estates showing generosity to the Quakers, a then unpopular form of charity. Petre was the head of a markedly clerical family with strong Jesuit connections. All were to some degree isolated. On the day following the committal of the five peers Oates declared that Lord Castlemaine, the Catholic husband of the King's former mistress the Duchess of Cleveland, had wished success to the Plot to gratify his desire for revenge on His Majesty. He, too, was arrested and sent to the Tower.

At the same time progress was made in regard to Godfrey's death. William Bedloe, a former servant of Lord Belasyse and recently discharged from Newgate, declared that he had seen Godfrey's dead body in the Queen's palace at Somerset House and was subsequently most helpful to Oates, amending his evidence so that it should coincide with that of his leader. For these services Bedloe received a reward of £500. On 24 November an accusation of high treason was made against Queen Catherine, who was declared to have consented to a plan formed by her physician Sir George Wakeman for killing the King by putting poison in his posset. Such a statement was a serious error in policy and the attitude of Charles II and the peers prevented the maintenance of this accusation.

At this stage Bedloe accused a silversmith named Miles Prance of Godfrey's murder and he in turn made a false confession accusing three servants at Somerset House, two Catholics and a Protestant. The accused servants were executed, as was William Staley, the son of a well-known Catholic banker in Covent Garden, on account of some French expressions of a treasonable nature which he was alleged to have uttered in a cookshop. Once the fever of the prosecutions had passed the innocence of all four men was not doubted. On 3 December Coleman, who had been tried and sentenced some time before, was executed and on the same day the Middlesex Grand Jury found Lord Arundell guilty of high treason. In the same month various Jesuit fathers, Mr. Pickering a Benedictine lay-brother and Mr. Grove a Jesuit laybrother were brought to trial charged with a treasonable meeting at the White Horse tavern in the previous April at which Oates declared that the details of the alleged plot had been discussed. Fr. Ireland, the Jesuit procurator and the two laybrothers were condemned and executed. After December a period of comparative peace ensued on the dissolution of Parliament and in April the Duke of York was persuaded by the King to withdraw to Brussels.

On 13 June, 1679, Frs. Whitbread, Harcourt, Fenwick, Gavan and Turner were tried for treason. All the priests were condemned and executed together on 20 June. The next trial was that of Richard Langhorne, a Catholic barrister of established reputation and con-siderable means who had acted for the last twenty-five years in the chief legal concerns of the recusants. He was now an elderly cultivated man, cheerful in spite of rheumatism, dividing his time between his chambers in the Inner Temple and his house in Sheer Lane. His position as legal adviser to the Jesuits made prosecution a certainty and at the end of June he was tried for complicity in the alleged Plot and executed on 14 July.

Nevertheless Langhorne's condemnation was a turning-point and the cause of uneasiness. Four days after his death Sir George Wakeman and three Benedictines were put on trial for the supposed attempt to poison the King and were acquitted. Belief in the Plot was almost over and when depositions were laid against Sir Thomas Gascoigne by the discharged manager of one of his collieries they were not credited. With the acquittal of Sir Thomas, his daughter Lady Tempest and Sir Miles Stapleton in January 1680 the agitation of the Popish Plot can be considered at an end. But Oates was to claim another victim.

The trial of the imprisoned peers had been fixed for 13 June, 1679, but was delayed through a second dissolution of Parliament until December of the following year. The case of William Howard, Viscount Stafford was taken first, for he was an old man (the trial opened on his sixty-ninth birthday), remote from the Court and dis-contented with it, disobliging in his attitude towards the King, hot-tempered and long-winded in argument and on distant terms with his own family. He was lame and broken in health and inevitably prolix and vague in his defence, although on some points he cross-examined with effect. A native slowness of mind threw into relief his courage and profound honesty. As a result of what was practically a trial of strength between the Opposition and the Court lords the former were successful and Lord Stafford was condemned by fifty-five votes to thirty-one. It is a curious fact that had the twenty Catholic peers, recently excluded from their seats, been enabled to take part the voting might have almost tied. On 29 December, 1680, Lord Stafford was executed. Castlemaine had been acquitted in the previous year, but the trial of the other four peers was not proceeded with. They remained imprisoned until 1684 when Lords Powis, Arundell and Belasyse were released. Lord Petre had died in the Tower.

Various questions remain unsolved, the nature of the activities of John Sergeant one of the secular clergy opposed to the Jesuits, the character of certain witnesses employed on the Catholic side and their relations with Shaftesbury and the Opposition, and the maintenance of the fever heat of public opinion. The details of the prosecution of Pepys, which have only recently been fully studied,[1] suggest the widespread ramifications of the political effort associated with the campaign of calumny. In this case Pepys, who was careful and even punctilious in his attendance at the Anglican services, suffered on account of his association with the Duke of York in the administration of the Navy. His wife, now dead, had been a convert to Catholicism; his musician, Cesare Morelli not unnaturally belonged to that faith; he himself had sat in Parliament for Castle Rising which was more or less at the disposal of the Howard influence. These were sufficiently slender contacts with the " popish interest."

In the background of the prosecutions there moved those ominous figures who were employed by the Opposition and who would hardly be credible as political figures at a later period. Colonel John Scott, for instance, had survived the most extraordinary adventures and as the climax of good fortune had been pardoned on account of " his hopefulness and brisk parts " when about to be hanged at St. Kitts for the murder of his master. A contemporary description

---

[1] In the admirably documented volume, *Samuel Pepys : the Years of Peril*, by Arthur Bryant. A delightful account of Colonel Scott is given in this book. It i interesting to note that as far back as 1673 at the Castle Rising election " Mr. Offle had . . . infused it into the whole country . . . that Mr. Pepys was a Bludd Papist," op. cit., p. 87.

gives an excellent impression of this " proper well-set man with a great light-coloured periwig, rough visaged, having long hair on his eyebrows, hollow-eyed, a little squinting." It is not only Dr. Oates who has to be borne in mind in considering the prosecutions, but also the " proper well-set " colonel as he moved about with his confederates in the bar of the *Dog and Dripping Pan*.

Throughout the country there had been a renewed attack on the Catholics. Once Oates had aroused opinion a proclamation was issued on the petition of Parliament " for the discovery and apprehending of all Popish Priests and Jesuits," and rewards offered. Apart from the London trials which have been recorded, eight priests were put to death[1] in 1679 in the provinces for their priesthood alone.

The execution of the Archbishop of Armagh, Oliver Plunket, was a sequel to these events. An apostolic prelate and very generous towards the English, he had been arrested on the outbreak of the Plot fever; after two years he had been brought to England and suffered on 1 July, 1681. His body was taken to Lambspring Abbey in Hanover and was eventually brought to Downside where it now rests. On the day of his death an informer named Fitzharris who had tried to work up a second Popish Plot alarm was executed also, since the King refused to grant him the immunity hitherto given to self-confessed accomplices in treason. Fitzharris' elimination marked the end of the fabricated conspiracies.

Charles II's attitude throughout all this affair is not easy to determine and it is difficult to assess his exact responsibility for the execution of these Catholics in whose guilt he did not believe. His action was at every turn conditioned by politics. For the reigns of Charles II and James II and the subsequent Revolution form in one sense a consistent whole in which that form of government and outlook known as Whig gradually attained through setback to mastery; a process clearly traceable in the years between 1672, when the hitherto inchoate opposition became focused, and 1689 which saw the final victory. The philosopher of the party was Locke; the first political leader, Shaftesbury. The tone of mind revealed was progressive in the general acceptance of that term; the social atmosphere depended upon privilege; the essential political

[1] Among these John Kemble, David Lewis, John Plessington, Philip Evans, John Lloyd and John Wall were beatified by Pope Pius XI in 1929. Archbishop Plunket was declared *beatus* in 1920.

structure was oligarchic. In the early period certain Republican
ideals were found linked with the conceptions of Roman, rather than
Christian virtue. A foundation of sound landed wealth was common
to those families who controlled the inner policies. An occasional
financial opportunism was displayed, but the great fortunes were
for the most part inherited and stable. A support for the maintenance of the *status quo* in regard to landed property was of the
essence of the Whig position and with this went a genial, uninterested and serene attitude towards the penurious classes.
Many elements combined to make up the Whig outlook and it
was perhaps anti-Catholic chiefly on account of the accidents of
English politics. The Venetian oligarchy had always been Catholic,
although often consciously anti-clerical : a carefully fettered State
Church is almost necessary to this form of polity. As it was, in
England a strong anti-Catholic colouring was present from the first
and the Catholicism of the Duke of York provided the rallying cry.
The efforts at the Duke's exclusion from the succession continued
through the period of the Popish Plot agitation and Shaftesbury
and his colleagues supported the idea of bringing forward Charles
II's natural son the Duke of Monmouth as a *roi fainéant* to be
managed by a camarilla. Given the English situation some development towards an oligarchy was probably inevitable. Passive
Resistance and the Divine Right of kings were ideas which no
longer received even a nominal assent from the rich landowners ;
they were antiquated authoritarian phrases. The sons of the
supporters of the Parliament mingled with the heirs of a Cavalier
tradition. This second generation took a suitable interest in
scientific invention and was addicted to general ideas of freedom
and even of toleration considered in a most restricted sense. Solid
mercantile opinion followed this leadership with good cause. On
the other hand there were wide sections of opinion, and particularly
those of the Tory squires and of the clergy of that temper which was
to become known as non-juring, which followed the Court, but this
was not the only period at which the ideas of the Court were out of
date.

Confronted by this Whig movement in its early stages, Charles II
acted with a quickly calculating supple mind determined upon the
preservation of his rule. It was a fixed principle of his action never
to interfere with the course of law and he never pardoned those who
were once convicted by due process. As a consequence he sacrificed

the lives of priests and of Langhorne and Lord Stafford, but he retained that freedom of action which he held essential. The break-up of the Whig caucus by legal means and the exile of Monmouth was perhaps only open to the King because he had not pardoned Lord Stafford. At the time of the Rye House Plot in 1683 he was thus enabled to quell the Opposition. In connection with the position of Catholics Charles II never forgot his weakness in face of the many penal laws standing against them on the Statute Book. The years of exile had aided him to sense the moments in which his position might seem precarious. In the last four years of his reign he did not summon Parliament, but, if he sometimes disregarded diplomatic privilege and parliamentary custom, he was determined to hold fast to the Common Law.

When dying King Charles expressed a wish to be received into the Catholic Church. Fr. Huddleston, the Benedictine who had saved his life after Worcester fight, was brought from Somerset House and the King made his confession, was anointed and received *viaticum*, the Blessed Sacrament being carried to him from the Queen's chapel. On the following morning, 6 February, 1685, he died at Whitehall and his brother the Duke of York was proclaimed king as James II.

THE REIGN OF JAMES II

At the outset of the reign great significance attached to the personality of the King's advisers. These were, however, overshadowed by the new Queen and the question of the influence she might exert with her husband and over the nation. Mary of Modena was tall and graceful, with jet-black hair and eyebrows against a complexion unusually pale for her Italian blood, pleasant in her manner and dignified. At this time twenty-six years of age, she had borne four children, who had died, and was now childless. She had always maintained her private chapel, but she was not reported unduly stiff in her religious outlook ; her marriage had taken place in Italy without a papal dispensation and her children had been christened by Anglican prelates at the late King's wish. A Catholic heir would have been most unwelcome in England, but it was nearly three years since her last pregnancy and there was good reason to hope that she would have no surviving offspring. Her relations with the Queen Dowager were cool, with the ladies of her household, both Catholic and Anglican, friendly, and with many of the King's advisers unsatisfactory. The Anglican Tories, such as Lord Treasurer Rochester, had supported the King's mistress, Catherine Sedley, since they considered that her Protestant or rather sceptical influence would act as a counterpoise to the King's Catholic tendencies. It was inevitable that the Queen should be alienated by this action. On the other hand she had no liking for Sunderland and positively distrusted Fr. Petre whom the King raised to the privy council. With the general public and the squires on the fringes of the Court she had little success, for her classic features and a regal manner, increased by her child-marriage to the heir to the throne, only tended to emphasize a certain coldness of character and determination. Both had been accentuated by the sudden transition from the convent atmosphere of Modena and she was in no sense a woman of experience. As a girl she had had a wilful childish affection for the Carmelites at Modena, whose life she wished to share, and in her later years she was to be devoted to the Visitandines of Chaillot. Her deepest affection was perhaps reserved for her friend Vittoria Montecucoli, who had come from Italy with her and remained always at her side.

The first months of James II's reign were marked by the attempt of the Duke of Monmouth on the throne and his defeat at Sedgemoor in Somerset. At one stage he offered to become a Catholic in the hope of obtaining pardon. This step would merely have implied a reversion to his childhood's faith since he had been brought up until the age of ten under the charge of Stephen Gough, a convert Oratorian in Paris. When he found the effort to save his life hopeless Monmouth gave up this suggestion of embracing the King's religion.

From the early days of his power James II's complete lack of judgment, where individuals were concerned, became apparent. Thus his confidence was increasingly given to Lord Sunderland, whom he found on his accession as Secretary of State, a politician of the clearest insight who has had as great an effect as any other non-Catholic on the fortunes of the old religion. Few men have had so pure an attachment to the art of political manipulation, an abiding content in the power to move the puppets and to discover the designs of rivals. A sceptical mind more suited to the eighteenth than to the seventeenth century needed in his period the veil of religious sentiment and Sunderland understood so perfectly the wishes of the sincere and clumsy King. He was bent upon the gaining and the retention of the confidence of those to whom he was interiorly profoundly alien. His father-in-law was Lord Bristol, that eccentric Catholic, and Sunderland was acquisitive of moods. Soft, quiet, careful, supple and infinitely dexterous he had the qualities, but also the satisfaction of a hooded cobra. And he knew so much about his victim's habits. In the events that followed he often counselled the extreme provocative course and he was right in believing that if he went where others would not go the King would lean on him. He joined in the consultations of the Catholic peers overpersuading these cautious ancient men who were still numbed from the prosecutions of the Popish Plot.

Meanwhile in the eighteen months before the full effect of Sunderland's influence appeared the King had acted with some prudence. He had been crowned in Westminster Abbey with Anglican Rites by Archbishop Sancroft, an act which, whatever its theological implications, aided him to establish his authority. At the same time he might reasonably have imagined that the favour he showed to William Penn and his release of Quakers and Catholics would not have been misconstrued. The case of his action after Monmouth's Rebellion, was, however, very different. Here the King suffered once again from his lack of imagination and his wrong choice of servants. Whatever Jeffreys' merits, and he had wit, courage and boisterous goodfellowship, he was the last man who should have been sent on the Western circuit to quell and pacify hostile counties. It was an error to carry through the executions and to send so many men to the plantations ; but James II was never able to appreciate the effect on public opinion of his ideas of discipline and as a consequence he could not sense the hostility which was aroused by his proposals for the formation of a standing army.

The reliance on the dispensing power was similarly unwise, for this went beyond the prerogative of mercy. In 1686 a case was brought by arrangement against Sir Edward Hales of Tenterden, a convert Kentish squire, who held the command of a regiment of foot guards by letters patent granted by the King notwithstanding the existence of the Test Act. The Lord Chief Justice, Sir Edward Herbert, and eleven out of the twelve judges held that the King might lawfully dispense from the effects of penal statutes in particular cases for an adequate cause. This decision was the prelude to the appointment of various Catholics, four new privy councillors, Lords Powis, Arundell of Wardour, Belasyse and Dover ; two judges, Sir Christopher Milton and Sir Richard Allibone ; certain military officers and a naval officer of flag rank, Sir Roger Strickland. At the same time permission was given to the Master of University College, Oxford, to hold office although a convert.

Nevertheless such changes as these were to be expected and the King had been fortified by an abundance of sound counsel from Rome. Cardinal Howard, who was now Protector of England, favoured a cautious policy and his views were represented by his former secretary, Dr. John Leyburn, who had been consecrated Bishop of Hadrumetum and sent to England as vicar apostolic, thus taking up an office vacant since the resignation of Bishop Smith in the reign of Charles I. Bishop Leyburn, who reached England in the autumn of 1685, was supremely acceptable ; a small man of north-country stock ; a capable administrator ; with the scholarship and Latinity then valued ; careful and silent. He was about sixty-five years of age, once a student at Douai College and sometime its

president, and deeply experienced in the affairs of England. He had
lived for several years as chaplain to Lord Montague in whose household he had won the confidence of the great Catholic squires.
Setting methodically to work, he settled communities and restored
chapels keeping entirely aloof from politics. Had King James
followed the advice of Cardinal Howard and Bishop Leyburn and
confined himself to a moderate use of dispensation he could have
staved off much danger ; unfortunately he had also to reckon with
his own temperament and with Sunderland.

Still the time of peace brought in converts, some peers and one
great name, Dryden. It seems probable that the character of these
changes of allegiance have been the subject of misunderstanding in
view of the doctrines of the old high Cavalier party which laid so
much stress on the position of the King, the Divine Right by which
he ruled and the passive obedience owed to him. A devotion to
order was inherent in such a standpoint and in this case the King's
personal Catholicism was bound to have a serious effect causing in
the majority of Tories a profoundly irritating dislocation of mind
and in a few cases resulting in the disintegrating of their outlook
upon the Anglican Communion. It was only a century and a half
since all England had adhered to the old religion and in many cases
the Catholic tradition had only recently become submerged. Thus
among the converts was Lord Peterborough, a distinguished soldier
and a confidant of King James when Duke of York ; an old
Cavalier. But Peterborough came of a profoundly Catholic family
which had only conformed to the Established Church in his father's
time and in which the former traditions were not yet extinguished.
The case of the poet laureate, John Dryden, probably developed
along not dissimilar lines. He was a gentleman of assured position,
closely related to adherents of the ancient faith, deeply interested in
political changes, with a real concern for the fortunes of the royal
family and moving easily among the Court party. Sharing the
interests of the Duke of York's supporters, he was essentially
romanticist and it seems that he came to see the chief hope of order
in that Catholic religion which the sovereign had adopted. *The
Hind and the Panther*, written the year after his conversion, would
seem to give support to such a view.

At the same time it is true that the conversions were confined to
the Court circle and to Oxford ; the squires were entirely unaffected.
It is a sign of the weakening hold of Catholicism that the new

freedom produced no favourable reaction comparable to the movement of open adherence to the old religion, which had marked the
slackening of official pressure under the early Stuarts. The absence
of any serious movement towards Catholicism was, however, less
noticeable owing to the extremely friendly attitude of certain
Anglican members of the King's entourage, such as Lords Ailesbury
and Middleton and the presence of a considerable circle of his young
relatives *à la main gauche* who were being brought up in his religion.
These included his own family by his former mistress Arabella
Churchill, the Duke of Berwick, Lord Henry FitzJames and
Henrietta who was married to a Catholic peer Lord Waldegrave,
Comptroller of the Household and among his brother's children,
the Duke of Richmond and Lennox, the Countesses of Sussex,
Lichfield and Derwentwater and Lady Barbara Fitzroy, who became
a prioress of the Benedictines at Pontoise. Allied with these among
the young Catholic courtiers were the Salisburys and their cousin
Kinnoull, all three little more than children. It was a small grouping
but not without significance as providing a stiffening for the
Jacobites of the future. Had the King really been contented with
his private chapels, his own Court circle, his occasional use of the
dispensing power, and had the Queen remained childless he would
have been able to live out his days in peace.

However in 1686 the King made his first serious error in a succession of tactical mistakes by his appointment of a convert Fellow of
Merton, John Massey, to the vacant deanery of Christ Church,
Oxford. This appears an indefensible action so long as the office
remained a part of the normal preferment belonging to the Church
of England. It was seized upon by his enemies and awakened
suspicions in regard to all his ecclesiastical nominations ; suspicions
as groundless as the accusations of secret Catholicism against Bishop
Cartwright of Chester and Bishop Parker of Oxford, but equally
damaging in their effects. The attempt to make provision for
Catholics at Oxford was all the more unfortunate as it alienated some
of the strongest royalist support. Each step, the dispensation for
Dr. Walker at University College, the Christ Church appointment
and the attempt in 1687 to force a president on Magdalen against
the statutes was increasingly ill-judged ; the men unsuitable ; the
occasion badly chosen ; the legal grounds for action insufficient.
Granted the vigilance of his enemies in turning each act to his un-
doing the King was still too stiff and brusque to retain support or to

gather fresh adherents. His action in the case of Fr. Petre seems marked by the identical defects.

, A loyalty to his friends was a dominant characteristic of James II. The Jesuits had aided him and suffered for him and among the survivors the most prominent was the vice-provincial Fr. Edward Petre. He had many advantages, zeal, good business sense and influential connections. He had succeeded his brother in the baronetcy belonging to the Cranham branch of the Ingatestone Petres ; he was a nephew of Sir Edward Gage of Hengrave, a notable Catholic leader ; his relationships ran through all the coteries of recusant families in southern England. A contemporary of the King, he had suffered imprisonment in the Popish Plot agitation and he had the powerful recommendation of Lord Sunderland.

The King was looking for an ecclesiastical leader and now he had found one. The first step was his appointment as Clerk to the Closet and then to be privy councillor. Against this move was ranged the feeling of the more conservative Catholic leaders and the implied disapproval of Roman opinion. But lack of appreciation of his friends only strengthened the King's attachment to them. In this case it seems that he regretted his action later and in his *Memoirs* there occurs a passage stating that the King " was so bewitched by the Earl of Sunderland " ; but there is no doubt that it was his own decision. He was rumoured to dream of appointing Fr. Petre to the see of York and he certainly pressed the Pope to raise him to the cardinalate, continuously—but without success. The whole course of action could only exacerbate the dogged prejudice of English Protestant opinion. It had been the same with the sending of Lord Castlemaine as ambassador to Rome and the reception of the Nuncio ; functions carried through with a great degree of formality because the King wished to make amends for the pressure of the unjust laws. Such actions were, however, inevitably repugnant to the legalism which is the inseparable background of the oligarchic frame of mind. The test came ; the Queen gave birth to a son and provided the throne with a Catholic heir and then King James found how complete was his isolation.

In the months before the Prince's birth various developments took place. There had been some changes in Catholic administration : three fresh titular bishops had been appointed as vicars apostolic and the existing missions were divided ecclesiastically into the

London, Western, Midland and Northern districts. Among the new prelates Bonaventure Giffard was a member of the greater squire-archy ; James Smith came from west country stock ; Philip Ellis was a Benedictine, chaplain to the King and a convert, the only bishop which Westminster School has given to the Catholic Church. These prelates were assigned incomes, but they were without political influence, careful in their actions and unspectacular. During this period the King's opinion had swung round in favour of co-operation with the dissenters rather than with the Church of England. He put forth a Declaration of Indulgence to be read in all the churches and Archbishop Sancroft and six bishops refused and remonstrated ; were sent to the Tower, then tried and acquitted ; the famous trial of the Seven Bishops. During this period the Prince was born and the Opposition declared the infant supposititious. There is no doubt that popular feeling, especially in London, was running strongly against the King ; but everything appears to have turned on the succession.

Until the first days of 1688 the line of succession to the throne seemed secured for that Protestant successor which the great majority of the nation desired. The heir-presumptive was the King's eldest daughter Mary, Princess of Orange, a woman of twenty-six, married since 1677 to her cousin the Stadtholder of the Netherlands, childless and dominated completely by her husband. The next heir was the King's younger daughter Anne, who lived in England and was married to a nonentity, the King of Denmark's younger son. She had already several children and the succession was expected to be continued by her line. Should both princesses die without issue, the Crown would have passed to William, Prince of Orange, who was the only child of the eldest daughter of Charles I. Even as early as 1685 the relations between the English and Dutch Courts must be described as not cordial ; the Exclusionist Whigs had looked to Holland ; Shaftesbury had died and Monmouth had lived there. The Princess had resented Monmouth's execution and the Stadtholder was the almost official defender of Protestantism in Europe, the life-long enemy of Louis XIV and as such a natural focus of opposition. Still, until the birth of a Catholic heir, the English politicians who were out of office could look forward con-fidently to eventual triumph. It was manifest that, even as a consort, the Stadtholder would be the predominant partner and the Orange reign would provide an opportunity for the complete victory of the

Whig ideal; a government oligarchic in temper, supported by the mercantile community and based on a political philosophy consonant with a Protestant social framework. On the other hand, different sections would be satisfied by the Princess Anne's government which could be anticipated as an ultimate eventuality in view of her sister's childlessness. This reign could be expected to fulfil the wishes of the Church of England party, that element among the landowners who had remained faithful to some version of the Cavalier tradition. By the birth of the Prince of Wales the hopes of both of the political parties were extinguished and an attempt to overthrow the existing régime was henceforward inevitable.

The success of such an attempt depended equally on the wealth and influence of the leaders in the enterprise and on the apathy with which the King was regarded even in the most traditionally royalist of Anglican circles. The chain of dates leading to King James' fall fits easily together. On Trinity Sunday, 10 June, 1688, the Queen gave birth to a prince christened James after his father. On 18 June the Princess Anne wrote to her sister suggesting that the child was supposititious and in July the Stadtholder signified his intention of adhering to this point of view by ordering the prayers for the Prince of Wales to be omitted in his chapel. From this time a Dutch invasion could be predicated. Negotiations went forward with the seven chief English leaders who were prepared to pledge themselves to support such action. Finally the Prince of Orange set sail with a considerable fleet and a Dutch army on 19 October, 1688. He landed at Torbay on 5 November and marched towards London. On 25th of the same month the Princess Anne left London with the intention of supporting the Stadtholder against her father and it became impossible to rely on the royal forces. King James II abandoned his capital secretly on 11 December, but was detained at Feversham and brought back to London. The Stadtholder and his guards were by that time in possession and the King left again, landing at Ambleteuse on Christmas Day; his wife and child had preceded him to France. Louis XIV granted the exiles the use of the royal château of St. Germain-en-Laye near Paris and the reign of James II was ended.

The King settled down to the life of a court in exile, surrounded by his former household and a series of devoted friends, developing a strong resigned religious life and making the necessary efforts to regain his kingdom. In these he was unsuccessful; there were the

Scottish campaigns associated with the battle of Killiekrankie ; his Irish journey which saw the defeat of the Boyne and led to Aughrim and the siege of Limerick ; one or two abortive English conspiracies. He never returned to England and he died in 1701 at St. Germain.

The departure of King James had a doubly serious effect upon English Catholics : on the one hand it destroyed their hopes for the future by permanently seating their enemies in power and on the other it removed a proportion of their leaders. The King-in-exile drained away some of the most active element among the Catholics ; Powis, Waldegrave, Caryll and Strickland and their families lived henceforth in France ; their territorial and personal support was lost to Catholicism in England. Not only that but the small section of the Anglican court party who were positively friendly to Catholicism became inevitably Jacobite. Their right wing formed the Protestant section at St. Germain and among these some, Ailesbury and Middleton serve as examples, became Catholics. But such converts were made and remained in exile and not only the Catholics themselves but also those friendly to their religion were effectually removed from public life in England.

At the same time the exile of the Stuarts brought a transient prosperity to the English religious establishments in France such as the convent in the Rue de Charenton in Paris, known as that of the " Blue Nuns " and especially to the Benedictine Abbey at Pontoise. Their communities, already aristocratic in character, benefited by the presence of the Court, numbers increased and Catholic colonies sprang up around them. The case of Pontoise provides an example. Here under two successive abbesses, Dame Anne Neville (1668–1689) and Dame Elizabeth Dabridgcourt (1690–1710), there was a stream of novices including daughters of Charles II and James II. The religious outlook of these adherents of the ancient faith was very remote from that of the Protestant English squires of the last decade of the century, so also was the organization of the Court.

The example of Louis XIV and the ideas represented by Versailles acted by attraction upon the European princes and by repulsion upon the new Whig oligarchy. Jacobitism in England came to mean not so much an active party in the country as a considerable, magnificent and impoverished Court. This centred on St. Germain with its great terrace by Le Notre, its outbuildings and dependencies, and outside lay the town with its society and English quarter. In practice the lives of the elder Jacobites were bounded by the territory which their master controlled, St. Germain with its gardens and high grottoes and the view over the hill-sides of the Parisis. The Whigs ruled in England and St. Germain was a Versailles *manqué*, a palace, a king, a large hierarchic court, without a nation.

THE WHIG VICTORY

MEANWHILE the Whig victory had been ushered in by a very different sovereign. Early in 1689 the Crown had been settled by the Convention Parliament on the Prince and Princess of Orange for their joint lives under the title of William III and Mary II. At thirty-eight the Stadtholder took up the government. He had practically no experience of Catholic things and still less interest ; he was before all else a soldier ; he had none of the cultivated interests or polite vices of the Stuarts. The new King was a thin, small man, serious and talented whose chilled manner provided an appropriate medium for the expression of somewhat morose antipathies. He was Calvinist, but with a frigid standpoint in religion which was a preparation for the eighteenth-century scepticism. His favourite, Lady Orkney, was English ; his friends and *protégés* Dutch. No sovereign has stood more remote from Catholicism.

It was a complete victory for the defenders of Protestant liberties and one which the Whigs knew well how to turn to the best advantage. Fortunately for them popular opinion was easily inflamed in regard to Popery. They soon found that a thorough search of all ranks in the army for possible papists was a sound strategic move ; for James II's popish militia had taken hold of the imagination of the respectable voting public. In consequence two trends are apparent in the anti-Catholic legislation, a determination to debar Catholics from profitable employment, as in the Act of 1695 by which the professions of counsellor-at-law, barrister, attorney and solicitor were closed to them, and a constant reference to suspected papists, a term intended to pander to the helpful sense of well-bred alarm with which this section of the population was regarded. In this second category is included the Act forbidding a suspected papist, who would not take the oaths of allegiance and supremacy, to keep arms and ammunition or a horse of greater value than £5. No person refusing the oaths of allegiance and supremacy was entitled to vote for the election of Members of Parliament and the former penal legislation was revived. An Act of 1700 incapacitated papists from inheriting or purchasing land ; but it does not seem that it was often carried into effect in England. Priests were made subject to imprisonment for life and a reward of £100 was offered to any informer who had secured the conviction of a priest for saying Mass. These last enactments were the basis of various prosecutions in the reigns of George II and George III and give the tenor to the action against priests during that period. Refusal to take the oaths of allegiance and supremacy, offered together, was the test of the penalties for recusancy.

In this connection the declaration against transubstantiation, which was also required, was probably beneficial to Catholics since it made the position clearer. The half-measures of the early seventeenth century were no longer possible, for the declaration could not be taken except by one who had determined on a positive abandonment of the sacramental teaching of Rome. Loyalty to the Church now subjected the Catholics to the long strain of inactivity.

Many of the more vehement Jacobites had gone abroad and the recusants in England do not seem to have been buoyed up by any illusion of a return to freedom. The letters of William Blundell of Crosby give an impression of resignation hardly tempered by hope. He and his friends could not but be aware of the deep hostility of the Anglican Tories towards them and even the defeat of the Whigs would not necessarily bring alleviation.

For once, too, those family contacts of political opponents, which are so striking an illustration of the homogeneous character of the old prosperous English life, had been broken down. The Catholics had now no friendships in the enemy's camp. Lady Jersey, the Lord Chamberlain's wife, their only coreligionist in the Court circle, was of little assistance and the numerous ex-Catholics were for the most part hardened against their friends and bitter. It is remarkable that the Dukes of Beaufort, Bolton, Norfolk, Shrewsbury and Richmond had all been brought up in the old faith, as had such lesser politicians as Scarborough and Rivers. But in these cases political bitterness was added to religious feeling. With the exception of Beaufort, who was a Tory, these men were regarded by Catholics as having betrayed both their King and their religion, a double charge which could not fail to rouse the indignation of the most lukewarm.

In consequence the Catholic life became more sharply differentiated from that of the remainder of the nation. The Court of St. James', which had played so considerable a part in their mental background, suddenly ceased to affect their calculations. St.

Germain was a source of subdued interest and Rome loomed on the horizon of the ardent or the artistic. The amount of travel increased and the beginnings of that faintly cosmopolitan character which marked the richest recusant circles in the period between the flight to St. Germain and Emancipation could already be discerned. Thus Charles Dryden, the laureate's son, became a papal chamberlain and James Gibbs, a young Scottish Catholic from the Links of Fetternear in Aberdeenshire, went out to study in Rome under Fontana. He was eventually to return to England and to be the architect of St. Mary le Strand, St. Martin's in the Fields, the Senate House at Cambridge and the Radcliffe Camera.

A curious correspondence of this period throws an interesting light on the close understanding of foreign affairs and personalities possessed by the more travelled Catholic gentry. During the year 1694-5 a series of newsletters were sent from London to Lord Derwentwater at Newcastle and Mr. Thomas Errington at Dilston. One of these contains a delightful commentary on contemporary social and religious standpoints. " An extraordinary congregation," says the writer,[1] " has been held [at Rome] to consider the means of putting a stop to the spreading of a sect which has sprung up, not unlike that of the Quietists whose sanctity and simplicity of life draw many proselytes, though they are persons of no great literature." Thus calmly, with poise and confidence, the Catholics awaited[2] the outcome of a regime which bore no hope for them.

Since the Crown had been settled on the Prince and Princess of Orange for their joint lives, the death of Queen Mary II in 1694 made no difference to the Catholics and was merely marked by the change in style of the regnal years. The Queen had had a cold, strong dislike for her father's faith. When dying she had imagined that a popish nurse was lurking behind the screen in her bedchamber at Kensington Palace to disturb her. She had all her life carefully avoided Catholic associates. During the remaining eight years of the reign of William III, until his death in 1702, the figure of the heir to the throne, the Princess Anne, became significant. Until 1700, when her surviving son the Duke of Gloucester died, it seemed that the succession was assured to the princess and her children. Her

[1] Cal. S.P.Dom., 1695, p. 340.
[2] An indication of the continued Catholic activity is apparent in an information lodged in March 1703 against John White, a popish priest who said Mass in the house of Mrs. Forster, a zealous catechist living near the Vine Tavern in Holborn. Cal. S.P.Dom., 1702-3, p. 646.

feelings were without her sister's rancour, but her strong religious
convictions made her a determined Anglican. She was a woman
who lived by and for her friendships as a relaxation to that strong
sense of duty which sprang from her ordinary and conscientious
mind and her common-sense instincts. She had various Catholic
contacts amounting in one instance to a minor friendship with Lady
Jersey. But for the old faith she had the remoteness of indifference
and it was natural that it should not enter into the scheme of that
essentially Anglican polity on which all her preconceptions were
based. From her accession to the throne the Catholics might expect
a lessening of hostility, but no further change.

ISOLATION

THE REIGN of Queen Anne represented a lull in the progressive disintegration of the fortunes of the English Catholics. The hostility which William III had aroused in Tory circles was succeeded by that atmosphere of contented, sober, widespread patriotism which has always been so well attuned to the English temper. The new Queen was a Stuart; Anglican; unimaginative and worthy; a sufficient monarchic figure. During the twelve years of her reign there was no possibility of the restoration of her young half-brother Prince James Edward. The Tories and Whigs manœuvred, pivoting about a government from which the Catholics were totally excluded. Public opinion, in so far as it was vocal, was ranged against them supporting Queen Anne calmly, unenthusiastically, but solidly. Besides, King James II had died in 1701 and his son could hardly claim allegiance of the same quality. The Catholics remained Jacobites, but with great placidity, reasonable fidelity and a certain slackening. The minority of the Prince, the established position of Queen Anne and the fact that even the Tories insisted on a Protestant Stuart all combined to sap their interest in politics.

The governments and the successive favourites, the Duchess of Marlborough and Mrs. Masham, were without concern[1] for the Catholics. Conversions to the Church were rare : Sir Henry Fletcher of Hutton in the Forest, who became a monk at Douai, is one of the few names recorded. At the same time there was a certain stability ; for all the middle-aged men had experienced a personal fidelity to James II. The pressure of the Hanoverian government, which was to be so definite, so obviously interminable, had not yet begun. It was among the boys growing up, not among their fathers now in possession, that secession from the Church would become common. Meanwhile the young Catholics of the wealthier sort were sent for education to the Low Countries or to France, where a

---

[1] The Duchess of Marlborough had a Catholic sister, the Duchess of Tyrconnell and Godolphin a Catholic brother, Sir William Godolphin, but these connections exercised no influence upon events.

knowledge of polite uses could be obtained in a region sufficiently remote from the Stuart Court. Thus in the years 1700–1703 the college for nobles at La Flèche in Touraine was frequented by twenty English youths. A description of this life given in the Marwood diary, kept by the tutor to Henry Bedingfield, throws a delightful light on a curious existence. The young Esquire (as he is always called) went to the college daily to study, but lived with his governor in apartments in the town. A mildly Jacobite atmosphere prevailed. There was a constant movement among the Englishmen and their tutors ; dinners at the respectable hostelry, the Lion d'Or ; shooting and fishing ; sermons from the Jesuits ;[1] an elegant company, some conversation and much hunting. It was all balanced, sufficiently prosperous and, as a background for a life of rural inactivity, somewhat unreal.[2]

Perhaps the general effect which this period conveyed was that of the late autumn of Catholicism in England with the changing leaves soon to vanish, hanging on the branches, heavy, unvital. For in the previous half-century secession had chiefly affected the very rich in contact with the Court and certain areas of the Catholics in the towns. During the period between 1660 and the death of Queen Anne there had been little change in the ranks of the country gentry merely a steady, very gradual decline. Such of the yeomen and labourers as were reached by the ministration of their chaplains also remained faithful. A study of the list of Catholic non-jurors in 1715 shows a considerable number of baronets, a class which was held in Georgian literature to represent the rustic gentleman of prosperity. The pressure of inactivity was to make itself felt in the rising generation of this section of the squires. Under Charles II it had been rather the families connected with the Court who had suffered the immediate limitation of action through the passing of the Test Act. The semblance of stability in the Catholic body was further preserved when three or four Mass centres, dependent upon great landed fortunes, were regained in the early years of the eighteenth

---

[1] Two entries from *Marwood's Diary*, for August 1701 will indicate the trend of this existence. " *Wed*. 10. *St. Laurens*. We were in the Morn at ye Filles Penitentes, & afternoon at ye Costeau, kild a 'Perdreau & a Tourter . . . . *Wed*. 17. This day Esqr was in Classe to compose for ye Generall Premium, & was there from about 7 in the Morn till about 6 at Night. *Thursd*. 18. We were afternoon a shooting towards Bire with L. W(aldegrave)." C.R.S., vi, p. 108.

[2] It is noticeable that they did not all return to this inactivity, for the three wealthiest of the youths at La Flèche, Lords Waldegrave, Brudenell and Montgomery abandoned their religion in later life.

century on the death of those leaders who had abandoned their religion[1] in the earlier reign.

Among the town populations, especially those in the south of England, there had been something approaching a landslide during the years of the Popish Plot agitation. At the same time those who had given way under this stress appear to have belonged for the most part to the residuum of careless Catholics whose children had in many cases been educated in the State religion. The now reduced numbers of the Catholic urban middle class increased in prosperity in equal proportion with their Anglican neighbours. As a result they formed a substantial element among the supporters of the colleges abroad and, as the eighteenth century progressed, the general body of the faithful grew in cohesion. The wine merchants, the corn factors and the mercers came gradually to fill the places in the ranks left vacant by the seceding gentry. Nevertheless these men of business were permitted for a considerable time to take their part in supporting the cause of religion without receiving a position of influence. Until the close of the period the oligarchic tendencies of the English governing class were faithfully reflected within the Catholic body.

This again marks a distinction between southern England, where the influence of London was felt increasingly, and the distant north. With certain exceptions the prevailing type of surviving Catholic family in the south was rather prosperous in character ; the wealthy landowner, the substantial merchant. For this reason there was from the first a quota of Catholics among those respectable circles of gentlefolk of restricted means which existed in their hey-day from the time of Queen Anne to the late Victorian age. In general these groupings were composed of the impoverished relics and offshoots of landed stocks ; at first living in the small houses in county towns ; later coming to benefit by the air of the new watering-places ; following a routine of circumscribed amenity. The wealthier portion of the congregation of the Winchester mission was of this character. Similarly the poor in the agricultural districts were most often linked by tenantry or service to some wealthy family of the old faith. To this rule the already great population of the poor in London and the smaller grouping in Bristol formed obvious exceptions. But the lesser towns had hardly any Catholic inhabitants, for the intimate

---

[1] Thus the Norfolk line was Anglican between 1684–1701 and Catholic from 1701 till 1786, and the Shrewsburys were Anglican between 1669–1718 and Catholic from 1718 till 1856.

relation between the townsmen of Shaftesbury or Cirencester and the farms of the surrounding country brought no contact with the old religion.

In the north it was very different, for the hold of Catholicism on the farming stock of Cleveland, for instance, would constantly reinforce the congregations in the seaports of the North Riding. Similarly under Queen Anne the northern Catholics showed a greater political optimism that the southerners and the Northumbrian gentry were to give to the rising of the '15 such vitality as it ever possessed.

The vicars apostolic acted prudently with a safe quiet Jacobitism, legitimist in character and hardly tinged by current politics. On Bishop Leyburn's death in 1703 Bishop Giffard succeeded as vicar apostolic of the London district, a cautious man, already old, very charitable, clear-headed in money matters, patient under suffering and perhaps too prudent to be inspiring. He administered the missions in the west of England for some time in addition to his own vicariate ; for Bishop Ellis had lived in Italy since the Revolution. Dr. James Smith was still bishop in the north ; formerly president of Douai and custodian of its traditions, a rugged character whose bronzed face and heavy, almost matted, black hair are familiar to all who know the portrait in the refectory at Douai Abbey, Woolhampton.

The whole *tempo* of the reign served to stress the remoteness[1] of the Catholics from current politics, the Sacheverell agitation, the High Church party, the Act of Union with Scotland, the coffeehouse and pamphlet war : such movements could hardly touch those whom the Whig victory had deprived of their rights so very completely.

---

[1] A curious impression of this remoteness is provided by Aubrey in his description of Mr. Howard's retreat. " On the west side of his garden," he wrote of Deepdene, " is a little building, which is (as I remember) divided into a laboratory and a neat oratory by Mr. Howard. Above the hill, on the west side, is a thicket of black-cherry trees, with which the walks abound, as does the ground with strawberries. The house was not made for grandeur, but retirement (a noble hermitage) neat, elegant and suitable to the modesty and solitude of a Christian philosopher," *Antiquities of Surrey*, iv, p. 164.

DECLINE

B Y THE Act of Succession passed in 1700 the Catholics in the line of descent from Charles I and James I had been excluded from the throne. In addition to James II's children and those of his niece the Duchess of Savoy, they numbered as many as thirteen ; some like the Regent Orleans and the Empress Wilhelmina Amalia were extremely wealthy, others impoverished and hardly even princely. It is curious to reflect as to what would have happened had any of the younger Countesses of Salm abjured Catholicism either before the passing of the Act or between that date and the death of Queen Anne. As it was that sceptical nebulous religious outlook which the Electress Sophia described as her Protestant Faith remained in possession of the field.

Although the Hanoverians, called in to preserve the nation from Rome, naturally proved themselves the most profoundly non-Catholic of English royal houses, they did not acquire the character of an honest, old-fashioned, narrow Protestantism until the middle of the eighteenth century. George I, as the Electress Sophia's eldest son, had been brought up at his mother's Court, which was dominated by her shrewd projects for matrimonial and dynastic advancement and diversified at one period by Leibnitz's drawing-room plans for Christian reunion. The Electress is said to have hesitated in her daughter's religious training, so that she could accept Catholicism easily if the good fortune of a marriage with the Dauphin might be contrived. She certainly encouraged the " political conversion " of her niece the Duchess of Orleans. Prince Maximilian, a younger brother of George I, had become a Catholic and the new sovereign had been brought up in an atmosphere of polite indifference which tempered the question of faith to expediency. The King was thus free from animus and one of the first and most lasting of his attachments had been for the Catholic Madame von dem Bussche. His marriage with his cousin Sophia Dorothea of Zell had proved a failure and had been dissolved. He was already fifty-four at his accession, an isolated phlegmatic man, speaking little English and entirely in the hands of the great Whig families. It is not surprising that his indifference towards the Catholics did not result in any active benevolence.

The first public event of the reign to affect them was the Jacobite rising in the north, known as the 'Fifteen. It took place in the year after King George's accession and was of more importance in Scotland, where James Edward landed, than in England. South of the Border it mainly affected the Jacobite gentry in Northumberland and Durham and to some extent those of Lancashire. Among the leaders were Lords Derwentwater and Widdrington, Catholic peers of medium importance and some landed fortune. After the rapid collapse of the Rising both these families were ruined and Derwentwater was executed for treason. He was a young man, rash, handsome, rather consciously romantic and had been brought up at St. Germain with his cousin the Prince.

In England as a whole it is true to state that the quiet lukewarm character of the Jacobitism of the Catholic gentry possibly preserved them from disaster, but in no way acted as a check on individual secessions from the Church. The wealthier among them did not risk their liberty in doubtful adventures and English Jacobitism developed in this country as a specifically Anglican growth, a political philosophy which was in time to develop into high Tory support for George III. Bolingbroke, as the author of the essay on the *Patriot King*, was in time to be its prophet : the present leaders were old, rich, established Anglicans, Lord Westmorland and the Somersets and Wyndhams. With such a section of opinion the Catholics had little point of contact ; but it proved on occasion a misfortune that they had not some political enthusiasm, even if ineffectual, to prevent the dreariness of apathetic inactivity which led so frequently to that act of " conforming to the Established Church " which opened the gateway to public life. Thus the second Marquess of Powis and Lord Waldegrave both abandoned Catholicism at this time. The latter who received an earldom and the Paris Embassy was pursued with particular detestation by the Jacobites, since he was a grandson of James II. In rare cases, as in those of Lords Gage and Montague, peers who had made a " political " conversion returned to their former faith on their deathbeds. Sometimes when the family was divided in religion its " conforming " head would still maintain a Catholic chaplain for his relatives and dependants. The household of Earl Fauconberg, Sterne's patron, provides an instance of this practice. Nevertheless, however they were masked, these defections steadily pulled down the Catholic strength.

For the Catholics this was a period of dispirited discouragement. A definite proportion of that generation of the surviving landed gentry which had grown to manhood in the reign of Queen Anne and in the first years of her successor had abandoned the old religion. The outlook seemed hopeless ; lacking even the stimulus of severe persecution. The vicars apostolic were for the most part elderly and there was a need for new blood among both clergy and laity. It was perhaps at this time that the hopes of the Catholics were at their lowest. Jansenist tendencies, with the inevitable official disapprobation that these implied, were reported from some of the English colleges abroad and there was a natural falling away of vocations. Conversions in England can hardly be said ever to have entirely ceased ; but at this period they were almost unknown. The reception into the Church in Spain of the young Duke of Wharton, profligate, bankrupt and *déclassé* in his own country in no way countervailed this impression. Lady Bolingbroke, a French Catholic, had become a Protestant on her husband's recommendation as a prelude to fitting in even with the Tory scheme of English society. Finally the life of Alexander Pope suggested the tenuous hold of Catholicism in some of the more intellectual circles.

The poet, small, wizened, limping, and coming from the restricted prosperous London Catholic middle class had brought his classic wit to the circle of the old Catholic gentry whom closeness to the Court had made sophisticated. Throughout his life he was bound by the closest ties to the Blounts of Mapledurham. The dramatist Wycherley in his last period familiarized the young Pope with those standpoints from which Catholicism was held most negligently. A great metrical skill and sense of poetic values were combined in Pope with a mature appreciation of the current civilized elements in a society which highly valued him. He was received wherever polite letters were considered and was fortunate in the opportunities made for his high talents. He rode easily through a period which for him held no serious controversies of the mind and, never denying his religion, died with the consolation of the Sacraments in a fashion which all his contemporaries would have regarded as seemly. During this period one factor might reasonably give encouragement. In the college at Douai the young Richard Challoner was growing up.

At the beginning of the reign of George II in 1727 a rather different tendency became apparent in the slow pulsation of the Catholic life : the situation was becoming static.   The new dynasty was firmly established and the position of the Stuarts already hopeless ; Prince James Edward lethargic ; the young Charles Edward still a child.   At the same time the strong Walpole administration, Whig and profoundly Protestant in its policy, was making its influence perceptible through every section of the national life.   If Walpole ever did maintain that "every man had his price " one point was obvious, he did not even trouble to buy the Catholics. At the same time strong as was the antipathy towards the old religion its weakness secured it from persecution, save of that passive kind which exclusion from all employments must imply.   The Court was now the centre of the sincerest anti-Catholic feeling, the tone being set by George II's consort, Caroline of Anspach.   At the same time the very definiteness of this attitude made certain social toleration possible.   The fact that this became manifest was the last sign of their complete weakness.   From the moment when the Howards abandoned the support of the Stuarts the beginnings of a very gradual recognition of Catholics could be perceived.   Thus George II's son, Frederick Prince of Wales, when at feud with his father, took refuge in Norfolk House.   At the same time the social privileges of the peerage were always recognized by the polite Georgian world and this secured a measure of consideration for the leaders of the Catholics like the ninth Duke of Norfolk and Lord Shrewsbury.   The defections among the gentry almost ceased in the mid-eighteenth century and the organization of the depressed remnant in the country districts into chaplaincies and spheres of influence of religious orders became perfected.

Among the less prosperous Catholics the numbers would seem to have fallen steadily ; but early in this period the decline had been considerably checked by the influx of Irish labour, particularly into London.   In Hogarth's time the Irish sedan-chair carriers had become recognized as a type.   A general slight lessening of hostility could be perceived throughout the country.   Thus in the War of Austrian Succession the Empress Maria Theresa was regarded for a time as a national heroine in England.   She was, perhaps, the first avowed Catholic to receive such recognition for two centuries. About the time of the vogue for Maria Theresa, Miss Ambrose, the Dublin beauty popularized by Lord Chesterfield, became a toast in

London and there are evidences in Chesterfield's writings that in his circle Catholicism was beginning to be considered as a not unsuitable religion for ladies of quality. Both Lady Lichfield and Lady Abingdon had their supporters. At the same time politically the Catholics never counted for less and in great areas of the new middle class they were extinct. In the country districts the landowners enjoyed the prestige which their estates brought them. Lord Arundell of Wardour kept a pack of foxhounds which remained in the possession of his family until they were sold in 1782 to Mr. Meynell of Quorn. There was a certain amount of large-scale building and Vanbrugh designed Gilling Castle for Charles Fairfax, an anticipation of the great houses of the next generation. Gradually the defection[1] of Catholics from even sentimental Jacobitism became complete. Such was the situation changing very little throughout the reign, from 1727 till 1760, and it was into this England that Challoner returned in 1741 as a bishop.

[1] A letter from Roger Strickland to the Duke of Mar, dated 26 October, 1718 reflects the beginning of his process. " I shall never," he wrote, " take the least step that may . . . have the appearance of a Whiggish Papist whom I shall always abhor as the most notorious villains," Cal. Stuart MSS. vii, p. 440.

CHALLONER'S ENGLAND

URING THIS PERIOD of acute religious depression it cannot be said that any very successful effort was made by the first series of vicars apostolic. As a race they were afflicted by an extraordinary longevity. From 1703 until 1734 the Catholics of the London district had been under the control of Bishop Giffard, now a very old gentleman of delightful manners and deep piety, who had been consecrated in the reign of James II. On his death at the age of ninety-two he was succeeded by his coadjutor Benjamin Petre, Bishop of Prusa, a prelate of great humility, urbanely mildly Jacobite, and constantly asking to be freed from the burdens of his office. In 1740 he was still only in his early sixties, but worried by responsibility and the necessity for decisions. Like most of the early vicars apostolic drawn from the secular clergy he came of ancient family and was possessed of private means. His time was divided unevenly between his London residence in King Street, Golden Square and Fidlers in Essex, a country house belonging to his nephew Francis Petre who had likewise embraced the ecclesiastical state and was to become a vicar apostolic in his turn. The succession in the Midland district passed in a similar fashion and the vicariate was now held by Bishop Stonor. He resided for the most part at the family seat of Stonor Park and was an autocratic prelate of fine address and determined character, realist in politics, and distinguished as an advocate of a vaguely favourable attitude towards the *de facto* Hanoverian government. This bishop had a certain claim on the consideration of the ministry as a nephew of that staunch supporter of the Protestant Succession, the Duke of Shrewsbury, whose house at Heythrop he sometimes used. On the same side in this conflict of opinion was the Abbé Strickland, who was said to have become Bishop of Namur through the good offices of George I; a busy churchman always meddling with the affairs of England. Opposed to them were Monsignor Ellis, now Bishop of Segni, who had been one of James II's vicars apostolic, and Mr. Laurence Mayes, a priest serving in Rome from 1708 till 1749 as agent for the English prelates and an active supporter of

the Stuart line.   As the years passed the Catholic support for the
Hanoverians became a little stronger, but the differences of opinion
between the vicars apostolic appear as vague and faint as their own
dim rule.   And then into this quiet not undignified existence there
came the strong consolidating power of Bishop Challoner.

Richard Challoner had been born in 1691 at Lewes in which
town his father had been a wine cooper.   Early left a widow, Mrs.
Challoner had entered the service of Sir John Gage of Firle from
which she passed to that of Lady Anastasia Holman of Warkworth
Manor.   Both households were considerable and penetrated by a
deep Catholicism, which led eventually to Mrs. Challoner's conversion while living at Warkworth apparently as housekeeper.   Her
son became a Catholic likewise and aided by the chaplain, Mr. John
Gother the well-known controversial writer, went out in 1705 to
Douai to be educated for the priesthood.   His early surroundings
were thus Jacobite, since Lady Anastasia was a daughter of the
martyred Lord Stafford.   From these days Richard Challoner
always retained an understanding of the old Catholic families coupled
with a sense of detachment from a circle to which he did not belong
and a conscious desire to spend himself in the work of strengthening
and reviving the faith in England.   At Douai he remained for the
next twenty-five years.   This college was then the chief centre of
the English secular students and already possessed of a long
tradition, rather poor in its material buildings, harassed by the wars
in Flanders and controlled by the religious but somewhat austere
regime of Dr. Edward Paston (1688–1715) and Dr. Robert Witham
(1715–1738).   The north-country origin of many of the students is
shown by a list of those examined at a visitation at this period.
Melling, Kendall, Haydock, Skelton, Boamer and Brown.   Challoner
made an admirable course of studies, took his doctorate of divinity
and served for the last ten years of his stay as professor of theology
and vice-president.   Finally in 1730 he obtained a long desired
permission to return as a missionary priest to England.   " He is
said," wrote Mr. Mayes the Roman Agent, " to be one of ye
brightest men ever bred in Douay College."

In London he stayed for seven years working incessantly, writing
on controversial matters in defence of Catholicism and above all
maintaining that solid devotional life through which his acts were
turned to the following of Christ.   This calm ordered devotedness
marking his days at Douai was yet more striking in a London

profoundly alien to any aspect of deep religion. In these missionary years the veneration which was felt for him in later life first took hold of the English Catholics ; a quite special character of reverence and restrained affection was to mark his people's feelings towards the only real leader which God then gave them.

In the course of time Challoner was elected to the Chapter, whose influence remained considerable throughout this period, and acted as vicar general to Bishop Petre. Then as a result of his sound firm criticism of Dr. Middleton, an apologist of the Established Church, he found himself obliged to retire abroad, since the penal laws might be invoked against him. Dr. Witham, now in failing health, welcomed him at Douai and asked that Rome should appoint him as his successor in the presidency of the college. A dispute for the privilege of his services was maintained between the college and the vicars apostolic until it was solved by Bishop Petre's request that he should come to London as coadjutor-bishop ; there were various further difficulties and delays and finally in 1741 he was consecrated as Bishop of Debora in the convent at Hammersmith.

Dr. Challoner was at this date just fifty years old, a tall man of medium build, with brown hair, a rather long nose and a serious attractive expression. Poor and unsupported, without the private means so frequently possessed by his brother-prelates, he began his long forty years of calmly and resolutely apostolic episcopate. Working incessantly and given with great regularity to prayer, he lived for the most part in London in a modest fashion lodging with a Catholic, Mrs. Hanne, who moved to various houses in the Holborn area, Devonshire Street, Red Lion Street, Lamb's Conduit Street and finally Gloucester Street, Queen's Square. He was for seventeen years coadjutor until he succeeded the old bishop in 1758 ; then for twenty-three years himself vicar apostolic. In later life he was accustomed to have two or three priests living with him and serving the Catholics of central London. An ascetic habit, constant recollectedness, a practice of prayer after the fashion of his own *Meditations*, a great generosity to the poor, a special compassion towards prisoners and a custom of preaching frequent simple homilies, such were the marks of his episcopate. No English prelate had led a life more truly evangelical than the greatest of the vicars-apostolic. His writings, too, *Think well on't* (a delightful title), the *Memoirs of Missionary Priests* and, above all, the *Garden of the Soul* did much to carry forward the solid sound tradition which seventeenth-century English Catholicism had bequeathed to a less dignified and exacting generation. He could be severe upon occasion, but a spiritual prudence marked his actions ; he kept remote from politics, and, although Jacobite in his private sympathies, eventually recognized George III as his *de jure* sovereign ; his consideration was always for his flock. A seriousness of disposition went with a touch of austerity in his relations with the regular clergy. This was marked during the long disputes over the question of the exemption from all episcopal control of those Religious serving parishes, a matter which was settled in 1753 by the brief *Apostolicum Ministerium*. Among the laity Challoner had from the first the love of the poor, but he did not gain in his early years the intimate confidence of the wealthy Catholics. He was rather remote and spiritual for those who lived on the edges of that polite world which Chesterfield's wit illuminated.

Much of the Catholic life of London centred at this period about the embassy chapels maintained by the Sardinian, Portuguese and Bavarian envoys with whom the Bishop's relations were not infrequently difficult. He was aloof from the mental atmosphere of that succession of suave and not particularly talented foreign noblemen who were for the most part profoundly uninterested in rubrics, immune from piety, hardened against scandal and sometimes sympathetic in a patronizing fashion towards the writings of Monsieur Voltaire.

In any case an age which saw the nominally Catholic governments moving towards the suppression of the Jesuits could not be free from painful friction. The expulsion of the fathers of the Society from the college of St. Omer and the transference of the property to the English secular clergy was carried through by the French Government in 1763. This measure caused fresh difficulties which only served to manifest the Bishop's sensitiveness of conscience. The question of education was one which always exercised him.

During the first half of the eighteenth century a school for the sons of the richer Catholics existed at Twyford near Winchester, but this had been abandoned in 1745. Six years later Bishop Challoner established another school at Standon Lordship, an estate in Hertfordshire which had belonged to the last Lord Aston, a Catholic. This school was subsequently transferred to Hare Street and in 1769 to Old Hall Green. The Bishop gave similar encouragement to the founding of a school at Sedgeley Park in Staffordshire in 1763. Close contact was maintained between the two establishments and the Rev. Hugh Kendal who became first president of Sedgeley Park was a brother of Richard Kendal who had founded Standon Lordship. Both schools met with success and served to encourage the depressed Catholics. Similarly Dr. Challoner's intervention was responsible for the reinvigorated life in the historic college at Valladolid which was amalgamated with the two other Spanish colleges at Madrid and Seville in 1767, after the work of the Jesuits had been crippled by the King of Spain's government. In this connection the particular flavour of English Catholic life in the eighteenth century is well brought out in the correspondence of the first secular rectors of Valladolid, Dr. Perry (1767–1774) and Mr. Shephard (1775–1796). Douai, the Bishop's old college, had provided the priest-founders of the schools at Sedgeley Park and Standon Lordship and had assisted greatly in the reorganization of the Spanish college. In regard to the ecclesiastical students in Portugal, Dr. James Barnard had been sent out to strengthen the English College at Lisbon. These activities, in addition to his ordinary episcopal duties in a gradually declining community, give an impression of the crowded, complex, unsatisfying years through which Bishop Challoner passed serene, faithful and recollected. It was from the side of politics that he was to suffer his last and gravest troubles.

BACKGROUND TO THE GORDON RIOTS

BEFORE CONSIDERING the legislative action in connection with Catholic relief it is necessary to refer to a change which was slowly coming over the outlook of a section of the wealthy laity; the beginnings of that spirit which, after Bishop Challoner's time, was to receive the name Cisalpine. Under one aspect this new spirit was a variant of seventeenth-century Gallicanism and it can be maintained that its later form developed as a result of the conditions of life in Georgian England. The rich Catholics enjoyed a measure of social freedom and consideration, while political action was still wholly denied them. The poor of all creeds were then politically insignificant and the rooted prejudice and polished scepticism of fashionable circles united in a refusal to welcome the middle classes and the clergy. The Catholic gentry were thus divided *politically* from their Protestant equals and separated *socially* from their less fortunate co-religionists. The change from a consideration of the activities of Bishop Challoner to those of the ninth Lord Petre marks an immense divergence. The position of the peer's chaplain perhaps tended to increase in significance; but on account of the lack of contact between their manner of life there grew up a certain coldness between the secular and ecclesiastical leaders.

In this connection two elements should be taken into account, the liquidation of the Jacobite movement and the new reign. The last attempt by the Stuarts to regain the throne, the rising known as the '45, had only a very transient effect on English Catholics. The landing of Prince Charles Edward, the fighting, enthusiasm and defeat took place in Scotland. Although the Prince penetrated as far as Derby, before he retreated northwards again, this invasion was a march of Scots. It was only in Lancashire that his cause received support and a few Catholic gentlemen of that county and Mr. Vaughan of Courtfield, who had ridden up from Herefordshire to join him, were the principal victims of this attempt. The vast majority of Catholics in England heard of the marching Highlander only in rumour, nor did they suffer from their defeat. It was true however, that until Prince James Edward died in Rome in 1765 the Popes continued to recognize him as *de jure* sovereign. No such recognition was accorded to Charles Edward, who survived until 1788, nor to his younger brother Henry Benedict known as the Cardinal of York, who lived on at Frascati as the last survivor of the Stuart line until 1807. His cardinalate at once secured him princely rank and eliminated his practical claims upon the throne. As a movement Jacobitism came to an end in 1745 and as a sentiment it hardly outlasted the death of " James III."

Meanwhile a considerable change had come over the English Court with the accession of George III in 1760. George II had been almost without Catholic contacts, old and careful about money, surrounded by a small political and domestic grouping and kept entirely free from tiresome religious complications. The question arose only on one occasion. In 1749 his son-in-law the Landgrave Frederick of Hesse Cassel became a Catholic and was at once cut off from the family circle. In place of George II his grandson, the young King, now reigned ; English in his preferences, obstinate, aware of his position, rather slow, profoundly honest ; a new rallying-point for the nation. In the year following his accession George III married a princess of Mecklenburg-Strelitz and established a decorous domestic atmosphere about the Court which was to endure for fifty years. Queen Charlotte's contacts had been confined to the still rigid Lutheranism of the lesser Baltic courts. A slight figure, almost a child, she moved stiffly in this new world with her small pale face a mask of dignity and clear light eyes which looked for German virtue. It was a counterpart to the rather lymphatic gaze and heavy forthright manner of the sovereign who would in time to come be Farmer George. But there was one quality of the reign by which the Catholics were deeply affected ; in their correspondence and diaries it is evident how sincerely they appreciated this king for his Christian sentiments and virtue. This fact dominates the negotiations which took place between 1760 and the King's final lapse into insanity in 1811. It had its part in promoting loyalty and strengthening intercourse and the King's friendship with the Welds of Lulworth, which developed during his summer visits to Weymouth, depended upon this affinity. Yet the King became in time the chief obstacle to the easing of the Catholic position ; for he felt so strongly that he could not grant concessions without violating his coronation oath. He was a traditionalist and all the more determined because of the comparative brevity of his tradition ; a maintainer of the Protestant religion. He was firmly opposed to any measure that would overturn " the fabric that the wisdom of our forefathers esteemed necessary " as he euphemistically described the penal laws. The first two mild Relief Acts were to get past him, Emancipation never. Yet he was so conscientious that the Catholics could not fail to admire him and he had a deep and naive attractiveness, for who could resist a man who could ask how the apple got into the dumpling ? But these more bucolic developments were in the future and the dullness ascribed to the Court also belonged rather to the sovereigns' middle age than to their youth. The opening of the reign, the Bute administration and the ministries which led up to Lord North's appeared full of movement ; a bustling régime and intensely non-Catholic. No figure of even secondary importance, not even a distinguished *littérateur* was to be found in the thin Catholic ranks, only their social freedom increased from year to year.

In the period of George III's reign between 1770 and 1778 the situation of the recusant peers and the great squires seemed stabilized ; the few secessions which had taken place in the seventeen-sixties like those of young Lord Molyneux and Lord Dillon's heir were now over, and an increasing measure of security is found reflected in the building plans of the rich Catholics.

There had been little building by the great Catholic families in the earlier portion of the century ;[1] but now such work developed rapidly partly due to the popularity of James Payne's designs. This architect was already known through the recent completion of Nostell Priory, which he had built for Sir Rowland Winn in the Italian style, when he was introduced to Catholic circles by Mr. William Middleton for whom he designed the new house at Stockeld Park. He soon gained an extensive practice in the Midlands and the north among families with such close Catholic associations as the Claverings of Axwell and the Fenwicks of Bywell, and in 1763 he began on the great house called Worksop Manor for the Duke of Norfolk. From 1764 till 1770 he was employed by Lord Petre on the construction of Thorndon Hall and from 1770 till 1776 on Wardour Castle. The Arundells were in different ways his patrons, but he was soon affected by the rivalry of the Adam brothers, who

---

[1] Gilling Castle, which was re-built by Vanbrugh for Charles, sixth Viscount Fairfax mainly between 1711-5, is a notable exception.

were called in by Lord Scarsdale to build Kedleston for which Payne had drawn up the plans. Still Payne has left the two chief monuments of late eighteenth century Catholicism in England, Thorndon and Wardour.

At the same time the increased freedom of the Catholics was manifest in the political field. The grant of toleration to their co-religionists in French Canada, which had been in English hands since the conquests of the Seven Years' War, must have given rise to some faint repercussion in England. Still from such changes it was the laity who benefited and not the clergy who were pressed by the unrelaxed penal legislation.

The entry of the Tory governments into power had brought the richest adherents of the old religion into some relations with the Court and to a faint interest in politics at second remove ; nor were the Whigs without their occasional supporter among the Catholic landowners, as in the case of Fox's friend Henry Howard of Corby. Yet such a case was rare and the majority of the wealthy Catholics of the second half of the eighteenth century were brought up in an atmosphere sympathetic to the political outlook of Lord North and George III. In this connection a certain drift in the political current is indicative of interest. By the time of the Napoleonic Wars the small section of the more important Catholic landowners had passed over from the Tories to the Whigs as shadowy but persistent supporters.

Meanwhile prosperity and an assured position had turned the attention of the greater squires not only to building but to collecting. Debarred from active politics and the army, they became in some cases connoisseurs and patrons of art. And with these interests there came at this level a novel form of toleration.[1] Catholics were regarded as not uncultured. The opportunity of travel, which they did not neglect, gave something of a cosmopolitan atmosphere to that section of Catholic life which is reflected in the Jerningham Letters. Henry Swinburne the traveller, with his sketch-books and his elaborate descriptive writings, was thus at home in the great northern houses viewing the marbles which Charles Towneley had collected or the octagonal hall of statuary and the galleries of

---

[1] A passage in the correspondence of Horace Walpole and Mary Berry illustrates this point. " Your partiality to the pageantry of Popery," he wrote, " I do approve, and I doubt whether the world would not be a loser (in its visionary enjoyments) by the extinction of that religion, as it was by the decay of chivalry and the proscription of the heathen deities." *Letters* xiv, p. 141.

Italian and Dutch paintings of distinction with which Henry Blundell was furnishing Ince's solid magnificence. The custom of a private travelling tutor had been growing more common as the century progressed and the education thus imparted was seldom conventional but not infrequently specialized. The influence of such a priest-tutor as Mr. John Needham F.R.S., noted for his microscopical discoveries, must have been remarkable amid the rather arid educational experiences of those who were excluded from the universities. Bishop Walmesley, too, was an admirable mathematician and the last member of the Catholic episcopate to receive the fellowship of the Royal Society. This cultivated priestly influence and the antiquarian and botanical studies of the clergy must have produced an effect upon their pupils and on those rich squires' sons in whose households they lived with so much intimacy. A line of influence would seem to run from these priests' rooms, where the clever son of the family would be stimulated to respectful study, to such men as Marmaduke Tunstall the ornithologist and to the work of Charles Waterton in the next generation. The effect of the teaching of such a master of the spiritual life as Jean Nicolas Grou, serving the chapel at Lulworth for the Welds, was manifest ; but the chaplains of the last Penal times passed on their interest in humane studies also.

The remembrance of all the employments from which they were excluded has tended to encourage an exaggeration of the degree to which the families faithful to the old religion suffered isolation in the Hanoverian reigns. In this connection a passage in the *Antiquities of Hengrave* gives a delightful glimpse of the extent to which a Catholic squire could fit into the period landscape. The short character sketch refers to Sir Thomas William Gage, seventh Baronet of Hengrave Hall in Suffolk, a Fellow of the Linnæan Society, who belonged to that section of the laity attached to the Jesuits and dying in Rome was buried in the Gesu under a memorial inscription composed by Charles Plowden. " Enthusiasm and delicacy," the passage relating to Sir Thomas opens, " distinguished his character and were blended in a manner as happy as unusual. His tastes and pursuits were all elegant. Whatever he said or did was marked by gentlemanly feelings. It was both from nature and from cultivation . . . that he possessed a tact, which, while it was essential to the pursuit of botany, his favourite science, rendered him tremblingly alive to the beauties of art and the more sublime charms of creation. In the most abstruse parts of the vegetable world he had laboured hard by the lamp, as well as by the sun ; studying the works of his predecessors in his closet, and exploring the objects themselves in the fields." It is obvious that, although debarred from more active pursuits, numerous Catholic gentlemen must have been fitted to secure a similar appreciation from their contemporaries. One curious fact is traceable to this form of recognition. It undoubtedly played its part in convincing a section of the principal laity that they could best hope for the alleviation of their lot by not permitting the intervention of the Catholic episcopate and instead negotiating directly with their Protestant fellow-countrymen who knew their personal worth.

Meanwhile an unexpected event hastened the first attempt at a removal of the Catholics' disabilities, for a minor persecution confined to the south of England broke out and aroused public opinion to the worst features of the situation. A series of prosecutions under the Statute of William III had been initiated in 1765 through the action of common informers anxious to obtain the reward of £100 granted to anyone who could obtain the conviction of a priest exercising his sacerdotal functions. The peak of these vexations, which resulted in the suppression of Mass centres, was reached in 1767 the year in which John Baptist Maloney was sentenced at the Croydon Assizes to perpetual imprisonment " for exercising the functions of a popish priest." Although to some degree a manifestation of popular anti-Catholic feeling, these prosecutions were undertaken without the approval of the government and in this case the sentence was commuted after four years to one of banishment. Subsequent acquittals on this charge were due to the Lord Chief Justice, Lord Mansfield who held that it was necessary to prove the fact of ordination before such a prosecution could succeed.

Nevertheless in spite of the general dissatisfaction with the state of the law, the occasion for a change was not provided until 1778 when Lord North's government was anxious to secure the enlistment of Catholic Highlanders for the war with the American Colonies and France. After preliminaries in Scotland, negotiations went forward with the English Catholics, although from the first Bishop Challoner foresaw the outbreak of that hostility which was to culminate in the Gordon Riots. Meanwhile a statement made by the Catholic lawyer, William Sheldon gives a prevision of the difficulties which would soon break out among his coreligionists.

" I strongly opposed," wrote Mr. Sheldon in regard to the discussions at this time " any application to the clergy in temporal matters the English Roman Catholic Gentlemen being quite able to judge and act for themselves in these affairs." In this spirit the negotiations went forward under the chairmanship of Lord Petre.

In June 1778 the first Catholic Relief Act received the royal assent. In consequence of this measure Catholics could legally purchase and inherit land and the prosecution of the clergy by common informers and the penalty of imprisonment for life were abolished. To gain the benefit of these concessions it was necessary to take an oath of loyalty to George III. During the whole progress of the matter the bishops, in the words of Dr. Challoner, " were nowise consulted." Very aged, the vicar apostolic was doubtful as to the future and his doubts were justified. They were within two years of the Gordon Riots.

The origin, course and suppression of the mob action, generally known as the Gordon Riots, was simple and predictable. There was a mass of anti-Catholic feeling steadily fanned. In 1779 there were riots in Edinburgh and in the following year the trouble spread to London, where a Protestant Association pledged to obtain the repeal of the Relief Act had been organized under Lord George Gordon, a Member of Parliament of bizarre mentality whose leadership showed the courage of a partly unhinged mind. It is notable that while the Londoners supporting his association had the most ingenuous hatred of Popery, a religion of which they had the slightest knowledge, Lord George had a fanatical distaste for the familiar. His home was in a Catholic part of Scotland ; his father the third Duke of Gordon had been brought up a Catholic ; his aunt the Duchess of Perth had been the mainstay of Scottish Catholicism. For a time he had a great success. Very earnest and rather mad, with his long red hair and solemn face, he harangued the poor of London almost as an equal.

The first reaction of the government to this agitation seems to have been irritated indifference at the tiresome result of their Relief Act towards which all parties had shown a desultory sympathy. The movement gathered in strength, a mass demonstration was held and a petition presented to Parliament. On the afternoon of 2 June, 1780, the demonstration with its petition turned into a riot and members of the House of Lords, who had supported the Relief Act, were attacked. Among those set upon was the Duke of

Northumberland (the first of the Smithson Percy line), an aged peer who had been baptized as a Catholic and brought up in childhood in the old religion. In the days before newspapers the crowd had long memories. The chapels of the Bavarian and Sardinian Ambassadors were destroyed and, later, Lord Mansfield's house. The following day Bishop Challoner was brought to a house at Finchley belonging to a Catholic merchant, Mr. Mawhood who had long been his devoted friend. The rioting lasted, with intervals, for five days and among the Catholic properties destroyed were the chapels in Moorfields, Bermondsey and Virginia Street, Wapping, the last place being the centre of an Irish congregation numbering about four thousand. The Catholics remained quiet under great provocation. On 7 June, Newgate prison was burned down and the mob began an indiscriminate destruction and was rapidly quelled by the military. Lord Petre and Mr. Langdale the distiller had their houses destroyed, but the greatest damage was done to business premises within reach of the city and south of the Thames. One of the facts revealed by the accounts of the riots is the large number of Irish already engaged in trade in London. In an incomplete list of forty Catholics who had suffered loss of property, fourteen names are Irish, four foreign and twenty-two English. This was a considerable change from the situation on Bishop Challoner's appointment. According to a report sent to Propaganda in 1746 the number of Catholics in London had remained more or less stationary at the figure of twenty thousand since the death of Queen Anne. This represented the declining English nucleus to which the immigration from Ireland was now adding.

In the provinces there was some repercussion of the disturbances and the chapels at Hull and Bath and the house of the vicar apostolic of the western district in the latter town were destroyed. Both in town and country the government's measures were effective in preventing any renewal of the rioting and many rioters were hanged. Lord George Gordon whose responsibility rested on his inflammatory speeches was, however, acquitted. He soon lost all public significance, supported various causes, declared himself a Jew and died eventually in prison undergoing a sentence for libel. Bishop Challoner did not long survive the riots and died at 25, Gloucester Street in January 1781. His last spoken word was " charity " in reference to some moneys given him for the poor on the morning before his last seizure. He was succeeded as vicar apostolic by his

coadjutor the retiring and rather colourless Bishop Talbot. Dr.
Challoner was buried in the family vault of the Barrets at Milton
in Berkshire. The veneration felt for him was well expressed by
John Milner, then a young priest in charge of the mission of Winchester. With his death there vanished the chief support for the
oppressed Catholics during the eighteenth century.

In the years between 1781 and 1790 the fortunes of the Catholics
in England reached their lowest ebb. The slight assistance from the
Relief Act of 1778, which had been the occasion of the Gordon
Riots, had done nothing to check the decline in numbers. The old
Duke of Norfolk had died in 1777 and had been succeeded by Mr.
Howard of Greystoke, a gentleman of a melancholy habit of mind
whose religious outlook was both depressed and submissive. In
his description of his father he appears to give his own opinion.
" He was,"[1] wrote Mr. Howard of Greystoke, " one of the few of
those days who held that religion should never be blended with
politics, further than as it enjoins a due submission to government,
and an attention to the peace and prosperity of society." This is an
unimpeachable sentiment, but not encouraging from the leader of a
persecuted minority.

Among the rising generation in the great families there had
indeed been one Catholic outstanding in character, if not in ability :
young Charles Howard. Combining developed eccentricities with a
substratum of political common sense, coarse, popular in speech,
proudly negligent in dress, convivial, impetuous, he possessed a
sincere ardour for the aristocratic whiggery to which he was a
convert. Such combination in this time and place could have done
much to mitigate the lot of the failing remnant. He was to have
great wealth and always a love of spending ; but, when he inherited
the Norfolk dukedom in 1786, he had already abandoned
Catholicism.

The laity were left almost without leaders and the episcopate
lacked talent. In the north Bishop Matthew Gibson was a strong
hardy prelate, but the Midland and London vicariates had passed
to the two quiet old brothers Thomas and James Talbot, pious, of
exalted descent and tolerably wealthy. In public life the Catholic
body was regarded not so much with hostility as with profound
indifference. Earl Nugent, otherwise Craggs, a minor politician of

---

[1] *Historical Anecdotes of some of the Howard Family*, by Charles Howard of Greystoke, 1769, p. 127.

unsavoury reputation, was reconciled to the Church on his deathbed in 1788. Two Catholics of little personal influence were introduced into the political circle, the Marchioness of Buckingham, wife of the Lord Lieutenant, and the young Lady Shaftesbury. *Vanity Fair* deals with a later period, but Thackeray was correct in suggesting that this age would not be greatly troubled by the religion professed by the Marchioness of Steyne. In 1785 the Prince of Wales, later George IV, married Mrs. Fitzherbert, a young Catholic widow of good family, by birth a Smythe of Acton Burnell. The marriage was private, illegal as contravening the Royal Marriage Act and its very existence was denied in Parliament. The atmosphere of condescension at this period is well borne out in the case of Edmund Burke, who for all his friendliness inevitably conveyed to the Catholics a sense of their political inferiority. Meanwhile almost every year some old family died out or some young squire seceded and each apostasy involved the closing down of support for poor Catholics as the rich landlords fell, Mr. Chichester of Arlington, Mr. Clifton of Lytham, Mr. Heneage of Hainton, Sir Edward Swinburne and Sir Thomas Gascoigne. It was at this unfortunate moment that divisions appeared among the Catholics themselves. These were due in great part to the Cisalpine spirit, which developed in a comparatively small but influential grouping.

THE CISALPINE SPIRIT

THE term Cisalpine is associated as closely with the eighteenth century as is that of Ultramontane with the nineteenth. These words are counterparts representing directly opposing points of view. They designate two parties or more accurately two types of mental outlook. The Ultramontanes looked, as the term implies, towards Rome *beyond the mountains*. They stood for an open, loudly proclaimed and selfconscious attachment to the Holy See and, in lesser matters, for a dutiful acceptance of each detail of the papal organization. They received gratefully all the encouragement and guidance which Rome would give to them and throughout gave the Papacy a keen support.

The Cisalpine spirit, with which we now deal, was the antithesis of the attitude just described. The name by which it is known, with the suggestion that it belongs specifically to the lands *north of the Alps*, gives only a very vague impression of its character. It indicated in the first place the adoption of a certain attitude towards the civil Government. Accepting the general tenets of Catholic dogma, the Cisalpines were accustomed to concentrate attention on their moral obligations towards the State. They were ready to receive the dogmatic teaching of the Holy See ; but they regarded all other forms of papal action with chill reserve. In practice they were very independent ; they made constant difficulties about appointments ; they were exclusive. Wherever they were gathered together there was always a strong sense that the clergy were exceeding their rights.

It may be suggested that the growth of the Cisalpine point of view can be numbered among the consequences of the development of sharply differentiated and nationally conscious states. Again, as far as the individual was concerned, it developed most easily among those who understood the actual workings of the civil government, who benefited by the particular political systems then in vogue and were in a position to influence the machinery of politics. In contemporary France the Gallican position, which was somewhat similar, affected most strongly those elements in the nation which had an appreciative understanding of the Bourbon absolute monarchy. It has been said forcibly, but rather inaccurately and crudely, that the Gallican and Cisalpine attitude implies the consideration of the interests of the State as paramount over those of the Church. It would be more correct to say that the Cisalpines held that the interests of the State should come before those of the Church organization ; and as a result they favoured government vetoes and the appointment of the national bishops by elective agencies functioning within the particular country. In England this attitude was modified by diverse trends. What Rome considered to be an essential freedom of action, they were inclined to look upon as foreign interference. The medieval ideal of the Church as a *Societas Perfecta* was entirely alien to their minds.

Taking this as a rough basis it can be pointed out that the full Cisalpine standpoint was found only after the complete victory of the Hanoverian government system. Once the Jacobites had ceased to be a serious political force attention was concentrated upon this successful government to whose changes and coalitions no permanent alternative could yet be found. A certain frame of mind tended to develop among those members of the privileged classes who were only debarred by the Test Acts from the exercise of power. The state of affairs in which their social prestige was unbalanced by political freedom brought many of the Catholic peers and greater gentry to a condition of permanent but unfruitful dissatisfaction. No restrictions were placed on the social intercourse and private friendship between the Catholics and the rest of the community. In fact the Voltairean atmosphere among the governing circles, the stereotyped but universal travel, the traditional popularity of Paris and the prestige of the French Court at Versailles all tended to dispel any narrowly Protestant outlook among the English ruling class. This Protestantism still characterized those engaged in commerce and the lesser squires emphasizing the remoteness of these elements from the inner circles, which had been touched by that aristocratic, sceptical, free-thinking spirit later associated with the eighteenth century. Religious feeling had been strained out from such men as Chesterfield to whom Catholics of sufficient politeness were individually acceptable.

It was just the freedom with which the wealthier Catholic gentry could range which induced some of them to attempt the removal of the obstacle of the Penal Laws. They understood and admired the governmental system and wished for that influence within it that their rank would normally carry. As a result they were anxious for some relief which would enable them to enter diplomacy or politics or the fighting services. They were ready to accept any compromise to this end provided that it did not offend against their sense of honour.

Some further characteristics marked the Cisalpines. For instance, an impatience with the clergy, which has proved a recurrent factor in self-organized lay opinion, reinforced their standpoint. A line of spiritual descent can, in fact, be traced leading down to them from the lay opponents of the Jesuits in the sixteenth century through the supporters of the oath of allegiance under James I. Similarly at a later date differing social origins and outlook were to complicate the struggle between the Cisalpines and their great opponent Bishop Milner. Again the suppression of the Jesuits in 1773 had led in certain quarters to the weakening of the tradition of strict religious allegiance and it seems also to have had the effect in certain minds of loosening the conception of a powerful Tridentine central authority. Finally it appears that to the Cisalpines the papal doctrine and Rome itself seemed, although true, extremely uninteresting.

Fortified as it was by writers of merit, the Cisalpine position was nevertheless not in any way intellectualist. Its supporters suggested a club rather than a coterie. As a group they were unbreakably sincere, generous and honourable. A certain colouring was given to Cisalpinism by the legal Catholics. Thus the few and often distinguished conveyancers of Lincoln's Inn tended to support it; for they found themselves against closed doors. The Cisalpine movement naturally included many of those who suffered most severely from this *carrière fermée aux talents*. But in the circumstances of its rise the inevitable eclipse was foreshadowed. In England the movement could not well survive Catholic Emancipation and the Reform Bill. Still, under varying names, the Cisalpines were a factor in English life for fifty years. But before considering their activities from 1783 till 1829 it is necessary to obtain an impression of their successful opponent Bishop Milner. A detailed description, even entering into trivial habits and traits, will be an aid in making the position which he held quite clear.

MILNER'S STANDPOINT

FOR THE first quarter of the nineteenth century the Catholic minority was dominated by the courageous personality of Bishop Milner. This prelate stood at the head of the long tradition of the parochial clergy in nineteenth-century England; he fully shared their firmness, their strong sense of reality, their independence. By descent a Lancashireman, by birth a member of the then restricted Catholic middle class, by education an inheritor of the Douai tradition, he was well fitted to defend the old religion. A lover of truth, preferably rather obvious truth, and of plain dealing he was ill at ease with the complex and the sophisticated. A deep interior simplicity coloured all his actions. Although a student, an antiquarian of some repute and an F.S.A. neither intellectual nor general society appealed to him. The period of his mission work was divided into two roughly equal halves, his pastoral charge at Winchester from 1779 till 1803 and his administration of the Midland district as vicar apostolic and Bishop of Castabala *in partibus* from 1803 until his death in 1826.

As a bishop he was always anxious to avoid either offending or consulting his brother-prelates; towards his flock he was paternal, to the interfering laity he was markedly severe. He had a singularly clear-sighted appreciation of all that concerned ecclesiastical prerogative. A filial devotion to the Holy See was always manifest and he had a strong sentiment of loyalty to George III. "Religion is all my politics" was an expression often on his lips. It is essential for an understanding of the pre-Newman Church to attempt to visualize John Milner. The well held but unwieldy figure, the short strong neck, that florid face and the open hazel eyes beneath the dark thick eyebrows inspired confidence in his trustworthiness and firm capacity. He was a familiar figure first in the streets of Winchester walking plainly dressed with his black velvet waistcoat and the white cravat folded carefully within his coat's straight collar, and later in the lanes of Staffordshire in his episcopate as he rode his black horse " Farmer " or drove his gig through the parishes round Wolverhampton muffled in a cape and a drab greatcoat. The

F

copious speech and the loud voice, contrasting curiously with a half-smothered lisp, were well controlled ; for he joined a deep personal humility with much common sense. His tastes were simple, remote from and alien to the more sophisticated Catholic gentlemen who met with the Prince Regent's tolerance. He had much more in common with Cobbett than with his own old school fellow the Duke of Norfolk. His appetite was hearty and he was particularly fond of boiled corned beef. He had a developed taste for the more plebeian forms of fish and a curious dislike for cheese. After these details it is no surprise to learn that he fasted conscientiously and with much discomfort. Puns did not appeal to him, but in other respects he had a fund of homely humour and had two songs which he was prepared to sing upon occasion. A rather insufficient knowledge of rubrics was offset by calmness in ceremonies, a loud but uncertain singing voice and permanent self-possession. He had considerable eloquence, perfect sincerity of expression and not very much literary taste. Italian plaster work appealed to him and he introduced stained glass even into his bedroom windows at Oscott. He liked white flowers for the altar or alternatively decorations made from gold and silver paper.

As a correspondent to the Press he was notably diligent enlivening the Catholic periodicals by many contributions, especially during his later years. When a bishop he generally used a pseudonym and his strongly worded communications were signed by names such as " Laocoon " and " Old Catholic Pastor " or sometimes " Aloysius Stanislaus." As this last choice implies he was particularly attached to the Jesuits. He made his daily meditations with great regularity, was a competent theologian and student of the *Summa*. His favourite prayer was the *Adoro te*. He was devoted to children and most successful with them, large-hearted, very charitable to the poor, perhaps a little suspicious of the rich. The Irish bishops gave him their complete confidence. Gallicanism he could not understand. At the root of his attraction lay a deep simplicity.

It is a part of Milner's great significance in Catholic history that he understood so completely the people's standpoint. Like the great mass of the Catholic body, he stood for the old core of England. He was as close akin to those who made the eighteenth-century conquests as he was remote from that restricted circle which reaped immediate benefit. The Sheridan side of literature, the " Bucks " of the Regency, Brighton Pavilion, the Corinthians were far from the

scope of Milner's world. He was closer to the great players with
their background of respectability and he had been at school with
John Philip Kemble. But here theological conceptions entered.
Perhaps as a boy he had known Kemble's sister Sarah, who was to
be the famous Mrs. Siddons ; but in his mature years Milner
certainly abhorred the stage. (This was perhaps not unnatural, for
the stage had taken much from Catholicism and given little back to
it : besides in one of its aspects it was the least respectable depend-
ency of the life of privilege.) His views on his contemporaries
were solidly grounded like his humour. Thus his own sympathies
went out to Grattan upon the one hand and to Wilberforce on the
other. It is particularly notable that in the lifelong struggle which
he maintained against the protagonists of the Cisalpine spirit in its
many forms he had the Catholic middle classes and the people on
his side. Against him were ranged sections of the wealthy gentry
and of the peers, a group of lawyers, some writers, clerical and lay ;
in fact the party of privilege.

This characteristic is again apparent in the reception accorded to
his polemical writings. " He was," in Provost Husenbeth's pleasant
phrasing,[1] " a great controvertist." To many he is chiefly familiar
as the author of the *End of Controversy*. But it would seem to
have been the average Catholic who most appreciated and benefited
by his work. His clear statements and a certain sturdy intransigence
gave back to the generality of the laity an intellectual confidence
which the long deadening eighteenth century had almost sapped.
In this he had the preacher's gift of familiarity. Whatever the effect
upon the apathetic general public, to the Catholics his words went
home. In another sense, too, his episcopal reign marked the beginnings of a movement which was to develop through the nineteenth
century. He realized vaguely the great future of Catholicism in the
towns.

His predecessors in the Midland vicariate had sprung from the
ranks of the rich landed gentry, Stapleton of Carlton, Berington of
Moat, Talbot, Lord Shrewsbury's brother, Hornyold of Blackmore
Park. Since 1752 the bishops had lived at Long Birch in Staffordshire, a house on the Chillington estate left to Dr. Hornyold by Mrs.
Giffard. Some of the prelates had lived upon their private fortunes
and the wealthy Dr. Talbot had been much interested in agricultural

---

[1] *The Life of Bishop Milner*, by Provost Husenbeth, is a mine of information on the
bishop's outlook and habits.

development. But Bishop Milner became definitely alienated from the circle favoured by earlier vicars-apostolic on account of the strong Cisalpine sympathies of the Giffards, Throckmortons and Beringtons who were bound together in a close and disapproving cousinage. Meanwhile, Bishop Berington's pupil, Peter Giffard, upon whom so much landed influence devolved, had conformed to the Established Church ; Lady Charlotte Giffard was a Protestant and Chillington had fallen. Milner determined to break loose. In 1803 he settled at Wolverhampton which had always contained a Catholic element.

It would be a mistake to read any advanced social or political ideals into this change. In some ways Milner was notably conservative ; but it was the conservatism of the rising middle classes, unconnected with politics,[1] in the last analysis neither Whig, nor Tory. This independence of judgment was reinforced by the responsibilities of authority. He was direct, logical, absolutely honest and sincere. Such a man would have no time for the refinements or the shades of feeling. Thus Milner's character only throws into relief the importance of the change, little noticed at the time, when the seat of ecclesiastical administration in the Midlands was removed from Long Birch with its coach-houses and stabling and farms to the main street in Wolverhampton.

[1] A letter from the Marquis of Buckingham to Lord Grenville dated 19 June, 1810 indicates the irritant effect of his independence on the ruling families. Writing from Stowe Lord Buckingham refers to " Dr. Milner whose conduct . . . is very reprehensible and his letter from Wolverhampton in Cobbetts' paper is that of a very dog," Cal. Fortescue MSS. x, p. 7.

THE PARTY OF PRIVILEGE

THROUGHOUT Bishop Milner's pastoral life the movement towards Catholic Emancipation had been gathering strength, but in the early years its driving force had come from the ranks of the Irish Catholics who also were responsible for the successful termination. Emancipation in England in the lines of its actual development was to a great extent the result of a struggle in Ireland which brought liberty for English Catholics in its train. It is natural, therefore, that the early efforts should hardly have impinged upon the consciousness of English life. Dr. Curry, Mr. O'Conor and Mr. Wyse laboured in their own country and it was only the occasional peers, who entered into the movement reluctantly and with a well-developed sense of their personal dignity, who were familiar to London society. In the early years of George III Lord Trimlestown had thus a restricted influence in those circles to whom he gave political allegiance. At this time Lord Taaffe, the veteran Austrian general, became an accustomed figure with this equipage and polite bravura when he came over periodically from Silesia to concern himself with the affairs of his co-religionists.

A few years later in 1773 Lord Kenmare accepted the leadership of a Catholic Committee, but in 1783 he found himself outvoted on account of his compliant attitude towards the government and for the remainder of his life was out of sympathy with the method adopted by the supporters of the new movement for Catholic freedom. This point has a bearing on the relations between English and Irish Catholics. The Kenmares and the young Earl of Fingall, who held that peerage from 1795 till 1836, were in familiar contact with the old Catholic squirearchy and one can thus readily understand the opposition of the English squires to the standpoint of the leaders of the Irish Catholic " democracy," John Keogh and later O'Connell. Throughout these years the vocal English laity saw the question from this point of view ; they applauded Fingall's loyal action against the rebels in '98 ; they fully entered into his anticipations as to the benefits of the Act of Union.

The bearing of this factor in the situation becomes clearer when the action of the English Catholics is considered. As early as 1782 at a meeting of laymen of affluence a Catholic Committee had been formed composed of ten members, five of whom represented the different ecclesiastical districts. No priests were elected to this body. This practice of using ecclesiastical divisions but without clerical representation was obnoxious to the bishops, and the vicars apostolic of the northern and western districts showed marked hostility to the Committee. Difficulties became intensified after 1787 when the Committee was re-formed and proposed to work for the passage of a Catholic Relief Act.

The Committee soon indicated a desire for the appointment of diocesan bishops, instead of vicars apostolic, and for the establishment of an English school in place of Douai. The conciliatory attitude of Bishop James Talbot enabled them to go forward and they received some support in their educational plans from Fr. Strickland of Liège. The moving spirit of the Committee was Mr. Charles Butler who had succeeded Mr. Sheldon as secretary. He was singularly well fitted to be their leader. He was at this time thirty-seven years of age, had been educated at Douai and was an eminent conveyancer of Lincoln's Inn. Through his wife, a Miss Eyston of East Hendred, he was connected with the old families. In temperament he was ascetic and his interests were chiefly liturgical. He was rather consciously high-minded, regular in his habits and serious. Entertaining did not appeal to him and he spent his leisure in the privacy of his family in Red Lion Square. (In most things he was the antithesis of his lifelong opponent Dr. Milner.) He kept the minutes of all the Committee's meetings and supplied a clerk when this service was required.

Very soon the Committee embarked on a series of proposals to restrain the influence of the Court of Rome and opposition naturally developed. The hostile feeling centred upon the Cisalpine leaders the chief of whom were Lord Petre, Mr. Throckmorton of Buckland and his cousin Sir Henry Englefield of White Knights. They were governmental in sympathy, Gallican by preference ; a close corporation of the polite unenthusiastic Catholicism of the Thames Valley. Sir Henry took a serious interest in the Antiquaries and was for a time president of that society and Mr. Throckmorton permitted Cowper to form a charming intimacy with his family. The amenities of a civilized life meant very much to them.

Meanwhile as soon as they found that feeling ran counter to their projects the Committee prudently elected three clerical members the most significant being Dr. Charles Berington, coadjutor of the Midland district. At this stage the situation was governed by the dates of the tenure of office of Dr. James Talbot as vicar apostolic of the London district from 1781 till 1790 and Dr. Thomas Talbot as vicar apostolic of the Midland district from 1778 till 1795. The close relationship of these bishops with the leading laymen prevented that acerbity which developed later with Dr. Milner ; while the position was complicated by the fact that the Cisalpine leaders maintained chaplaincies, were sometimes almost wholly responsible for the support of the Church in their counties, were the chief mainstay of many charities and had all suffered severe disabilities for their religion.

This in part accounts for the manner in which the bishops allowed the negotiations with the government to be controlled by the Committee and accepted eventually a protestation dealing with the deposing power of the Pope and designed to satisfy Pitt's administration. This protestation, although it could be regarded as Cisalpine in tone, was signed by three vicars apostolic and the leading clergy and laity. Some form of assent was obtained from Bishop Gibson of the northern district. Fr. Charles Plowden alone gave a categorical refusal. The total number of signatories was above fifteen hundred including two hundred and forty priests.

Meanwhile the bishops had taken alarm and in 1789 had condemned a proposed form of oath, a condemnation which was repeated in rather stronger terms two years later. The Committee had concerned themselves with the introduction of a measure for the relief of Protesting Catholic Dissenters and the bishops had likewise refused to accept this curious description of their flock. At the same time the situation had been radically altered by the death of Bishop James Talbot and the failure of the strong effort made by the leading laymen aided by Monsignor Christopher Stonor to obtain Bishop Berington's appointment as his successor. The attempt was defeated mainly through the influence of the aged vicar apostolic of the western district, Bishop Walmesley, and the consecration of Mr. Douglass, the priest at York, marked a new trend in Catholic policy. A few months later Monsignor Stonor, who had been agent in Rome since 1749, died at an advanced age and with his death the generation of effective rule by Talbots, Beringtons, Hornyolds and Petres, the prelates of the squirearchy, passed away.

In the following year the Catholic Relief Act was passed partly due to the efforts of Bishop Douglass. Catholic chapels became legal on registration and Mass could be celebrated by all priests who had taken a form of oath (the Irish Oath of 1774) acceptable both to the vicars apostolic and the government. The celebration of Mass was forbidden in any building possessing a bell or steeple. It was, however, permitted in a private house if not more than five outsiders were present. No Roman Catholic ecclesiastic was allowed to exercise any of the rites or ceremonies of his religion except in such a private house or in a registered chapel. The habits of religious orders might not be worn in the streets.[1] These were the main provisions. With the passing of the Relief Act of 1791 the acute difficulties within the Catholic body diminished. Lord Petre busied himself with good works as appears from an account of the building of a Catholic chapel at Monmouth which was opened in 1793. " On these now legal establishments," he wrote,[2] " the Catholic Religion must ultimately depend. The middling classes will find themselves more independent, and the Gentlemen will feel themselves at liberty to consult their own convenience in the expense attending chaplains. I shall therefore willingly subscribe."

The personal advantages were, however, felt rather by the richer Catholics in the towns than by the squires, for the double land tax was still exacted and the Test Act still prevented them from holding offices of profit under the Crown. On the other hand the restrictions imposed by the Act of William III, which precluded Catholics from practising as barristers and solicitors, were removed and Charles Butler became the first Catholic barrister to practise since the fall of the Stuarts. In April 1792 the principal members of the Committee, which had been dissolved on the passing of the Relief Act, formed the Cisalpine Club which existed until 1830 but with diminishing influence. Lord Shrewsbury joined Lord Petre as its leader, but after the death of Bishop Berington in 1798 the group had little significance in regard to the details of Catholic life in England, although it gave a certain tone to the habits of thought of the generation which was brought up in the first years of the nineteenth century.

Meanwhile in other quarters opposition to any veiled Gallican

---

[1] The last minor disabilities of this character were removed by the Catholic Relief Act of 1926.

[2] Clifton Archives, vol. iv, printed in Bishop Ward's *Dawn of the Catholic Revival in England*, i, p. 204.

standpoint had been steadily gathering strength. Mr. Milner of Winchester had taken a leading part in supporting the views of the bishops in the past five years and he had behind him the bulk of the solid Catholics engaged in commerce who combined to oppose a movement which was based on privilege, impatient of Rome and remarkably amenable to the point of view of the English government. The bulk of the northern Catholics agreed with Milner and were quite unmoved by the wishes of a London Committee singularly unrepresentative of their own strength. The representative of the northern district on the Committee, Sir John Lawson of Brough, was himself unsympathetic to the standpoint of Petre and Throckmorton and on various occasions demanded a stronger policy. This solidarity in the north was emphasized by the firm rule of the two brothers Bishop Matthew Gibson, who was vicar apostolic from 1780 till 1790, and Bishop William Gibson, who was vicar apostolic from 1790 till 1821. They were among the twenty-two children of Jasper Gibson of Stonehouse and his wife Margaret Leadbitter and came of strong Catholic stock with an hereditary attachment to the Dominicans. They had been brought up at Hexham, a centre of recusancy, and had close contact with the people. Their rule was vigorous and paternal and marked by directness of thought and action. They had no use for Lord Petre ; neither for his ordered hierarchic life at Thorndon ; nor for his sympathy with the un-orthodox ; nor for his careful fashionable hair and his flowered silk waistcoat.

Another influence and in this case more consciously ultramontane was that of Fr. Charles Plowden and the friends of the Jesuits, the old pupils of the gentlemen of Liège, Mr. Weld and Lord Arundell and Lord Clifford. Among these names that of Mr. Thomas Weld of Lulworth had a high significance, for in this generation his family had accumulated great estates which were later dispersed among his children. He was said to have been the second largest landowner in England. Lulworth, Chidiock and Pylewell in the west, Leagram and Stonyhurst in Lancashire and Britwell in Oxfordshire, together with the provision for their Catholic population, depended upon him. In the years that followed it was these sections, the northern Catholics, Mr. Milner and the wide body of his supporters among his poorer coreligionists, and Mr. Weld and his friends, who took the most active part in the changes which the French Revolution brought to Catholicism in England.

THE FRENCH REVOLUTION

THERE can be little doubt that the French Revolution was of great benefit to Catholicism in England by bringing back the schools and colleges, so long established abroad, to English soil. Throughout the seventeenth and eighteenth centuries the places of higher education which were most accessible had been the colleges at Douai and St. Omer; but in 1762 the Jesuits who controlled St. Omer had been expelled from France and in 1773 the Society of Jesus had been suppressed. The college had gone forward under the secular clergy, but without great success; still the pension was not considerable and had attracted one youth of promise, Daniel O'Connell. The bulk of the supporters of a Jesuit education had, however, transferred their sons to the house at Liège, known as the English Academy, where the fathers of the suppressed Society continued their work through the favour of the prince bishop, who was a temporal as well as an ecclesiastical ruler. In 1776 the " gentlemen of Liège," as they were known, had as many as one hundred and fifty pupils under their care. Their misfortunes only increased the sympathy with which they were regarded by a large section of the Catholic body and they had an influence on affairs which was much more extensive that that of the other communities of regulars engaged in education. In regard to the houses for students for the priesthood the English College at Rome had lately passed through a series of misfortunes under unsuitable foreign superiors, while the colleges at Valladolid and Lisbon were to remain unaffected by this stage of the Revolution.

In August 1793 the secular college at St. Omer had been sequestrated. This was followed in October of the same year by the expulsion of the priests and students at Douai, in the Benedictine houses of St. Gregory's, Douai and St. Lawrence, Dieulouard and in the Dominican house at Bornhem. The " gentlemen of Liège " realizing that the prince-bishop was no longer able to protect them had sent their students home in the previous August. Convents in France and Belgium had also been involved in this disaster.

The existing school at Old Hall Green near Ware was reinforced by students from Douai, but the vicar apostolic of the northern district was anxious to concentrate the studies at Tudhoe in his vicariate. The Cisalpine element among the laity had obtained a school, building Oscott, which they subsequently ceded to Bishop Talbot, and this led the northern gentry to a solid support for the Tudhoe scheme. But in 1794 it became clear that the Liège Academy could not continue and the fathers there accepted Mr. Weld's offer of Stonyhurst. Much of the more influential lay support for the Tudhoe scheme collapsed and Bishop Gibson opened a college at Crook Hall under Mr. Thomas Eyre, a professor at Douai. Dr. Lingard, the historian, then a young man of twenty-four, became vice-president and both remained in office for fifteen years from 1795 till 1810 including the whole of the period at Crook Hall and the establishment at Ushaw in 1808. Dr. Stapleton, the President of St. Omer, was given charge of Old Hall, which had been dedicated in 1793 to St. Edmund and was subsequently known by this title. A legacy of £10,000 enabled a large college to be built at Old Hall, which now shared with Ushaw in the heritage of Douai. The presence of these buildings, the college at Stonyhurst and the establishment of the English Canonesses of the Holy Sepulchre at Liège in the magnificent Tudor palace at New Hall gave in time an entirely different character to the material background of the Catholic body. To these centres Oscott was soon added. When the Oxford Movement broke on the Catholics half a century later they were already in a strong and entrenched position. But the changes were carried out quietly, evoking little suspicion and less hostility, for the French Revolution caused in England a wave of vague benevolent sentiment towards every form of Christianity and the establishment of the English refugees was masked by the enormous invasion of French royalist clergy.

Almost immediately after the passing of the Relief Act of 1791 there occurred a great influx of priests into England. As a result of the French Revolution a very large number of priests, amounting at one time to over five thousand, took refuge across the Channel. Many of them were lodged in the King's House at Winchester, while the prelates and a great body passed on to London. At their head were nineteen bishops and they were accompanied by a considerable section of laity for the most part connected in some way with the Bourbon Court.

For various reasons the influence of the French priests was not proportionate to their numbers. They did much to break down prejudice ; something to establish permanent missions (the London parishes of Holly Place, Hampstead, St. Aloysius', Somers Town and St. Mary's, Cadogan Street were founded by them) ; little to bring a knowledge of Catholicism to the English. They were in the main chaplains to an allied garrison and after the Concordat of 1802 their numbers decreased to a few hundreds. The dealings of the Holy See with Napoleon and the French Church had their repercussion among the *émigré* priests in London and a small group, known as Blanchardists, followed the Abbé Blanchard who was suspended for his writings against Pius VII. A Gallican trend was notable among a proportion of the *émigré* clergy and the relations between the French bishops in England and the vicars apostolic were strained at periods. On the other hand the prelates were very well received particularly in Tory circles. It was felt that they had shown an exemplary loyalty to their sovereign and had carried through their whole duty as lords spiritual. Throughout the country the French priests awakened sentiments of respectful compassion. They bore their sufferings with a dignity in keeping with their respectable character and it was understood that they encouraged their flock in their moral duty by lofty considerations. On the other hand the very generosity of the sentiments which animated their hosts prevented the English from contemplating the possibility that these priests had a religious message for England.

At the same time this influx undoubtedly contributed greatly to the internal strength of the Catholic body. Monseigneur de la Marche, Bishop of St.-Pol de Léon proved in many respects an admirable leader ; while among the refugees who were received at Lulworth was Père Jean-Nicholas Grou, the author of *Maximes Spirituelles*. Several of the priests attained in time to a considerable personal influence in England and, perhaps, the most notable in this respect were the Abbé Carron and the Abbé Voyaux de Franous, who both worked in London, and the Abbé de la Rue who strengthened the existing mission at Gosport. The French laity numbered nearly six thousand in 1797, according to the Duke of Portland's returns as Home Secretary. Throughout the nineteenth century a proportion of the Catholic business community in London was composed of their descendants. The formerly wealthy families attached to the late French Court lived somewhat apart and generally married within their own circle. Corisande de Gramont, Lady Tankerville, wife of the Treasurer of the Household, was one of the few French Catholics to obtain influence by marrying into an English political family.

Another very different line of foreign Catholic influence requires some reference. Through the artistic world of London there had passed a succession of sculptors, painters and engravers who had come from Italy or Germany or sometimes from France where they had been trained under the secure patronage of cardinals and prince-bishops. It was a long list beginning more than a century earlier with Verrio and Laguerre and continued until the time of Zoffany, who had been brought up in Rome at the Buon' Fratelli where he had been sent by his father who was in the service of the Prince of Thurn and Taxis. A nominal Catholicism often characterized these men who had in general that power of adaptation to their social environment which the age fostered. The negligent religious affiliation of Nollekens the sculptor was of this kind. On the other hand Angelica Kauffmann was deeply Catholic and had a definite influence in a restricted sphere, as had her cousin the architect Bonomi[1] and the ardent Mrs. Richard Cosway. There was a tendency for this artistic community to centre round the chapel of the Sardinian Embassy in Lincoln's Inn Fields, where Nollekens was baptized and where Dr. Arne, the composer of *Rule Britannia* had been accustomed to perform his devotions. To this earlier period belonged Signor Gabriele Piozzi, that Catholic musician who so prudently married Mrs. Thrale, and Bartolozzi the engraver. But any movement from Europe belonged to the high eighteenth century and the French Revolution brought it to a standstill and left only the *émigrés*.

A vivid impression of the Anglo-Italian life at this period is given in the *Wynne Diaries*, a record very naive, grown-up and cosmopolitan, written by the young daughters of Richard Wynne, one of whom married Nelson's subordinate, Admiral Fremantle. They were determined in their adherence to their religion, but they were the nieces of the Countess Wynne von Rosenberg, a woman of doubtful character grown devout, and combined a rooted

---

[1] In Bonomi's house died the unfortunate painter James Barry. In referring to his death Farington reports a conversation which he had with Carlisle the surgeon. " He sd. had Barry been bled at any early period of his disorders he might probably have been saved. He sd. he was surrounded by Roman Catholics," *Farington Diary*, IV, p. 34.

Catholicism[1] with a somewhat sceptical attitude[2] towards the clergy. There was a casualness in the outlook of the fashionable circles of the *Ancien Régime* upon religion and the survivors became more attached to religious values after the collapse of the pre-Revolution world. The casual half-sceptical adherence to the Catholic faith which had formerly been accepted without comment tended to pass away as the conditions of the eighteenth century vanished.

[1] Two typical entries will give the impression. " Christmas Day, 1789. We heard three Masses at the Muniglie Vechie the Capucin was very slow." " 6 April, 1792. Yesterday the *Cure* of Roschach was very polite to us and gave us candles at church (Tenebrae). I think that very amiable of him, more so that he cannot stand us," *Wynne Diaries*, edited by Anne Fremantle, I, pp. 26 and 126.

[2] In reference to a financial transaction the young diarists allude to their uncle's " adviser and assistant, a disgrace to the cloth he wears, the greatest villain on earth, Monsignor Barola, Bishop of Famagusta," ibid., I, p. 315.

TOLERATION

AFTER THE REFUSAL of George III to entertain any project for Catholic Emancipation, when that question was raised by Pitt in 1801 and by the ministry of all the talents in 1807, hopes for any progress during his reign were gradually abandoned. The long Tory administration of Lord Liverpool, which continued from 1812 till 1827, also contributed to defer a solution, for the Prime Minister was personally opposed to full concessions. But the movement in favour of political freedom gathered momentum and was assisted by the sense of unity induced in the nation by the long Napoleonic Wars. The Whigs were the chief supporters of the Catholic claims and the Duke of Norfolk did much to assist them. The eleventh Duke, who held the title from 1786 till 1815, had himself conformed to the Established Church, but he exercised all his influence on behalf of the religion to which his relatives adhered and which he felt to be in a manner within his protection. His idiosyncrasies were invariably generous ; his dress and carriage ostentatiously democratic, a plain bluish purple coat and his own hair worn without powder ; his taste was for building and for heavy dignified potations ; he has left us Arundel Castle.

Among his *protégés* was Thomas Creevey, a young conveyancer whom he introduced as member for Thetford, a seat which was in the joint gift of the Duke and Lord Petre. It is through this contact and from the Creevey Papers that so much light is shed on the great Whig Catholics, their political reactions and election plans. One letter provides an illuminating commentary. At a subsequent election Creevey was not offered the seat and wrote in anger to the new Duke of Norfolk. " I am justified on this occasion," he declared,[1] " in reminding you of the fact . . . that you and Lord Petre, the only Catholic peers with parliamentary patronage, are the only peers of the Whig aristocracy who turn out their old members upon the express grounds of pecuniary arrangements with new connections, and the members you so sacrificed, viz. Romilly and myself happen to be persons who themselves sacrificed in 1807 every

---

[1] Letter dated 3 August, 1816, to the twelfth Duke of Norfolk, who was a Catholic ; printed in *Creevey's Life and Times*, ed. Gore, p. 113.

interested consideration for no other object than that of serving yours, the Catholic cause." Whatever may have been the basis of this disagreement it clearly emphasizes the experienced contact of the leading Catholics with the management of the boroughs of the unreformed parliament.

In this connection two further episodes will indicate the friend-ship between the Catholic families and those which had eventually conformed after a long tradition of resistance. There seems to have been none of the wrench of apostasy ; relationships were seldom severed and acceptance of Anglicanism for the purpose of entry into public life was considered as a weakness like a somewhat doubtful moral character or a taste for extravagance and strong liquor. This would, however, only apply to a single Catholic grouping that allied to the Whig oligarchy, where the Gallican leaven worked perceptibly and the idea of the point of honour imported a slight unreality to moral questions.

In the first case Creevey transferred his alliance to Lord Sefton, a Whig supporter of the Catholic claims who maintained at Croxteth a venerable Jesuit, Fr. Emmett who had been his father's prefect of studies at St. Omer. In the second case an abortive measure of Catholic relief was sponsored in Parliament during the Liverpool administration by General Mathew, a son of the " conforming " Lord Llandaff.

The widespread atmosphere of co-operation at this period was also fostered by the interest taken in horse-racing by such leading Catholic owners as Edward Petre. John Gully the prize-fighter had married a Catholic and had a rather loud friendliness[1] towards the old religion ; while John Nyren of the Hambledon Club, the author of *The Young Cricketer's Tutor* was a mainstay of rural Catholicism as were other members of the sides which played at Broad Half-penny and Windmill Downs. It is pleasant that these early days of cricket owed so much to the country chaplaincies of the Home Counties. On the other hand the formation of the Mary-le-Bone Club appealed to a much wealthier grouping and Mr. Stonor was one of the rare Catholics in the original list of members. Thomas Lord was another of Nyren's coreligionists.

An impression of the expensive town life during the Napoleonic Wars and the years following the peace is provided in the Jerning-

---

[1] " I shall try old Lomax," wrote Gully, " to say Mass for me. What will he charge ? " *John Gully and his Times*, Bernard Darwin, p. 89.

ham Letters, a correspondence carried on during thirty years between Lady Jerningham of Costessey and her daughter Lady Bedingfield, who was a woman of the bedchamber to the Duchess of Clarence. The mother was a vital character; brought up by the Blue Nuns at Paris; shrewd in her outlook; cosmopolitan; Whig in politics and Hanoverian in sentiment; Whig in her consciousness of her position and with sympathies far wider than the Catholic grouping; Catholic in religion and undemonstrative in devotional practice; well-disposed towards the persons of quality who frequented the London chapels and generously condescending to her less fortunate neighbours. It was delightful to live in such a world as an equal, with the point of honour and the calm extravagance; it was perhaps less easy for the chaplain.[1]

To this coterie the difficulties between the prelates came muffled and there was an unwillingness to concede any significance to the wishes of the Irish episcopate or to be unduly influenced by Dr. Milner's vehemence or the charges of Gallicanism against the French clergy. Lady Bedingfield would travel to Bath and note the presence of " over eighty English and Irish Catholics of quality."[2] An interest would be manifested in Mr. Turnerelly " a most famed sculptor and excellent Catholic ", who taught modelling to the royal princesses, and in young Mr. Novello the composer and old Mrs. David Garrick, and in the memory of Dr. Arne who had so tastefully embellished the music of the Catholic chapels. For the rest as they came up from the country to stay at the Royal Hotel in Pall Mall, then a rendezvous for their coreligionists, they entered fully into the amusements and the political excitements of the day. They admired the Duke of Wellington, although opposed to his views, and had an instinctive distrust of that emotional approach which they still termed enthusiasm. Lord Rocksavage's conversion at Palermo in 1812 awakened little interest and his subsequent adoption of Methodism no surprise.[3] There was a general atmosphere of

---

[1] Cf. Letter from Sir William Jerningham to his daughter, dated Cossey, 19 June, 1786. " The Abbé Plowden as I hear is ill and cannot live long. I shall not be sorry for him upon two accounts; the first is that I shall have a friend in Heaven to pray for us, and the second is which is a more worldly wish that the annuity I pay him of £300 *per annum* I shall give to your Good Mama for pin money," *Jerningham Papers*, i, pp. 40–1.

[2] The senior of the " Ladies of Llangollen," Lady Eleanor Butler was a vague Catholic linked with this circle.

[3] The change from Catholicism to Methodism made by Lord Rocksavage in 1817 was perhaps responsible for the marked coolness shown to Fr. Ignatius Spencer on his conversion. Thus Lady Bedingfield expressed her fear of " Mr. George Spencer's enthusiasm," ibid. ii, p. 313.

accommodation with the age. As early as 1822 Sir Richard Acton and his brother, the future cardinal, were entered at Magdalene College, Cambridge, where Henry Jerningham was sent because "Mr. Neville the Master does not require any attendance at the chapel."[1] The vote and the degree were still denied to them; but the *mondain* Catholic circles were determined to take the fullest possible share in the life of their equals.

It is interesting to compare with these passages the changing attitude towards Catholics at this time. In the literary groupings alone at least three tendencies were apparent. The new freedom to which Shelley was pledged would hardly find inspiration in the Church of Rome. In his boyhood he had been very familiar with the quasi-Catholic *ménage* at Arundel; but neither Hogg, nor the Godwins, nor Leigh Hunt belonged to circles which had any contact with the Roman Catholics. Lerici, a conservative town, traditionalist and sleepy, was hardly an angle from which to survey the free untrammelled movements of Catholic life and thought.

But Claire Clairemont, Godwin's stepdaughter, who went to Italy with the Shelleys was eventually received into the Church and Byron sent her daughter Allegra to be educated at a convent in Ravenna. Byron himself had always the potentialities of dramatic conversion, sudden, probably ultimately sincere and possibly even permanent. There were aspects of his mental outlook which were not remote from those of certain of the Catholic Romanticists and it seems possible that he might have submitted to the Church had some Franciscan, clad in the habit, ardent and a patriot come to him as he lay dying of the marsh-fever at Missolonghi. He had not been fortunate in the Catholics with whom he had been intimate. Teresa Guiccioli was not *pratiquante*; neither was Lady Blessington, that doubtful character romantic, magnificent as the term was then regarded, a little tawdry in the night sky; nor was Count Alfred d'Orsay.

These people were not in contact with even the most worldly of the English Catholics and it is curious that when those authors are considered who really were accustomed to move with some familiarity among the adherents of the old religion their standpoint is found to be even more remote. After these centuries the spirit of Catholicism eluded them. In the case of Sir Walter Scott there

---

[1] ibid. ii, p. 226. The fact that the nomination of the Master of Magdalene was vested in his father Lord Braybrooke perhaps enabled Mr. Neville to take a more independent line.

are several facets ; for his genuine interest in the Middle Ages and
his romantic buoyant enthusiasm for the picturesque were crossed
by Scottish Presbyterian generations. He certainly familiarized
the reading public with many of the external phenomena of Catholicism and he showed some feeling for that religion in his correspondence with Byron. " I would rather," Sir Walter declared[1]
in 1815, " look to see you retreat upon the Catholic faith and
distinguish yourself by the austerity of your penances. The species
of religion to which you must, or may, one day attach yourself
must exercise a strong power on the imagination." But the
dislike of " Popery . . . a mean and depraving superstition,"[2]
was firmly rooted in ancestral prejudice and Sir Walter was more
than ready to commit himself to the facile optimism which characterized the more conventional opinion of his later years. " Un-
opposed, the Catholic superstition may sink into the dust," he
declaimed[3] in satisfied rhetoric, " with all its absurd ritual and
solemnities." Here he approached the standpoint of polite, but
somewhat insular circles. The Court supported, as he would have
wished, this unimpeachable sentiment.

In this connection Madame d'Arblay, the chronicler of the Court,
has an illuminating passage concerning the last illness of her
husband who lay dying in Great Stanhope Street after having
consented to receive the Last Sacraments. The priest had returned
for a second visit. " I sent them word," she wrote[4] " that a
Protestant myself . . . they must not expect me to make a
persecution for the performance of a Catholic rite that might
impede all chance of restoration by its appalling solemnities."
And Madame d'Arblay, so well known as the author of *Evelina*, was
not unrepresentative of her generation, very kindly, quite tolerant
and without the gift of understanding. The life of rural England
was still severely divided into compartments. Jane Austen, for
instance, seems to have had hardly any Catholic contacts although
there must have been a considerable number in her geographical,
if not her social area. For Miss Austen died and was buried in
Winchester and in the Catholic cemetery of the town are the graves
of Mrs. Challoner and Mrs. Milner and Mrs. Lingard.

[1] Cf. Letter, printed in the *Life of Sir Walter Scott*, by John Gibson Lockhart, V, p. 35.
[2] ibid., IX, p. 270.   [3] ibid., p. 270.
[4] Madame d'Arblay, *Diary and Letters*, vi, pp. 365–6.

EMANCIPATION

THE BACKGROUND of this life of privilege was, however, profoundly uncongenial to that dominating figure in Catholic life Dr. Milner, who ploughed his way with perfect determination and an accustomed courage now supported by the weight of episcopal authority. From 1803 till 1826 he ruled the Midland district. His successive colleagues in London, Bishop Douglass, who ruled from 1790 till 1812, and Bishop Poynter, who held office from 1803 (as coadjutor) till 1827, failed to satisfy his ideal. Their friendship with some of the Cisalpine laity was abhorrent to him; their contact with the Gallican priests disturbed him; nor could he tolerate their efforts to pacify the former friction in the Catholic body. Milner was always ready to bind up his sheaves and he had a sure instinct for the cockle.

Early in his episcopate an opportunity for action came to him largely as a consequence of his determined opposition to the Cisalpines. As a result of the passing of the Act of Union in 1800 the Irish demand for complete Catholic relief became insistent, and for the first time the views of the hierarchy of Ireland were brought forward. The promises made to the Catholics had not been implemented and emancipation in its Irish rather than its English aspect and as a concomitant to the dissolution of the Irish Parliament had become a national issue. In these circumstances the Irish bishops felt that it was necessary to have an agent in England and this post was filled by Milner. Both they and he valued the civil government. Archbishop Troy, a Dominican long resident in Rome as prior of San Clemente, who ruled the see of Dublin from 1789 till 1823, had favoured the Act of Union; but the Irish prelates and Milner were alike opposed to the Cisalpines, to privilege and to cultivated Whig sentiments emptied of their religious animus They were downright and so was he, very determined, very firm and utterly opposed to sophisticated tolerance. It is not difficult to see in this agency the source of much of Bishop Milner's firmness He was convinced that he had behind him the strength of the millions of Catholics in Ireland. He felt that the great body of English

Catholics the middle classes and the poor were on his side and it was only the five hundred wealthy Catholics whom he regarded with invincible repugnance. Charles Butler remained the enemy and the Catholic Board which had risen phœnix-like in 1808 to represent the old Cisalpine standpoint.

Thus Milner became adamant on the question of a proposed royal veto on episcopal appointments, and regarded Grattan's Catholic Relief Bill of 1811 with suspicion. He attacked Canning's clauses, which were introduced into the Bill to provide a modified form of veto, and on this subject he won his point. " I shall be baited like a bull," he wrote,[1] " but I am ready to encounter the white bears of Hudson's Bay . . . rather than yield." And this was only one of other similar triumphs marked by a keen attachment to Rome. By Ireland he was supported and by those whom Lord Petre called " the middling sort of Catholics " ; while the fashionable adherents of his faith remained aloof and indifferent as they attended the routs in London and their curricles rolled along the Brighton road.

The restoration of the Society of Jesus throughout the world by the Bull *Sollicitudo omnium Ecclesiarum* promulgated in 1814 found Milner among the supporters of the " Gentlemen of Stonyhurst," who could now resume their designation. He was friendly to the Jesuits in their difficulties with the vicars apostolic and defended them against the bluff lack of cordiality of Bishop Gibson. A phrase of Milner's dating from this period indicates so well his personality. " I have been found in the end to be right," he wrote[2] of his positions, " and my Right Rev. brother to be wrong, owing to his pursuing the *Utile*, and myself the *Honestum*." The very spirit of Cobbett is in these words. In addition Milner had an understanding of the rising town Catholicism, for he would not live in the country " as a gentleman farmer like Thomas Talbot," as he described his predecessor. He sympathized with the immigrants and in his good relations with the priests and people of Ireland foreshadowed what was to be one of the most fortunate aspects of Cardinal Manning's policy. It was during his retreats with the Benedictines at Caverswall and in the care of his own Midland

---

[1] Letter printed in Husenbeth's *Life of Milner*, p. 231. For all this period a most careful and detailed account of the various negotiations is given in Bishop Ward's volumes.

[2] Gradwell Letters from the Westminster Archives printed in Ward's *Eve of Catholic Emancipation*, III, p. 11.

district that he was seen to best advantage.[1] But he was still
active in general questions, denouncing the suggestion for some
modified form of the oath of supremacy, opposing Plunkett's
Relief Bill of 1821, supporting O'Connell's Catholic Association
two years later and opposing Sir Francis Burdett's relief measure
of 1825.   All through his later life he was determined not to accept
emancipation, unless it should be granted unconditionally freed
from all oaths and vetos.   " Recollect that you are in sacred pre-
cincts," declared O'Connell when visiting the aged bishop, " the
terror of the Vetoists has made Wolverhampton holy."   In March
1826 he died and the spiritual leadership of the Catholics passed
into more cautious hands.

.   .   .   .   .   .

The years between 1820 and 1829 covered almost the whole of
the reign of George IV and during that period the movement
towards Emancipation was a dominant issue in home politics, but
one which was to prove as distasteful to the new sovereign as it
had been to George III.   When he was Prince of Wales the situation
had been very different ; for George IV had little personal antipathy to Catholicism and his bad relations with his father had led
him to mock at the old-fashioned narrow Protestantism when
obtruded in a fashion hardly consonant with the air of a man of
breeding.   The bucks had small concern for the Church of England.
Then had come the Prince's support of Fox and the Whigs on the
Catholic question and that secret marriage with Mrs. Fitzherbert
which had introduced him into the intimacies of the lives of the old
Catholics.   He had been generous to the exiled nuns and to Mrs.
Fitzherbert's *protégées* ; but the union had taken place in 1784 and
they had been separated by 1811.   Now his interests had moved
away from this relationship ; there had been the catastrophe of
his royal and legal marriage to Caroline of Brunswick and a succession of other influences.   And the caricatures of Mrs. Fitzherbert as the " abbess of Brighton " had wounded his vanity.
The Prince was markedly susceptible to criticism and was very ready
to change his views on subjects about which he cared but little.

[1] Thus the following passage from the same letters indicates clearly the light and
shade. " My whole hopes of supplying Pastors to my extensive District," wrote
Milner, " centre in my little Seminary and College of Oscott and the confined resources
which I myself can provide for supporting it (the Holy See withholding its 2000 crowns,
the King of France alienating our funds in his dominions, and our Nobility and Gentry
not contributing a shilling for such a purpose)."

It was his friend Fox who had described him, perhaps unjustly, as " an uncommon pleasant fellow, but as hollow as a pear."

It is at any rate clear that between 1806 and 1812 he passed from support to opposition in regard to the Catholic claims. For some years after this date the issue was in doubt and the Marquess Wellesley, who was married to Mrs. Patterson, an American Catholic, pressed him for a favourable decision. But finally, under the influence of his friendship for Lady Hertford, the Prince Regent, now George IV, adopted a position of clear hostility to Emancipation. When the matter came to a head he was already in his later sixties and had been for practical purposes the head of the State since his father had become insane in 1811. The earlier stages of his predominance with their keen interest in Nash's building, in Regent's Street and Regent's Park, were behind him. Now he was tired and very corpulent ; driving with Lady Conyngham in a little phaeton ; fishing in the Virginia Water ; happy about the quality of his claret ; disliking Windsor Castle ; thinking back on an imaginary past of " how he won the Cup at Goodwood by his own riding." Into this world there came Daniel O'Connell.

The public career of the Liberator does not fall within the scope of this subject except in its effect upon the fortunes of Catholicism in England. Emancipation was an Irish victory, fought out in Ireland and decided when O'Connell won his seat at the Clare election. This was a well-timed contest coming towards the end of a decade in which this cause had seemed becalmed. Various circumstances had contributed to this delay ; the long Liverpool administration ; the open hostility of the heir to the throne, the Duke of York ; the hopes set on Canning, and finally the doubt as to whether it would not be wiser to allow the matter to rest until the issue of parliamentary reform had been settled. Then in 1827 Liverpool, his successor Canning and the Duke of York had died. O'Connell was faced by new conditions and found himself an un-questioned leader in Ireland strengthened by the great power which had come to him as a result of the organization of political sentiment by means of the Catholic rent, a monthly contribution of one penny per head.

Nevertheless, even after the Clare election, the reluctance of the King delayed the matter, as did the gradual character of the change of mind on the part of the leaders of the Tory ministry, the Duke of Wellington and Sir Robert Peel. They had formerly been opposed to such measures of relief for Catholics as the Whigs had been prepared to favour ; but the natural fear that the government might be unable to control the situation in Ireland decided Wellington on a change of policy.   Two factors had enabled the demand of the Catholics to be brought forward in Ireland by constitutional means ; the extension of the franchise to include the forty-shilling freeholders and the grant of the vote to Catholics, both measures which had been passed in 1793.   Now concurrently with the introduction of relief from religious disabilities the forty-shilling freehold was to be abolished and the former property qualification reintroduced.

In the parliament of 1829 the Catholic Relief Bill was brought forward ; it was foreshadowed in the speech from the throne in February ; it received the royal assent in April.   Catholics received the right to vote and sit in Parliament and to occupy nearly all the offices of State.   As a concession to Protestant feeling bishops were, however, forbidden to adopt the titles of sees in use by prelates of the Established Church, and religious celebrations were forbidden outside churches and private houses.   By another clause restriction was placed on the freedom of religious orders and their increase ; but this section remained a dead letter.   Before he was allowed to take his seat O'Connell was forced to seek re-election from the now restricted body of electors.

It has frequently been pointed out that O'Connell received little gratitude[1] from his wealthier English coreligionists for his great services.   This was partly because there was much in his outlook which was bound to be uncongenial to those among whom the Cisalpine tradition still lingered.   Such men would recognize his position at the Irish Bar, but they often detested his political principles and were by no means favourable to the Catholic rent and to the reliance which he placed upon the poorer voters.   His manner and his open references to his religious principles were peculiarly unsympathetic to the cold oligarchic mind.   O'Connell was sensitive to the coldness displayed towards him by some of the rich English Catholics ; but few leaders have received such gratitude from their own countrymen.

[1] Cf. Letter of Daniel O'Connell to James Sugrue, dated Bury Street, London, 17 May, 1829. " Have you heard of the conduct of the English Catholics towards me ?   They have a club here called the ' Cis-Alpine,' a bad name you will say.   They had been much divided amongst themselves and were now about all to reunite.   I agreed to be proposed into it, when, behold ! they met the day before yesterday and *black-beaned* me."   *Correspondence of Daniel O'Connell*, ed. W. J. Fitzpatrick, i, p. 186.

The effect of the Act only became clear gradually and the Catholics were slow in attaining the posts now open to them. The Earl of Arundel, eldest son to the Duke of Norfolk, took his seat as Member of Parliament for Horsham and became a solid supporter of the Whigs and uninterested in religious questions. Quiet settled down upon the Catholic body as William IV succeeded George IV upon the throne and the national interest was concentrated on the Reform Bill. The vicar apostolic of the London district, Dr. James Yorke Bramston personified the cautious spirit. A convert and a member of Trinity College, Cambridge and Lincoln's Inn, he was at this time advanced in middle age, delicate in health, very charitable, sensible and gifted with sound judgment. For twenty-three years he had worked as a parish priest at St. George's-in-the-Fields ; phlegmatic, generous and dignified. He possessed much of the poise and care of his predecessor Dr. Poynter and had inherited his dislike for precipitate and ill-considered action. Under the circumstances it was a wise caution.[1]

The same train of thought could be traced among the leading clergy of this time, notably in the cases of Cardinal Weld and Dr. Griffiths, the president of St. Edmund's College, who was to succeed Bishop Bramston in the London district. The generation of priests who had been ordained in the years before Emancipation manifested a similar reserve which went with an independence of mind and some insularity. The names of Dr. Rock and Provost Husenbeth and Mr. Tierney, the church historian, sufficiently indicate this pre-Wiseman world. Part of the stillness of this time was due to the pause in ecclesiastical affairs following upon the premature death of Dr. Robert Gradwell, a Lancashire priest of great energy of character who had been Rector of the English College in Rome from 1818 till 1828 and had re-established that great foundation. He had been brought back to London as coadjutor and it was a serious loss to Catholicism in England when he died in 1833 in the Bishop's house in Golden Square.

The life of the old faith in London had a special character of its own ; churches were being built, rectangular buildings with plain windows and a gallery supported by iron pillars ; beadles walked

[1] An entry in Lord Colchester's *Diary* under 1 May, 1828 gives an impression of the feeling in some responsible political circles. He is speaking of the Concordat concluded with the Holy See by George IV as King of Hanover. The Concordat, he writes, "if established in England with the spiritual authority therein reserved would be tantamount to a counter reformation," *Diary*, III, pp. 558–9.

the centre aisle in their gold lace and three-cornered hats; the members of the Italian Opera House sang in the Sardinian Chapel on the great festivals. From these centres the maintenance of charities and the care for the education of the poor developed : the life of the commercial circles progressed : the numbers of the Catholic poor mounted unceasingly.

THE JESUIT SCHOOLING

PERHAPS THE PRIMARY element in the Catholic tradition in the early nineteenth century was a conscious Englishness. The rather aggressive cheerful quality of insularity fostered by the Napoleonic Wars was fully reflected among the adherents of the old religion and the return of the boarding-schools to English soil, consequent on the Revolution, provided an appropriate frame for the Old English picture. As a school Stonyhurst and as a man Charles Waterton perhaps represented between 1808 and 1830 the perfection of this type.

The Jesuits had been fortunate in receiving the mansion of Stonyhurst from Mr. Weld on their departure from Liége in 1794. Within five years they had added the building known as Shirk and had received a warm support from a large and influential body of the Catholic laity and a cold shoulder from the local vicar apostolic. The school and its dependent activities had sunk deep roots into the countryside north of Blackburn. From St. Omer and Liége there came that tradition of robust and unemotional devotion to religion which was to characterize the boys of the new foundation. In the early years of the new century Fr. Wright carried out the duties of minister with the contacts with the outside world which that post involved. " A straightforward John Bull gentleman he was,"[1] records Richard Lalor Sheil, " a very old man with long white hair falling on his shoulders going his rounds upon a mule of dun colour with a black mane running back to its tail." It is a pleasant picture and one which goes easily with that of the Weld boys posting in a coach and four from Lulworth to Lancashire. Mr. Weld would come up every year for the festivities and in 1810 he brought his six sons with him and died from a fit of apoplexy at the college after singing " I am mad Tom, behold me."

The description of the arrival of the news of Trafalgar is entertaining. " The students," Sheil writes,[2] " were assembled in order

---

[1] Account quoted in Gerard, *History of Stonyhurst*, p. 125, a book which remains the chief authority for the development of this school.
[2] Quoted in Gerard, ibid., p. 231.

to witness some experiments in galvanism, which a gentleman who had brought to the college a philosophical apparatus had been employed to perform. In the midst of profound attention a person rushed in and exclaimed that Nelson had won a great victory." Even the gentleman with the philosophical apparatus gave way before the news brought by that person. And there was non-Catholic patronage. Admiral Lord St. Vincent, a friend of the Jerninghams, sent £50 for Stonyhurst because, as he observed, " the education of several of my young friends among the Catholicks appears to me so very defective." The Duke of Northumberland, too, sent money and was satisfied[1] with the result, for he was interested in a Portuguese boy at the school " poor little Ramos."[2] Already Stonyhurst was taking root and the Duke's phrase brings to mind that succession of " poor little Ramos'," so characteristic a feature of nineteenth-century Catholic education.

Then there was the solid work of Jesuit instruction and the inspiring presence of Fr. Charles Plowden in old age. A sympathetic description of Fr. Plowden has been left by Richard Lalor Sheil in which the filial respect is manifest against the delightful background of that serious period. " He was," writes[3] Sheil, " a perfect Jesuit of the old school : his mind was stored with classical knowledge ; his manners were highly polished ; he had great natural eloquence . . . and with his various accomplishments he combined the loftiest enthusiasm for the advancement of religion and an utter immolation of himself to the glory of the order." Sheil was impressed by " his command of lofty diction ; his zealous and forcible delivery ; the noble port he assumed as the herald of intelligence from Heaven ; and, more than all else, the profound conviction which he manifestly entertained of the truth of the doctrine which he interpreted."

So much for the teacher, now for the pupil. Among the manuscripts at Stonyhurst is a note in the handwriting of Fr. Edward Walsh and intended for a young gentleman setting out for France. " I would advise you," it runs,[4] " when abroad to lay yourself out to obtain the goodwill of some persons of consideration ; a little docility and engaging manners will soon procure it. You have all

---

[1] " The persons," wrote the Duke in 1809, " have expended the moneys subscribed with every proper attention to elegance and convenience," Stonyhurst MSS., A.11.29, f. 37.

[2] Stonyhurst MSS., A.11.29, ff. 36, 38a.   [3] Quoted in Gerard, ibid., p. 123.

[4] Stonyhurst MSS. A.11.24, f. 40.

the requisites to succeed ; youth, sprightliness, a prepossessing form, and a competency of means to produce yourself in the best companies." How pleasant is this passage suggesting that combination of a certain *savoir faire* with profound simplicity and bringing back Lord Arundell and Charles Langdale and Joseph Weld, who was one of the original members of the Royal Yacht Squadron and won its first cup race with the *Arrow*. There were, however, other sides, that of the antiquaries like Canon Oliver and of the fathers who joined the English Province and the tastes of the rich merchants. And then, binding all together, it is recorded in a college diary under 15 March, 1821, that " on this day the scholars were amused by the wonderful sagacity of an Italian swine." It was at the beginning of the century that Charles Waterton sat reading the *Metamorphoses* of Ovid in the branch of the tree.

From 1806, when he inherited Walton Hall at the age of twenty-four, until his death in 1865 Charles Waterton remained a striking figure in the life of his community and was, perhaps, symbolic of the insularity, security and strength of the old Catholicism. He was a naturalist and a traveller and unscarred by experience. With his friend Captain Jones he ascended the ball on the cross of St. Peter's ; his adventures in South America were numerous and on one occasion he rode on a cayman " which had swallowed an immense hook baited with raw meat and was being pulled along by several natives." A brave painting of this operation with Mr. Waterton astride the alligator, which is seen being drawn across the yellow sands against a background of palms and cheerfully coloured sky and mountain, is one of the most valued possessions of the Natural History Museum at Stonyhurst.

Waterton had a deep affection for his home and guarded all wild life on his estate except what he called the Hanoverian rat. As this phrase implies he was a man of strong political feeling ; his sympathies were Jacobite and he had a profound distrust of the Whig lords. " He was a staunch Conservative," writes[1] his friend and biographer Dr. Hobson, " Taxation of every kind and the National Debt were the odious and virulent sores with Mr. Waterton." He had that attachment to place which was typical of the old squire-archy, to the square house, the four sycamores on the north-west, the Lombardy poplar, a gift from Burghwallis planted by his father in 1756, the park, the heronry. He was full of homely devices and

---

[1] *Charles Waterton*, by Richard Hobson, M.D., ed. 1867, p. 157.

had constructed " a cast iron bridge which affords a most convenient communication from the park to the mansion, whilst it forms an ornamental object in the scenery." Such was the background to his work as a naturalist.

A devotion to the Jesuits and a strict and ascetic Catholic outlook were as marked as his charity. One passage will serve to complete this brief impression. " Mr. Waterton's personal apparel was," according[1] to Hobson, " of so peculiar a character . . . that he was now and then addressed by strangers as a person very much below his own grade in society. He usually rejoiced in a blunder of this kind, and was greatly delighted to carry on the misconception in apparent earnestness, by cleverly personating the man of poverty." Very tenacious and honest, Waterton stands at the end of a period ; henceforward the history of Catholicism in England was to a great extent that of the struggles of " the man of poverty."

Contemporary with Waterton and a schoolfellow of his at Stonyhurst was James Everard, tenth Lord Arundell of Wardour. In him another class was represented, wealthier and more sophisticated, the summit of Catholic life at the period of Emancipation. He was an antiquary and a patron of the arts, in the inner circle of the Grenville interest in politics and a brother-in-law of the Duke of Buckingham. He had a certain aloofness based on the secure respect which his generation accorded to a peerage supported by riches. " I cannot say," he wrote[2] to his cousin Hugh Clifford, " that I have ever felt or encouraged confidence in the wisdom or liberality of Parliament." He busied himself with his library and building plans and the collections for Sir Richard Hoare's *History of Wiltshire*. His grandfather's great house at Wardour with the heavy grey façade and the fluted Corinthian columns had come to him by inheritance and the chapel was his especial care. Lord Arundell himself describes Sir John Soane's designs and the gallery for the family supported by pilasters of Siena marble and the altar by Quirenza with " the tabernacle[3] in the form of a circular monopteral temple . . . the cupola of porphyry, supported by columns of jasper, with silver gilt capitals upon which is fixed an emblematical image of Religion." Within the house were an *altarino* from the Aldobrandini collection, sweeping landscapes by Salvator Rosa ; in the saloon a head of the Virgin by Carlo Dolci, more landscapes and snow-pieces ; in the gallery

[1] ibid., p. 163.   [2] Stonyhurst MSS. A.11. 24, f. 27.
[3] *History of Modern Wiltshire*, Hundred of Dunworth, by James Everard, Baron Arundell, p. 169.

and the music-room family portraits and a beautifully painted ceiling after Guido's " Aurora." Such was the great house, intimidating to the delicate cultivated Newman world, attractive to Manning's robust appreciation and infinitely remote from the vast incoming tides of Irish labour.

THE IMMIGRATION FROM IRELAND

THIS RECRUITMENT of Catholic strength from Ireland was no new thing and had developed through the eighteen century forming the basis for new centres of population in London, Bristol and, perhaps most of all, in Liverpool, for that port was the gateway into England for the harvesting. Then the building of the docks drew them to Liverpool and the industrial expansion and the development of the cotton towns. Estimates of varying reliability give some impression of this increase. In 1821 there was said to be a Catholic population in Liverpool of twelve thousand; by 1832 they are said to have numbered sixty thousand; by 1840, according to a manuscript note at Stonyhurst, eighty thousand in the city and its suburbs. These congregations were partly English from rural Lancashire, but were largely and increasingly Irish and this was before the immigration after the Famine. Out of the fifty-one parishes at present existing in the city of Liverpool eleven were already established before the great influx, while the move eastward is reflected in the six Catholic parishes in Manchester and Salford.

The navy and, to a still greater degree the army had contained large numbers of Irish Catholics and throughout the first half of the nineteenth century they came over as builders' labourers and dock labourers, weavers and spinners in the textile towns and wool-combers in Yorkshire. It was a fairly well defined road of entrance, Liverpool, the South Lancashire towns, then Leeds and the West Riding. Some went on down into the Potteries and the Staffordshire coal-field and in the heavy work of the puddling furnaces their fine physique was a great asset.

At the same time they penetrated to the little towns working in the navvy gangs during the great railway boom. Once they reached London they met with friends in the strong Irish settlement in Wapping and came again to their own people in the Irish lodging-houses. Poor and unwelcome, they met with open hostility in Lincolnshire in 1831 and on the railway workings. Their friends and support were the tavern-keepers of their race, who gathered them together and in many instances aided them in the practice of their religion. From the time of Cornelius Murphy, who kept the Sun in Golden Lane during the Gordon Riots, the keepers of licensed houses have maintained a fine tradition which has been inadequately recognized. In the smaller industrial towns especially, these houses were often the cradles of revived Catholic worship, where the leader of the people was the publican, stout, knowing the world, full of sense and generous. The Faith illumined the struggle of these difficult years and the keepers of the little railway hotels and the inns gave their parlours for the Mass and their sons to the priesthood.

To refer to the potato famine is to anticipate, for its effects were not seen in England until 1846; but it is just as well to mention it at this point to fix the Irish increase and the Irish flood as a background to the theological discussions of the Oxford Movement. Coming into England in this misery the Irish followed the tracks which normal immigration had prepared for them; they swelled the industrial populations which in the period of expansion were in time able to receive them. The agonies of the typhus and cholera passed and they settled down to reinforce the newly significant body of industrial Catholicism. A few figures will indicate the immense change. In 1841 as a result of a period of constant immigration the numbers of the Irish-born population in England stood at 224,128; in 1851 this figure had risen to 419,256.[1] In February 1847, 26,348 deck passengers from Ireland landed in Liverpool and by July of that year a total of over three hundred thousand had arrived, although a considerable proportion of these died in the epidemics in the overcrowded city and many others made only a temporary stay in England on their way to the United States or Australia.

The miseries of that time established a close union between the people and their priests, eight of whom died of fever caught while ministering to the sick in Liverpool. Among the young priests working there was Fr. Bernard O'Reilly who was in time to be the first really Irish member of the hierarchy. But this was in the future and the masses coming from Ireland were perhaps insufficiently considered during the first half of the century. For some time a section of the prosperous Irish families had been accustomed to send their sons to Stonyhurst or the Benedictine schools, but the growth of the Irish town populations was hardly perceived by the English Catholics

---

[1] Owing to the prevalence of seasonal employment and other reasons these figures for 1841 and 1851 cannot be considered really accurate.

on their estates. The vicars apostolic grappled with a problem of increasing magnitude and after the famine years a normal immigration recommenced to the new industries on Teesside and Tyneside, to the shipbuilding and the steel-works. It is one of Cardinal Manning's greatest services that he appreciated the problem of the new town Catholicism and that he brought to it his quick, persistent social sympathy. In the discussion of the very crowded events of the next thirty years it is hardly possible to refer to this factor, those great masses of town populations, largely Irish in origin, who gradually transformed the Catholic scene.

Far from the scagliola columns of Wardour chapel, remote from the careful high-minded discussions of the Oxford common rooms or the sober London houses of the substantial Catholic merchants and attorneys there gathered the tidal development of Catholic labour. In this matter one factor in especial served to keep the two sections of the community apart. There were hardly any adherents of the old religion in the first group of industrialists and contractors. Among the great figures of this period only Sir Marc Isambard Brunel, the engineer of the Thames Tunnel, who had begun life as a church student at Gisors, had any contact with Catholicism. The country and town parishes were very separate and few of the old squires who were dismayed by the nests of factory chimneys could discern a new Catholic life developing behind the smoke and the iron wheels.

BACKGROUND TO THE NINETEENTH CENTURY

WITH THE OPENING of this period a rather different line of treatment becomes essential. The great figures associated with the Oxford Movement require a more biographical method which is inevitably a little repetitive. As a result of the breakdown of isolation the Catholic community became to a considerable extent merged in the general life of the nation and it becomes more difficult to follow a strictly chronological order in tracing the development of a body whose members came in touch with the public life at so many points. Again, figures of national importance are only considered in those sometimes very restricted aspects which brought them transient contacts with Catholicism in England.

Various influences can only be indicated briefly and it is curious to remember that Edward Gibbon, whose place was now well assured, had become a Catholic for eighteen months in his youth. The first part of Dr. Lingard's *History of England* had appeared in 1819 and had greatly influenced the publicist William Cobbett, who produced his *History of the Protestant Reformation* in parts during 1824 and 1825. Cobbett sold forty thousand copies of this work, came into personal contact, friendship and conflict with O'Connell and seems to have chosen to contest Preston in 1827 partly on account of the political weight of the Catholic townsmen. Known in his own day through his *Political Register* and the *Rural Rides*, his book on the Reformation came to have increasing significance in the background of Catholic consciousness. Few men have had more joy in conflict. On his way back from Preston he referred to himself as " an old man, recollect,[1] who can travel five hundred miles, make speeches of half an hour long twice a day for a month ; put down the saucy, the rich, the tyrannical." It is small wonder that he was regarded by the prosperous classes with mixed feelings.

Four dates, all close together, indicate the rapid change of values in the general background of English life. In 1829 there came Catholic Emancipation ; in 1832 the passing of the first Reform

---

[1] An interesting account of Cobbett's activities in regard to the Catholic question is given on pp. 286–305 of the *Life of William Cobbett*, by G. D. H. Cole.

Bill ; in 1837 the accession of Queen Victoria ; in 1839 the Queen's marriage to Prince Albert of Saxe Coburg and Gotha. Gladstone entered Parliament in 1832 and Disraeli in 1837, while the transitional administrations of Sir Robert Peel and Lord Melbourne, who between them held office from 1834 till 1846, prepared the way for the Victorian age. The men who supported Catholic Emancipation were themselves, in most cases, very remote from any appreciation of Catholicism. Lord Melbourne came from a family which had only risen to the ranks of the affluent gentry in the Protestant atmosphere of the early Hanoverians. He had been brought up in the circle of the great Whig houses and combined the scepticism of the late eighteenth century with a respect for spiritual privilege and the Establishment.

Tolerance of all recognized institutions carried with it a measure of cordiality towards the States of the Church and their ruler. This point of view is well expressed in Greville's urbane and measured statements[1] as he moved about the Rome of 1830 with his *laquais de place* carefully avoiding the " more vulgar " English in the papal capital. Charles Greville, whose *Memoirs* are a primary source for this period, had indeed the discrimination of the inner Whig circle. It was inconceivable that his judgment should be stampeded by sentiment or recognizable prejudice. There was all the difference of an epoch between his standpoint and that of Gladstone.

Under such circumstances Catholics entered without difficulty into the diplomatic service and Henry Francis Howard and the brothers George and William Jerningham figure among the minor instruments of English foreign policy.[2] To this world, quite tolerant of all religious manifestations expressed with delicacy, belonged Mrs. Augustus Craven, the author of *Le Récit d'une Sœur*. The most successful career of these early years of emancipation was made on the border-line of diplomacy and the army by Sir Justin Sheil, the minister at Teheran.

In politics there was no influential Catholic leader and no adherent of the old religion could be regarded as a national figure. The twelfth Duke of Norfolk was deeply Catholic ; a Whig ; personally

---

[1] As an instance Greville wrote of his stay in Florence : " 26 March, 1830. Yesterday to Mass at the Annunciata ; the Mass beautifully performed by his (the Grand Duke's) band. Tacchironoli singing and Manielli directing," *Memoirs*, I, p. 308.

[2] For the details of the careers of the first Catholics in English diplomacy and for those of the fourth Lord Holland and Colonel Caradoc, later Lord Howden, the Ministers at Florence and Madrid who became converts to Catholicism, cf. *British Diplomatic Representatives*, 1789-1852, Camden Society, vol. I (1934).

opposed to O'Connell ; very old and not without some pleasing eccentricities. His heir Lord Surrey, also a Whig, was merely nominal in his adherence to the Church. But there seemed little prejudice with the Tories out of office and the pressure of the middle class was not yet felt severely by the government. Melbourne would support any man who was sound in his political opinions and moved within a well-defined social grouping. Thus five peerages were called out of abeyance during his administration ; four of them held by Whig squires of solid fortune. Among these new peers three were Catholics, Mr. Stapleton of Carlton, Mr. Stonor and Mr. Mostyn of Kiddington. Beaumont, Camoys and Vaux of Harrow-den represented a harvest for the peerage lawyers. Already Catholicism was gaining the flavour of a romanticism with which Scott's novels had been so liberally endowed. Melbourne gave two Catholics minor ministerial office: there was a general impression of mild well-being.

Such was the situation when the young Queen, who had succeeded her uncle William IV two years previously, married Prince Albert. Queen Victoria's character had been formed young. She was positive ; simple in her patriotism, dignity and sense of position ; unimaginatively strongly Protestant ; impressing and securing the middle classes. In spite of her early reliance on Lord Melbourne she had nothing of his detachment. As far as the Catholics were concerned it was the supersession of a casual indifference by a slightly puzzled dislike. Added to this there was the Prince's influence.

Prince Albert's influence over the Queen was as profound as it was manifest. Together they discovered the implications of the Christian virtues in a German setting. They had revolted from the Queen's wicked uncles and from the disordered domestic *ménage* of Coburg and the Prince had taught his bride enlightened virtue, duty and service. Together they took shelter in an ordered rather doctrinaire fairyland where the landscape of privilege was touched with sentiment like " beloved Rosenau." Throughout their life together the most sympathetic approach to the Church of Rome was in the intimacies of family affection, as in the relationship between the Queen and Prince Albert and their Catholic cousin, the Duchess of Nemours ; it was only under sentimental veils that Catholicism appeared acceptable.

It was not, however, that Queen Victoria and the Prince Consort had too few Catholic relatives, they had too many. For the Coburgs were the adventurers of post-Congress of Vienna constitutional sovereignty with a nineteenth-century Liberal acquiescence in religious change and this solvent of Liberalism produced some morally questionable figures. Leopold II of Belgium and his eldest daughter, to explore no further among the nominally Catholic relatives, fell below the Queen's standards of royal Christian virtue and womanly modesty. She was happier in a Lutheran atmosphere following out the *minutiæ* of genealogical data and succession among the rulers of the little German states and their princesses, who were so pure minded, *hausfrau*, Bible-reading and Protestant. Throughout life the Queen was constantly fortified in her own opinions.

The idea of secession was always distasteful to her as was evident in her relations with her own Court circle. Her reaction to the Oxford Movement and to the conversions to Rome, when these came, was a foregone conclusion. The weakening of the National Church was obviously deplorable and to a direct, strong, positive cast of mind, like Queen Victoria's, the acceptance of Catholicism was a sinning against the light ; especially in the advanced state of knowledge of the mid-nineteenth century. These facts had their importance which was emphasized by the Queen's personal integrity and her devoted faithful life. Determined, with a vein of hardness, susceptible to emotional influences only at a certain level, she became increasingly the symbol of her own great reign. Respected and eventually revered by her Catholic subjects she maintained the prestige of the monarchy as a bulwark of the Protestant Faith.

In the general field it seems not unreasonable to pivot the change of attitude, which affected the outlook on the Catholic Church and all other institutions, around the Queen's marriage and the fall of the Melbourne administration in 1841. It is not that these dates have intrinsic importance, but they synchronize with the emergence of the new forces ; industrialism ; the agitation about the Corn Laws ; free-trade doctrine. The country had long been conscious of the Evangelicals and now the conception of evangelical churchmanship and neo-liberal principles penetrated even the circles of privilege. It was in this period that the practical influence of the middle-class franchise came into action. Under the guiding idea of progress a direct development had led through the years of the railway mania to the Great Exhibition of 1851 and the legacy of the Crystal Palace.

As far as the Catholics were concerned the half century from 1791 till 1841 had formed one whole. A close corporation of the governing families had received their wealthier members on terms of hospitality. The Whigs had constituted themselves the champions of Catholic liberties and had received such support as Catholics, themselves excluded from Parliament, could muster in the boroughs under their control. Socially no wide gulf separated the Whigs from the Tories and in the case of both sections of the ruling class a genial attitude had marked their relationship with their social inferiors and some care was taken to ascertain the standpoint of men of substance among the middling sort. These and the poor, both Protestant and Catholic, had remained in their respective stations. In political circles a casual support for the Established Church was balanced by a careless indifference towards the professors of the ancient faith.

The new order on the contrary was built upon clarified certitudes. Positiveness came in with the belief in material progress and a degree of bitterness towards Catholicism developed. For, as the question of extending the franchise became more actual, the political potentialities of Catholics increased and at the same time the Oxford Movement, so essentially remote from Whig indifference, introduced a new and disturbing factor. Everything was seen clearly and with distortion. Danger was apprehended from the people in the Chartist disturbances; revolution was feared; the increase of popery appeared a menace. One representative of this new age was Mr. Gladstone, who first entered the Cabinet in 1843 and remained an active political force for fifty years. His political and religious position took a little time to clear; but he emerged in middle life as a national figure, Liberal in his principles, profoundly ethical in his outlook, deeply attached to High Anglican churchmanship, opposed to Rome, with a great moral courage and an openly expressed conscientiousness which secured him respectful support. Added to this he had the power to lull if not to satisfy the Liberalism of intellectual and academic circles.

In this connection the contrast with Disraeli is suggested. The latter did not attain Cabinet rank until 1852; but he had long been known as a writer of political novels who had imported the exotic vehemence of his Italian-Jewish strain alike into parliamentary debate and private life. The statue in Parliament Square in the peer's robes and with the Garter suggests him ; always the foreigner, very consciously the squire of Hughenden ; never establishing complete ascendancy over the Conservative party which he led for thirteen years. His unusual reactions have therefore less significance. For Catholicism he had an appreciation quite divorced from Christian theology and derived in part from a spurious romanticism. He was to commit himself to certain hostilities in *Lothair* ; but the higher ranks of the English peerage seem to have cast a magic for him on all that they might inherit or adopt. He was, perhaps, the last Prime Minister to be impressed by the Catholic representation in the House of Lords. But there seems to have been sincerity in Disraeli's appreciation of the great English peers and even his criticism of peerage lawyers, as in *Sybil*, is the satire of refracted affection. His superficial contacts were with a Catholic circle, sophisticated, *mondain* and not erudite. His flamboyant and in some respects impoverished imagination led him to concentrate upon externals ; but it seems probable that in his heart he admired in the Catholic Church the venerable and enduring qualities of his race.

WISEMAN AND ULLATHORNE

IT IS REMARKABLE that those who were now to appear as the Catholic leaders should have been such close contemporaries, a fact not without its influence in the clash of personalities. Cardinal Newman was born in 1801, Cardinal Wiseman in 1802, Archbishop Ullathorne in 1806 and Cardinal Manning in 1808. Then Cardinal Acton was born in 1803, Archbishop Errington in 1804, Ambrose de Lisle in 1809, Pugin and W. G. Ward in 1812 and Faber in 1815. It was, too, a period when comparatively young men were in control, even among the hereditary Catholics. Thus Dr. Griffiths, who was vicar apostolic of the London district from 1836 till 1847 had become a bishop at forty-two. Cardinal Acton was raised to the Sacred College at thirty-nine and died at forty-four ; Wiseman was consecrated at thirty-eight and Ullathorne at forty.

The Catholics were led by vigorous men of magnanimous temperament and subdued energy, still in early middle life. It is, perhaps, best to consider their influence first, since they played so great a part in dealing with the influx from Anglicanism that the Roman obedience was so soon to receive. From the first meeting between Wiseman and Newman in 1834 the former loomed in the imagination of the High Anglicans offering them Rome's dangerous friendship, and it was by Ullathorne that this hope of friendship was to be fulfilled. The expectation aroused by the one and the fulfilment given by the other were alike inevitable ; for Wiseman represented an Hispano-Irish background lit by the Catholic romanticism of nineteenth-century Europe and Ullathorne the yeoman reactions, the stolid, prosaic, humorous character and the long-rooted traditions of Catholicism in England.

There had been church-building and consolidation, but the Catholic Church in England had on the whole lain in the Doldrums through the 'thirties and the early 'forties. In 1840 there returned from Rome as president of Oscott and bishop-coadjutor the future leader Nicholas Wiseman, a priest still young and gifted with erudition, enthusiasm, emotional power and imaginative vision, who had held since 1828 the key position of rector of the English

College. He had been in the college as student and vice-rector since he was sixteen, in atmosphere he was almost *Romano di Roma*, the special *protégé* of Cardinal Mai and favoured by Gregory XVI the reigning pontiff. His name brought back associations with Braddocks and constancy under Elizabethan persecution, but he himself had been born in Spain where his father was a partner in the firm of Wiseman Brothers trading between Waterford and Seville. He had gone to Ushaw at the age of eight and stayed there till he had been sent to Rome in 1818. His life falls into two distinct sections, the phenomenal and rapid success of his early years and the constructive action but also the disappointments of his late maturity.

Tall, slight, pale with black hair, the young rector carried a vast linguistic erudition in the Mezzofanti tradition with a nice sense of humour which foreshadowed that of *Pio Nono* and a decorously youthful gravity. He had published his *Horæ Syriacæ* at twenty-five ; he had that devotion to Rome which had characterized the generation of de Maistre, a sympathy with the full tide of the Romantic movement, enthusiasm for Lacordaire, a fondness for happy Latin jests and a welcoming Irish impulsiveness towards each generous suggestion which might advance the Catholic Church.

To Wiseman, with his delight in Roman magnificence and his decorated style, came in 1830 a recently converted clergyman the Rev. and Hon. George Spencer, ardent, ascetic and very generous. The new convert, a son of Earl Spencer, had cut loose from the Whig traditions of Althorp and was consumed by an apostolic desire for the conversion of England. This he believed to be at hand and he fired Wiseman with his belief. Spencer, better known as Fr. Ignatius, C.P., from his name in religion, had shared with Ambrose de Lisle and Kenelm Digby in the activities of the small Cambridge movement. These new Catholics were warmly enthusiastic and romanticist, very different in temper of mind from the austere-minded, delicate, careful, inhibited outlook bred in the common rooms of Oxford. " I am disposed," wrote de Lisle to Spencer at this time, " to see in the events in Poland so glorious for Catholicity a fulfilment of Sister Antonia Ponte's prediction concerning Pentecost." This was very remote from what was to be Newman's approach ; but in Wiseman they found their own ideas reflected.

From this time the centre of Wiseman's interests shifted. He became the leader of the still small group who believed in the rapid return of England to Catholicism. He gave himself to lecturing and preaching rather than to research ; he spent a year in England and assisted in founding the *Dublin Review*. The *Lectures on the Blessed Eucharist*, which date from this period of his life, give an excellent impression of his work. In 1840 there was a redistribution of the English Catholic administrative areas and three new vicariates were created, the Lancashire, Yorkshire and Welsh districts. At the same time the former Midland district was divided into two sections, the Central and the Eastern. Monsignor Wiseman was chosen as bishop coadjutor of the Central district and president of Oscott College ; he returned to find a curious situation among the English Catholics.

The first group of converts, joined since 1834 by the young architect Augustus Welby Pugin, formed a small compact body united by family ties to that section of the old Catholics which was most familiar with Rome. Their activities were centred in the Midlands : they comprised patrons of the arts and gentlemen of literary attainments and Pugin, but no dons, no clergymen, nor any members of the philistine middle class. Ambrose de Lisle, the heir to considerable properties in Leicestershire, had recently founded the Cistercian abbey of Mount St. Bernard's and built from Pugin's design a Tudor manor house at Grace Dieu. He had married a Miss Clifford and spent his leisure translating works of spirituality from the Italian. Sir Charles Wolseley, a squire of radical principles from South Staffordshire, had also lately become a Catholic and was married to another Miss Clifford ; while their cousin Lord Clifford of Chudleigh, who took an interest in archæological investigations consonant with his rank, lived for the most part at Tivoli and was one of Wiseman's intimates. Dominating the others was de Lisle's chief friend and Pugin's most considerable patron the sixteenth Earl of Shrewsbury, who held that title from 1827 till 1852, combining an external Gothic magnificence with a life of extreme personal poverty ; individualistic ; a warm champion of the *Ecstatica* of Caldaro, equally at home in Rome and England, but in some ways very much the early-Victorian nobleman ; intensely generous and a builder of churches throughout the Midlands. On the literary side the group was represented by Kenelm Digby's *Mores Catholici* and his more celebrated work *The Broadstone of Honour or the True Sense and Practice of Chivalry*. On one side these new Catholics can be held to have had affinities with that transient mood in one *stratum* of English life which is associated with the Eglinton

Tournament, Disraeli's earlier period, the Young England party and Lord John Manners. Certainly these friends of Wiseman could hardly have been more remote from the old reserved English Catholics or Newman's more intellectual reticence.

The character of Wiseman's spontaneous and warm associations does something to explain the isolation which came upon him during the years at Oscott from 1840 until 1845. He welcomed Newman's publication of *Tract XC* and the trend of his followers towards Rome ; but in the period preceding Newman's submission to the Catholic Church in 1845 Wiseman's position was very difficult. Not only the Milner succession, but also Dr. Lingard the historian and the elder priests were opposed to his enthusiastic interest in the High Anglicans. The Catholic peers as a body felt that he had placed an undue value on enthusiasm and the country gentry had small confidence in the usefulness of these novel approaches. The clergy became distrustful of his preoccupation with those who were not yet, and might never be within the Church. They complained of his prolonged absences, his lack of method, his ignorance of Oscotian matters and his insecure command of detail. (The Oscott boys were growing up with a great admiration for him, but they were the future not the present generation.) All his life Wiseman was sensitive and the clergy did not take easily to sensitive men, even superiors. And then there was always the great sweep of his ideas, the trailing clouds and the cherubs of a Roman " glory " to dismay them. At this time all the seeds of his later miseries were sown just as his triumph was approaching. He had an essential greatness ; he was magnanimous ; he had an European scope ; he had the strength to carry through his programmes, everything except the capacity to make them acceptable. And to make the contrast with the old generation clearer there was working in the Midland district in charge of the mission at Coventry Dr. Ullathorne, who in 1846 joined Wiseman as a bishop.

William Bernard Ullathorne was to be for forty years the standard of reference for the Catholic tradition in England. Few men have filled the pastoral office with such success, unalterable devotion and common sense. Surrounded by the meteors men felt at home with him. His father, who was of old Catholic yeoman stock, traded at Pocklington in Yorkshire as a grocer, draper and spirit merchant. The background of his childhood had been this York-shire home and the rather greater prosperity of his Uncle Langstaff's

house in the Polygon, Somers Town.   At fifteen he went to sea as
a cabin boy, which in his case was the equivalent of a modern
apprentice, in the *Leghorn* sailing to the Baltic and later in the brig
Anne Resolution of Scarborough, whose owners the Craythornes
were Catholics and friends of his family.   During this second voyage
he determined to enter religion while hearing Mass at Memel with
the mate, Mr. Craythorne, who had been a boy at Stonyhurst.   He
entered the noviciate of the Benedictine house at Downside when
he was nineteen and received the name of Bernard.   Here he
remained for seven years and was ordained.   In 1832 he was sent
out by his superiors as vicar general of Australia and in this position
his firmness of character and virility of decision were first tested.
He was always direct and rather blunt, a forceful preacher.   His
celebrated sermon on " The Drunkard," which dates from his
Australian days, could hardly have been more vigorous and successful.   He had a great share in terminating the system of transporta-
tion of convicts and he returned home in 1840 with his reputation
for executive capacity made.   He came back to Coventry in the
early days of industrial expansion and he was to live in Birmingham
for forty years.   There was nothing of the Whig about him and he
understood the iron age of the pre-Chamberlain Midlands.

In politics he was a Tory of the old school ; addicted to snuff-
taking ; forthright in his speech ; with a hearty distrust for Mr.
Gladstone.   For over forty years he measured men and policies by
the sound Catholic tradition.   He knew the faith of the West Riding
and the Midlands, that adherence to the old religion maintained by
the townsmen and the farmers.   He shared all the intellectual background of the Catholic squires, for they had been brought up on
those works of devotion which had influenced his own formation.
He gained and held the implicit confidence of the laity.   After a
brief period in the Western district he returned to Birmingham and
was bishop of that diocese from its formation in 1850 until 1888.
He was throughout in a position to observe.   Wiseman he seems
to have regarded with independence, friendliness and some surprise.
When the Oxford converts were received into the Church he
brought to bear on them a singularly impartial and clear judgment.
Newman was long his subject.   He gave him a real sympathy
which went with a considerable understanding and he successfully
interpreted the gist of his position to the old Catholics.   A profound
honesty had enabled him to win his way to Newman's sensitive

friendship. Foreign devotions were distasteful to him and hampered his relationship with Faber. Manning he regarded with the determination and the courage, but also the suspicion of a mastiff.

Among the episcopate his intimacy was reserved for Bishop Grant. He had a lasting attachment to Canon Estcourt, an Oxford convert who was to be his constant companion from 1850 till 1884, and he had a deep appreciation of the energy and the spirituality of Mother Margaret Hallahan. Ullathorne was in all ways representative of the old Catholicism, its common sense, strength and toughness ; the spirit of the English Benedictine congregation religious and missionary. No one could doubt his integrity or the force of his character. As he lay dying in extreme old age he spoke rarely. Once he said " the last of the vicars apostolic is passing " and again during the prayers for the dying he interjected characteristically " the devil's an ass."

It seems appropriate to describe Ullathorne at this point since he was to hand on the old tradition ; but the centre of the stage was reserved for Wiseman who played his part magnificently, while Ullathorne led the unimpressed and rugged chorus of the old English clergy.

Two new major problems required solution and Wiseman treated them along large lines. In 1845 a stream of converts followed Newman into the Catholic Church and he had the responsibility for their welcome and settlement. In the following years the Catholic population was multiplied by the waves of immigration from Ireland where the failure of the potato crop had produced famine. The question of the converts is considered in the next chapter and the vast increase of the congregations in the cities belongs properly to the subject of town Catholicism. But both problems had a suitability for Wiseman appealing to his urgent and apostolic spirit which responded so readily to such challenges. In financial detail he was no great expert and his concern was always for the wider structural planning. He was in no way dismayed by the complexity of any question but carried his plans forward with an ardent confidence. It was for others to work out the application and the *minutiæ* of the problems which he was called upon to solve. At this period of his life Bishop Wiseman was truly *maiestuoso*.

Both the conversions and the Irish influx tended to the encouragement of a plan which had been foreshadowed when the four vicariates were increased to eight in 1840. Seven years later there had been tentative suggestions for the restoration of the national hierarchy and in 1850 this became an accomplished fact. A few months previously Wiseman had become vicar apostolic of the London district and Ullathorne had succeeded him in Birmingham. Then on 29 September, 1850, Pope Pius IX restored the English hierarchy by the Letters Apostolic *Universalis Ecclesiæ* and erected one metropolitan see and twelve suffragan bishoprics.[1] Nicholas Wiseman became Cardinal Priest of the title of Santa Pudentiana and Archbishop of Westminster.

His return from Rome was leisurely and splendid as his cardinalitial carriage with the arms on the panels rolled from the States of the Church into Tuscany ; to Florence where the footmen met His Eminence with torches ; then through the Lombard plain and into the Austrian dominions. It was at Vienna that he first saw the *Times* leader which dealt with the appointment. His letter from the Flaminian Gate of Rome had been published in England before he was aware of the storm which the restoration of the hierarchy had aroused. Its rich and enthusiastic phrasing, while angering the Protestants beyond measure, caused disquiet among the reserved, tenacious, careful Catholics of the older school. In London there were public demonstrations and effigies of the new cardinal were burned in the streets. Lord John Russell, the Prime Minister, took up the agitation naturally determined that capital should not be made out of this event by the Opposition. The Cardinal's immediate return and the publication of *The Appeal to the English People* did much to restore the situation. In this letter his apostolic charity for his own flock and especially for the poor was shown clearly in all the capably worded and coloured writing.

The Duke of Norfolk supported the public agitation, while his eldest son Lord Arundel and Surrey, the friend of Montalembert and Faber, came forward in the Lower House in defence of the Cardinal. Another Catholic peer protested against " this edict of the Court of Rome " and in 1851 the Ecclesiastical Titles Bill was passed. This measure imposed a fine of £100 upon any Catholic bishop who assumed the title of a territorial see. It remained a dead letter and was repealed some twenty years later.

[1] The eight districts of 1840 had been the London, Western, Eastern, Central, Welsh, Lancashire, Yorkshire, and Northern ; the sees of 1851 were Westminster, Beverley, Birmingham, Clifton, Hexham (later Hexham and Newcastle), Liverpool, Newport and Menevia, Northampton, Nottingham, Plymouth, Salford, Shrewsbury and Southwark. The title of Beverley disappeared in 1878 when the diocese was divided between the new sees of Leeds and Middlesbrough.

The indignation subsided rapidly and public interest faded. A considerable section of opinion, to which Greville gives expression, had always viewed the matter calmly and had deplored the introduction of the Bill. The stream of converts flowed again after the Gorham Judgment and the new hierarchy held their first synod at Birmingham in 1852. But with the successful meeting of this assembly the happier period of Cardinal Wiseman's life closes. His unconsidering optimism and a certain careless authoritarian temper made him enemies and he was inclined to consider that the supposed "rights" of others thwarted the progress of his ideals. The diocesan clergy were unsympathetic towards his public gatherings and lectures[1] when these were compared with his few domestic contacts. Command of detail is essential to successful autocracy and this he could not achieve. The bishops were opposed to him, mindful of the mutual independence of the vicars apostolic, while the northern prelates and especially Dr. Goss of Liverpool, wielding "the crozier hook and point" could hardly tolerate his quick generous expedients. The strain of artistic taste, moulded to ecclesiastical uses, was strong in the Cardinal. He regretted the loss of so fair a church as St. George's Cathedral to Southwark ; he would not leave Bishop Grant his independence ; he made difficulties about the Southwark funds. It was impossible for him to conciliate the old Catholics, although individuals were strongly attached to him.

The virtue of his plans lay in a largeness of vision and the failure of his remedies was due to their wide and drastic quality. Thus to cope with the diocesan work he persuaded Rome in 1855 to grant him a coadjutor, Bishop Errington of Plymouth, who was given the right of succession and promoted Archbishop of Trebizond *in*

---

[1] The old-fashioned point of view on this and kindred subjects is well expressed in four letters written by Dr. Lingard.

"I do not know," he wrote in 1839, " the Hon. and Rev. Mr. Spencer. From his recent doings with Mr. Philips and the mad baronet I should fear that he is not a man of very sound judgment."

Again : " I have had the Rev. and Hon. Mr. Spencer begging for the new convent. I never met with so methodistic a looking man."

At the same date he wrote that " if I am not allowed to wear my white cravat, I will as a Douation start the Douai collar. Alas, alas the days of fun are over, and therefore, to be serious, accept Dr. Wiseman's invitation. You may learn something new, at least how to wear purple stockings and silver buckles."

Finally in February 1850 he suggested as a subject for discussion at Dr. Wiseman's *soirées*. " How to send away those swarms of Italian congregationists who introduce their own customs here and by making religion *ridiculous* in the eyes of protestants *prevent* it *spreading here.*" *Life and Letters of John Lingard*, by Martin Haile and Edwin Bonney, pp. 10, 309 and 353.

partibus infidelium. By this measure he hoped to conciliate the bishops, the senior clergy and the laity of old-fashioned views. George Errington had been Wiseman's vice-rector at Rome and had assisted him at Oscott ; a fine old lion ; weather-beaten, rather grim ; well read in theology, exacting, determined ; of old Catholic stock from High Warden in Northumberland. There was, however, unfortunately no question upon which Wiseman was ready to delegate authority without right of appeal. The collaboration did not work. The Cardinal was a sick man suffering from diabetes and constant heart attacks and the situation was complicated because he had at last found an understanding friend.

Henry Edward Manning is only considered here in so far as he altered Wiseman's life. For from the moment of his reception into the Church the Cardinal felt a deep confidence in him and from 1858 he made him his chief adviser. In Manning he found all that he had laboured for in his long effort for the conversion of England. Here was the convert Anglican as he had pictured him. Manning and Errington were incompatible and it was clear that the coadjutor must go. He went, and worked in humility for many years. His cousin Lady Arundell of Wardour preserved until very recently the memory and the characteristics of Errington's England.

The Cardinal had suffered many disappointments, but now he found peace in Manning's strong friendship. His ill health increased upon him ; he became somnolent and could no longer concentrate. But he was at peace, confident that affairs were in good hands. " I have never cared for anything but the Church," he said[1] in his last illness. " My sole delight has been in everything connected with her. As people in the world go to a ball for their recreation, so I have enjoyed a great function." Again he would think of his happiness in Rome as a young man and of the villa of the English College at Monte Porzio. " I can see the colour of the chestnut-trees," he said[2], " and Camaldoli and the top of Tusculum." In 1865 he died. He had made the paths of the early converts smooth. He had provided in some measure for the new great congregations ; he had restored the hierarchy. Perhaps he had overestimated the influence of the Catholic body, even as extended, in English life. His view of the Church of England was naive and colourful and

---

[1] Quoted from the statement of Canon Morris in the *Life and Times of Cardinal Wiseman*, by Wilfrid Ward, II, p. 510.

[2] ibid., II, p. 511.

there was something of a child's optimism in his mounting hopes. Yet he did great work, which would not have been possible save for his vision and he left a legacy of high importance to the Church in England : Provost Manning.[1]

[1] An important factor in the gradually changing attitude towards Catholicism was the part played by the Sisters of Mercy from Bermondsey and the Sisters of the Faithful Virgin from Norwood who went out to work in the hospitals during the Crimean War. Among these Crimean ladies was Fanny Taylor who became the foundress of the Poor Servants of the Mother of God. With all these works Provost Manning was closely connected and he had been Florence Nightingale's adviser in the period when she was drawn towards the Catholic Church.

The educational work of the nuns was developing. Mother Cornelia Connelly had established in 1848 the first school of the Society of the Holy Child Jesus at St. Leonards. In 1856 Sister Mary of St. Philip Lescher opened the training school of the Sisters of Notre Dame at Liverpool. The Society of the Sacred Heart had founded the convent at Roehampton which will always be associated with the names of Mother Digby and Mother Janet Erskine Stuart.

NEWMAN AND MANNING

NO CONVERSION IN England has had a deeper significance and few have been more clearly foreshadowed than that of John Henry Newman in 1845. During two years his submission to Rome appeared inevitable. The doubt centred rather upon the number of followers that the great leader would bring with him and the place that he would occupy within the Catholic body. The early details of that Oxford Movement with which his name is linked inseparably, belong rather to the history of Anglicanism. Although he had met Wiseman at Rome in 1833, during that Mediterranean journey which led to the production of *Lyra Apostolica*, it was not until he was forty that his conversion could be regarded as in any sense probable. This development was a result of the condemnation in 1841 of *Tract XC*, one of the series of treatises from which the name Tractarian sprang. In this he had attempted to attach a Catholic meaning to the various Anglican formularies. Until the condemnation his desire for the *via media*, which he believed Anglicanism to provide, and the vast influence in Oxford of his preaching as vicar of St. Mary's had appeared to bind him firmly to the Established Church. His dual attachment to Trinity and Oriel and the whole tenor of his mind had seemed to favour a spiritual renewal within the limits of his own communion. His early associations had been Evangelical and the sound church-manship of his collaborators of the Hadleigh meeting phase was never to turn Romeward. None of his three chief associates in the period of the Oxford Movement from 1833 to 1843 were to submit; Hurrell Froude died in 1836 and Keble and Pusey survived to gather together those Tractarian forces which Newman's submission to Rome had left leaderless. It was only in 1843 that his close association with Catholicism developed. In that year he resigned his living of St. Mary's, retracted his anti-papal utterances and retired to solitude at Littlemore near Oxford. He was already in isolation, disturbed by the promotion of Alexander to the new Jerusalem bishopric and deeply wounded by the Bishop of Oxford's charge condemning his work. After two years' consideration he was received into the Catholic Church on 9 October, 1845, by Fr. Dominic Barberi, an Italian Passionist. It is interesting to consider how the Catholics regarded the new leader upon the eve of this event.

In the first place Dr. Newman's personality was in fact but little known. The University was without a Catholic element and Newman did not go out into general society. An element of curiosity, very painful to the sensitive, was therefore almost inevitable. The very matter-of-fact tone of hereditary Catholic opinion only made this the more obvious. A most illuminating phrase appears in Newman's private journal in which he refers to himself as treated " as some wild incomprehensible beast, a spectacle for Dr. Wiseman to exhibit to strangers as himself being the hunter that captured it." What exactly was it that Wiseman had " captured " ?

Newman combined the possession of a mind of wide range and extreme sensitiveness with a detachment from the grosser contacts. He breathed in almost unconsciously the Tory traditions with which he was surrounded. He had no concern with the new commerce, while his temperament and his home background at Ealing deprived him of interest in or experience of sport. An habitual deep-rooted shyness was allied to a singular integrity and independence of mind. A delightful familiar intimacy, such as he experienced at Oriel and more perfectly at the Oratory in his later years, went with a deep affection which he reserved for such a chosen friend as Ambrose St. John. But a corollary of his intimacy was the stiffness that he experienced with those who did not share his mental background. In addition he was unsympathetic towards colleagues who failed to maintain his exacting and rather Oxford standards ; standards which his future companions would sometimes neither appreciate nor accept. His mind, although deeply sensitive, was in some respects unresilient. He was singularly human, easily cast down and capable of inspiring an unique and reverent love.

It could be predicted that he would be misunderstood in certain quarters. It was only nineteen years since Milner died. But before describing Newman's Catholic life it is easier to mention briefly the influence of those who made their submission with him, some as friends and some as disciples. It will then be simpler to embark on his difficult history.

The immediate Littlemore grouping followed Newman into the Catholic Church as did those members of his outer circle who still remained in close dependence. Among these Frederick Oakeley, a Prebendary of Lichfield who had long represented a reserved traditional clerical opinion in the Balliol common room, was perhaps the most notable. His cast of mind was scholarly ; he had a rather impersonal charity of outlook ; he was not a fighter. He had a particularly Oxford distinction ; not intimate with Newman, he yet gave him the support of a detached sympathy.

From Balliol, also, came Oakeley's junior colleague Ward ; temperamentally poles apart from Newman, positive in manner and expression, very stout, untidy, impetuous, varying stretches of the most rigorous absorption in theology with a jovial and undonnish uproariousness. In contrast to so many of the early leaders he was a married man and soon to be wealthy. It was typical of his career that he should have produced a theological work which secured his expulsion from Balliol as a favourer of Romanists. His energy was always overflowing ; as long as he lived his influence was a permanent factor.

The significance of " Ideal " Ward, as he was known from his famous treatise, was not minimized in his own day. His layman's intense preoccupation with theology (he was even to teach this subject at St. Edmund's) was characteristic of an aspect of his period, while his clear-cut conceptions were always trenchantly expressed. His friendship with Tennyson indicates one of the most considerable of the contacts between the Ultramontanes and the outside world. Ward's chief legacy was the *Dublin Review*, a quarterly whose serious reputation was unquestioned and in which the expression of the standpoint of orthodoxy became increasingly eirenic with the years. He transmitted something of his position to his second son and the mental outlook and, indeed, the whole social history of the higher *strata* of Catholic life in the late-Victorian and Edwardian periods could hardly be seen more clearly than in a detailed study of the three brothers of the second generation, Granville, Bernard and Wilfrid Ward.

After Ward : Faber. Huguenot by descent, Frederick Faber possessed as an unwelcome heritage the eighteenth-century Erastian ideals of princely Anglican episcopacy. He had been brought up as a child at Bishop Auckland, where his father was chaplain to Shute Barrington, a prelate who enjoyed both the Palatine powers and the great unimpaired emoluments of the see of Durham. Harrow and Balliol, an educational *milieu* which he shared with Manning, hardly prepared him for reaction ; but, once ordained, Faber, like Hurrell Froude, turned vehemently against every aspect of Erastian domination. He was a poet, an enthusiast, an ascetic. On Newman's submission he was rector of Elton in Huntingdonshire and he followed him.

Like Ward, Faber was quick to find his Catholic niche. His monument is the London Oratory of which he was to be superior for fourteen years, but it is in his devotional writings that we may perhaps best catch his spirit. An excellent memory and an avid study both of the Fathers and of the authors of the Catholic tradition were found combined with a balanced, but in some ways rather limited, critical faculty and a perhaps slightly unoriginal literary talent. His great energy acting on these qualities and aided by an ardent desire for souls made him a copious and successful spiritual writer. His style had a popularity in many Catholic circles, which served to differentiate his adherents rather sharply from the reserved, silent, old fashioned grouping among his coreligionists. The wide dissemination of his works on the Continent was assisted by a literary manner which was particularly convincing in translation. His active Catholic life was comparatively short ; he was towards the end an ailing man and died in 1863. Thenceforward the London Oratory represented not the influence of a single leader but a trend of thought, the grafted Oratorian tradition of St. Philip Neri. When finished the great Brompton church symbolized in a sense the amalgam of diverse groups of upper-class Catholics. If the calm Roman Baroque satisfied Disraeli's rather elaborate taste for the romantic, it was to gain the prestige which still attached to a familiar London landmark standing greyly dominant above the hansoms and broughams and landaus, a sign of a complete social acceptance. But this is an anticipation, a tracing out of some remote effects of the conversions of 1845. It is a prelude to the necessarily brief and carefully tentative consideration of Newman's life and influence as a Catholic.

After his departure from Littlemore Newman went first to Maryvale, Oscott and then in 1846 to Rome. At Oscott he renewed his slender acquaintance with Dr. Wiseman, now a bishop and president of the college. Their relationship was friendly but not easy. Fired by his long work for the High Anglicans, seeing his hopes realized by this conversion Wiseman was both diplomatic and sanguine, qualities which were not possessed by Newman to whom they made no appeal. The conversion of England seen along large too hopeful lines, the immediate problem of the restoration of the hierarchy, the material and administrative details and the strategic placing of the Catholic viewpoint engrossed the Bishop's quick attention. Newman's thought was concentrated almost wholly on the solitary processes and adventures of the God-seeking mind. In Rome the same divergence was apparent in Newman's dealings with the English Catholic community.

Thus Lord Shrewsbury, who lived chiefly in Rome combining a cosmopolitan appreciation of aristocratic circles with a taste for curious unacademic knowledge, was not very far from Newman in outlook ; •but not near enough for contact. Again, since the eighteenth century the highest Catholic social *stratum*, such as the Jerningham Letters represent, had been at least bi-lingual, very frequently *mondain*, but almost never intellectual.

At the same time at the opposite extreme Newman, on his return to England as a priest, was difficult of approach by the clergy of the robust Milner tradition. He judged by standards very different from their own ; he displayed no urgent interest in their poor, nor in the humdrum details of the pastoral work which was their life. Yet, as at Oxford, he possessed a compelling attraction for certain natures, both among the hereditary Catholics and the converts. Most notable of these was, perhaps, the fifteenth Duke of Norfolk who was educated under his charge and whose father had been an intimate of Fr. Faber.

With these facts mentioned the external detail of Newman's life can be considered. He became an Oratorian and on his return to Birmingham in 1848 founded the Oratory, where he passed the whole of the remainder of his life, except for a prolonged stay in Ireland between 1854 and 1858 in connection with the rectorship of the Dublin Catholic University. He was not very deeply interested in the developments which brought Wiseman the archbishopric of Westminster and a cardinalate and he had an instinctive and rather insular distrust of the processes of ultramontane thought. Many differences of method tended to reduce the sympathy between Newman and Wiseman and this attenuated friendship changed under the growing influence of Dr. Manning with whom relations were at first uncordial and later frigid. Still Newman possessed what chiefly mattered, the encouragement and strong support of his own diocesan, Ullathorne.

The Achilli trial in 1853, when he was prosecuted for exposing an Italian ex-Dominican, brought him anxiety and trouble, as did the abortive Irish rectorship, the failure of the plans for an Oratory and a Catholic college at Oxford, and the controversy with Charles Kingsley which led in 1864 to the publication of Newman's *Apologia pro Vita Sua*. This book, the corner-stone of his writings, luminously sincere and marked by a deeply sensitive clarity of expression, gained him a great position in the world of English letters. Due to this and to his other works there were latterly three streams of his disciples, the religious, the philosophical, the purely literary. At the same time the school founded at Edgbaston aided the establishment among a section of the laity of a Newman tradition ; cultivated and essentially English, stretching out towards the older universities. It must be said however that he remained unsympathetic not only to the rough qualities but also to the robustness of Philistia. In 1877 Newman received an honorary fellowship of Trinity, a mark of peace with Oxford, and in 1879 he was created by Pope Leo XIII a cardinal priest with the title of San Giorgio *in Velabro*. He continued to live at the Birmingham Oratory and there he died in 1890 ; perhaps the greatest English influence on Catholic thought.

．　　　．　　　．　　　．　　　．　　　．

As this description has indicated, Newman's convert following centred upon the cultured, thoughtful circle based upon Oxford. His friends enjoyed that atmosphere of quiet, leisured scholarship made possible by the unaggressive gentle spirit which characterized one early-Victorian clerical grouping. An influence of wholly different character was also to play upon the Catholic body, that of Henry Edward Manning, a prelate of action. It was in 1851 that the Archdeacon of Chichester submitted to Rome as a consequence of the Gorham Judgment which emphasized the latitudinarian character of the Anglican bishops. This was a conversion which heralded many others. Its subject was quite remarkably remote from Newman's *ethos*. Archdeacon Manning had been early noted for a strength of will, a single-minded devotion and a singularly positive cast of mind. As a young man he was athletic, interested in politics, ecclesiastical and lay, and already singularly capable. He was a Tractarian of somewhat neutral colour, an archdeacon at thirty-two, possessed of certain Court connections, probably marked out for the episcopate. Although others were to follow him, no one so close within the *official* Victorian Church had ever before become a Catholic.

His personal qualities, noted before his conversion, developed rapidly with his Catholic life. They made an immediate impression both on the Archbishop of Westminster and the Pope. The ecclesiastical changes in 1850 had left Wiseman with a bench of bishops some of whom inherited the reserved careful outlook of the vicars apostolic, while others emphasized the strength of northern Catholicism, now reinforced by the Irish immigration and industrial development but utterly unaffected by the new conversions. At Westminster a confidential assistant was required who would take the place which Dr. Errington had failed to fill. The Cardinal's ill health emphasized this need and he turned to the strong-minded convert with his clear thought and readiness for responsibility. Trusted in Rome, unswervingly loyal to his superior, Manning, now a priest, was advanced within seven years to be a canon and provost of the Westminster Chapter. A disregard of passing unpopularity and a strong curbing self-denial marked his tenure of this post. He supported Cardinal Wiseman in his successful application for Errington's removal and from 1861 till 1865 was, perhaps, virtual ruler of the archdiocese. In the latter year the Cardinal died and Provost Manning was chosen to succeed him on the Pope's direct initiative. He ruled from 1865 till 1892, being raised in 1875 to the cardinalate. In the general affairs of the Catholic Church he was noted for his championship of the immediate declaration of the dogma of Papal Infallibility. At the deliberations of the Vatican Council he was one of the leaders of the majority who favoured this action. His intense devotion to the Holy See, his practical and positive mind caused him to rejoice in the decision. The same qualities appear in his dealings with the clergy, in the work which he accomplished for Catholic education and in especial in the negotiations leading to the Education Act of 1891. At the same time his impatience with the academic *nuances* and his lack of interest in secular scholarship *per se* were in part responsible for the early failure of his Catholic college in South Kensington. He always envisaged education primarily as it affected his pastoral duties to his struggling flock. Here he was aided by his deep sympathy for the poor and by his understanding of their pressing spiritual and material needs.

He was in general a friend of Ireland, sympathetic to the Irish hierarchy, and welcoming the Irish priests whom he brought over to work in his diocese. Many of his ideas of the priestly life can be studied in the history of the Oblates of St. Charles whom he established in London. In his private life he kept up a detailed mortification of every appetite, while the high standards which he expected from the sacerdotal state are well reflected in *The Eternal Priesthood*, the literary work of his old age. Ready as he was to understand all practical difficulties he was, perhaps, constitutionally unfitted to follow with sympathy the intellectual problems of others. Thus he was seldom at ease with Newman's ranging and hovering intelligence. In this regard he lacked imagination.

The atmosphere of Harrow and Balliol, then so valuable, remained with Manning throughout his life. The *milieu* from which his family came was not necessarily higher than that of the young Newman : but it was in much closer contact with the governing class. Government in its different forms and in all its aspects appealed to him. He had an understanding knowledge of the modes of official action, which he turned to good account in his relations with the Vatican and Whitehall and even in the London Dock Strike. His appearance in extreme old age, that transparency of texture, that asceticism were consonant with the unrivalled public position which he gained in the last years of his life. He fulfilled almost perfectly the popular ideal of a great churchman of the 'eighties, combining an appreciative knowledge of essential English institutions, like the Crown, with a firm and dignified political Liberalism and the realization of the need for much social reform. His death in 1892 at the age of eighty-three closed an administration singularly successful and firm and increasingly tranquil. It is only necessary to notice further that he suffered and his reputation eventually survived two posthumous misfortunes, the misuse of his correspondence with the naive Monsignor Talbot and the mismanagement through which Purcell obtained the charge of his official biography. In the development of Catholicism in England Cardinal Newman and Cardinal Manning were complementary.

THE SUBSEQUENT CONVERSIONS

IN THE SAME way a rough parallel can be made between Newman's converted disciples and Manning's converts. A very definite distinction is apparent between those who were drawn partly by affection for the Master and those who were assisted towards the Church by Dr. Manning's clear rather arid arguments and forceful piety. One consequence of Manning's predominance was that the focal centre of the movement towards Catholicism gradually shifted from Oxford to the less intellectually exigent atmosphere of London society ; for the former Archdeacon of Chichester came from the class which sent its sons to the university, not from that group which supplied the membership of the senior common rooms. It is, of course, impossible to generalize on such a subject ; but at Oxford, while the high tables and the clerical circle of the city had been most affected by the secessions of the 'forties, it was rather the section in which Blenheim impinged on undergraduate life that was affected by the conversions of 1868.

The dons and learned clergy of the Oakeley-Faber period were replaced in the stream of converts first by men from the younger serious element in the professions, like Hope-Scott, Serjeant Bellasis, William Monsell, and then by such aristocratic rather *mondain* incumbents as Lord Charles Thynne, Lord Henry Kerr, Sir William Molesworth. These in turn came in with a small section of the peerage of medium fortune, Feilding, Campden, Norreys and Orford, and with this group the wealthy antiquarian Dunraven ; while behind them, almost snuffing out the intellectual aspects of the movement in their crinolines, stretched the long line of the convert peeresses. It was a strange ending for the Oxford conversions which had begun with the celibate austerity of Newman and his intimates. The Duchesses of Argyll, Buccleugh, Hamilton and Leeds (but in this case it was a reclamation), Elizabeth Lady Londonderry, Lady Queensberry, the unfortunate Lady Waterford, the saintly impetuous Lady Lothian might bring zest and a certain influence, hold receptions, pray, fast, build chapels ; but as a rule their sons and husbands passed their religion by. Polite literature was represented by Lady Georgiana Fullerton. Immense charitable energy was expended, especially in London, and the Church increased. Then after a lull between 1855 and 1868 the stream of conversion began again.

The peak period of this second movement lasted from 1869 till 1874 but a gradual flow continued throughout the century. Various points may be noted briefly. In the main these converts of what we may for convenience designate the Manning period were practical men of the world and they contained a definite proportion of figures of public distinction. Lord Ripon, the Liberal cabinet minister who was to be Viceroy of India, was a man of a deep self-forgetful charity and particularly congenial to the Cardinal whose political preferences he also shared. Lord Bute's conversion made sufficient stir to provide a basis for Disraeli's *Lothair* ; Lord Albemarle had been Treasurer of the Household ; Lord Lyons was actually Ambassador in Paris. Meanwhile the Duchess of Newcastle had taken Lady Londonderry's place as a Catholic hostess and Lady Herbert of Lea with her devout and unremitting enterprise had come within the Catholic fold. There were gains from mixed marriages among the peerage and no spectacular losses save the return to Protestantism of the erratic Lord Robert Montagu. In the whole situation there may have seemed something a little over-sugared ; for the feminine element predominated in this convert circle with its wealth and enthusiasm, its warm devotional spirit, its absence of general literary interest and the close relationship maintained with the " black " or papal Roman aristocracy. It was a special " world " within the wider social unit, differentiated from and yet merging into both the hereditary Catholic element and the wide and now tolerant general political circle. Many of the leading converts had, indeed, been assimilated to the older Catholic grouping by choice or the accident of inter-marriage preferring the colder restrained fashion in devotion, the rejection of intellectual pretension and the frankly out-of-door existence to the rather heightened *tempo* and the more emotional expression of religious values which characterized the Catholic great ladies and their dependants, as they moved against a background of elaborate and still formal hospitality. At the same time the trickle of clerical converts never ceased. The writer Thomas William Allies was, perhaps, the most notable figure, and others were received in their old age like Richard Waldo Sibthorp, who had become a Catholic in 1841 and returned to the

Church of England, and the poet Robert Stephen Hawker who joined the Catholic Church at Plymouth on the day before his death. Sibthorp is interesting as an extreme Tory without intellectual interests who was also bitterly anti-ultramontane. Such overt opposition to the Vatican Council as can be traced among the Oxford Movement converts was usually linked with a Liberal distaste for the *Syllabus Errorum*. This was the case with Richard Simpson, the former editor of the *Rambler*, whose difficult life ended in 1876.

In this period a Catholic element was rising gradually to the higher places in the Diplomatic Service and the Law. The appointment of Sir William Shee, who was raised to the Bench in 1863, had broken a tradition dating from Stuart times and by the last years of the century the representation had been strengthened by the elevation of Lord Russell of Killowen, Lord Justice Mathew, Mr. Justice Day; while the Colonies had received Catholic governors, Lord Gormanston, Sir Frederick Weld and Sir John Pope-Hennessy. As to the political parties, the Conservatives, who could always count on a body of Catholic support, had given the Home Secretaryship in the second Salisbury Administration of 1886–1892 to Lord Llandaff. Courtesies had been exchanged between the English Government and the Vatican on the occasion of the Queen's Jubilee. Cardinal Manning could draw comfort from this great strengthening of the Catholic community. He himself had scientific interests of a general nature and in these matters his coreligionists were fortified by the assistance of a biologist of marked distinction, St. George Mivart, who had been one of the original converts of 1851. It is worth noting that the literary figures of this period as a rule stood rather apart from the rest of the general Catholic body. Within one man's priestly life the Church in England had been brought from the " Catacombs " to the place which it occupied in Edwardian England. The Cardinal Archbishop of Westminster had survived Newman and Ullathorne : he lived into the changed world of the 'nineties to the beginning of the failure of Victorian certitudes. He had had a high talent for administration, an understanding knowledge of the rich, a deep attachment to the poor.

To the Cardinal, as to all who penetrate to the realities of Catholic life, the poor were indeed his stand-by and encouragement. The rich were generous but also exacting and too prone to demand their pound of consideration. There was a sameness about the piety of the ladies of the devout circle and the prim pig-tailed children after Mass on Sundays in the Brompton Road. This was very different from the surging Catholic congregations in East London and throughout the industrial areas. For half a century their numbers had been growing and the position was now consolidated. A network of Catholic elementary schools had been spread across the English towns and the non-provided schools under the provisions of Forster's Education Act of 1870 and the Elementary Education Act of 1891 formed an integral part of the educational system of the country. The free, uncovenanted generosity of the poor had built up their churches and schools week by week. They were determined and loyal ; ready to defend themselves ; forthright. The churches had been paid for stone by stone out of the small wages of the faithful and this in part accounted for their eager attachment to the parish unit which remained their spiritual hearth. The old dominating priests of the fine Irish tradition received reverence and affection from a people who looked for strong leadership and handling. At the same time the Ushaw clergy led the ancestral northern congregations throughout the era of an industrialism whose grimness was not perceived by the sheltered classes. Far apart from the figures who influenced the restricted governing circles of the Victorian age there moved the great body of the Catholic workers.

VICTORIAN CATHOLICISM

DURING THE REIGN the great body of the Catholic poor increased and suffered much misery and perpetual discomfort. The great influx of the industrial revolution had been landed on the foreshores of the large cities and then almost confined in quarantine. They were housed in the streets which arose on the barren verges of the towns corroded by industrialism. The lines of railway and the warehouse structures hemmed them in, and two generations were brought up in the crowded and insecure buildings which had sprung from that first careless energy of the industrial age. Beyond the narrow streets were the coarse grasses of the waste ground which had never suggested profit even to the most stout-hearted building speculator. The cheap paper peeled from the damp bedroom walls and through the uncurtained windows the flecks of paper could be seen turning on the pavement while in summer the sun's rays lit the broken glass on the wall copings. At night the trucks grinding by on the railways were often within earshot and day and night the small streets lay still with little traffic. Behind the street front there opened out the tiny courts with uneven grimy paving and small houses tumbling towards one another, crowded and insanitary.

The families of the old faith in these areas found their chief support in the Catholic priesthood and it is in this connection that the work of the missionary priests from the Continent joined that of the English and Irish clergy and the new convert leaven. The most successful of these foreign missioners were perhaps those who were most closely in touch with the poor like Fr. Aloysius Gentili, one of the members of Rosmini's Institute of Charity, and Fr. Dominic Barberi the Passionist who was to receive Newman into the Church. These were both men of remarkable energy and sincerity and were responsible for establishing their respective forms of missionary activity in this country. Both died comparatively young in 1848 and 1849 ; both had companions and followers. It is probable that they landed in England at a time when foreign clergy were likely to meet with a more favourable response than at any period before or since. In spite of the prejudice against foreigners there was in those early-Victorian years a general consensus of opinion upon certain theological doctrines and an openly expressed admiration for dignity of character and moral worth. This moral worth the new-comers possessed in striking measure. It is just possible to suggest some of the characteristics of Fr. Dominic which made him such an appealing figure in the religious life of his adopted country.

He had been born at Palanzana near Viterbo and grew up with a profound attraction to prayer in the simplicity of Italian farming life. At twenty-one he entered the Passionist congregation as a lay-brother, since he knew no Latin. He had a delightful naturalness and was soon transferred to the choir, became a priest and a lector at the Roman house ; then later a missioner. As a postulant he had met Bishop Milner who was making a retreat with the Passionists and in later years he knew Sir Harry Trelawny, an English convert. Trelawny introduced him to George Spencer and Spencer to Ambrose Phillipps. In the spring of 1830 Phillipps would walk every day with Fr. Dominic in the garden of SS. Giovanni e Paolo, looking down through the cypresses on the Coelian, talking of England. Fr. Dominic's missionary desires were strengthened and he had a strong and developing sense of his particular vocation.

In November 1840 he landed at Folkestone and worked for the last six years of his life in England inspired by a pure charity. Monsignor Searle has left a description of his appearance. " He was," he wrote,[1] " short and rather stout of body and his voice was squeaky, but he had an eagle eye. . . . His countenance appeared to be grieving and was often unshaven." He worked chiefly at Aston and Stone relieving the many Irish who passed through on their way to the Potteries in the famine years. His life was austere and on a journey from Birmingham to Ese in Belgium he ate nothing except a twopenny pork pie[2] which he bought at Paddington and a pennyworth of bread. He travelled on his longer journeys with a large trunk, the " thronc " of his vivid and inaccurate English. A deep holiness and an interior gaiety of spirit marked him and he had a profound and attaching personal influence. On one of his mission-ary expeditions he had a heart attack in the train and died at the Railway Hotel at Reading.

---

[1] This is printed in the first *Life of Father Dominic* by Fr. Pius Devine, C.P., pp. 181–2. For further details cf. the recent work of Fr. Urban Young, C.P.

[2] Fr. Pius' book contains many other similarly delightful touches.

During the generation which followed the coming of these fathers, the work of the Capuchins and the Friars Minor developed and the converts of the Oxford Movement provided their own strengthening element to the English religious life. The Jesuits and Redemptorists probably received proportionately the largest share of such vocations to the regular clergy and these new converts thus took up work which had its roots in labour for the poor. In the case of the Society they formed an important element in the English Province whose influence was notable for half a century through those years of expansion which, developing from Stonyhurst, saw the establishment of Farm Street and Manresa House and Beaumont College. Such priests as Frs. Purbrick and Coleridge brought in this new element of English convert influence, while Fr. Gallwey in particular carried the contacts of the Jesuits into wide circles in London as the Society moved forward under the wintry sun of Wiseman and the frost of Manning.

The great influence of the Jesuits on Catholicism in England developed as the reign progressed while the established colleges like Stonyhurst and Mount St. Mary's were reinforced by the great day-schools in the north which provided a means by which sections of the industrial populations could reach to a less inadequate economic level. The representative figure in these earlier years of the revived life of the Society in London was undoubtedly Fr. Peter Gallwey, S.J.; an Irishman from the south; son of Lord Kenmare's agent; brought up at Stonyhurst. In 1857 he was made superior of the church and residence at Hill Street (the predecessor of the Farm Street house) and in 1877 after holding offices in other parts of England he returned to London where he was to live for the last thirty years of his long life. He was known for his talents as a preacher and was most sought after as a director; very earnest and devout; a tall stout man with a fringe of white hair; very determined. He was a channel for the distribution of much almsgiving and no man was better fitted to uphold the rights of his Church and Order. It has been said that " by the help of a certain combative instinct, well seconded by a masterful will, he seemed to command every situation." He had something of the prudent severity of the old tradition and a devotion which in his last years found expression in his work on the *Watches of the Passion*. Fr. Gallwey was known, too, by his occasional addresses. " Such," we are told,[1] " was the

---

[1] In notes provided through the courtesy of the Very Reverend Father Provincial, S.J.

H

collection of separate discourses spoken by him beside the remains of certain highly respected and well-known Catholics, the lessons of whose lives he gathered together under the general title of *Salvage from the Wreck*, a species of oratory in which he was more than usually felicitous." He was a commanding figure and well fitted to enhance the veneration in which the Jesuits were held by Catholic society.

Living in the same house and his colleague for many years was Fr. Henry Coleridge. A brother of Lord Chief Justice Coleridge and a convert of the Oxford Movement, he was the author of a *Life of Our Lord* and other devotional writings ; a delightful companion with something of the restrained gaiety of the Oxford common rooms ; patient and cordial. At that prosperous period of the reign, the first Jubilee, in 1887, Fr. Edward Purbrick, who had done so much as rector of Stonyhurst, held the office of provincial. He again represented another section and was a convert from the Midlands educated at King Edward VI's Grammar School at Birmingham. Fr. Richard Clarke, who had been a Fellow of St. John's College, Oxford, and was destined to found Campion Hall, was the editor of the *Month* ; the novices at Manresa were under the austere guidance of Fr. Morris. The English Province was equipped to play its part.

The Redemptorists had likewise received considerable reinforcement and much of their early development was due to Fr. Robert Coffin, who had been vicar of St. Mary Magdalen's, Oxford, and was to establish their headquarters at St. Mary's, Clapham. The names of Fr. Ryder, Fr. Gaisford and Fr. Vassall Phillipps indicate the influence of converts and of the convert families, while probably the work of Fr. Bridgett best suggests the nature of the Redemptorist achievement. He came from the very centre of the sober English Victorian world, the son of a silk manufacturer in Derby, from a Baptist family on his father's side and of Unitarian stock upon his mother's. In 1850, on leaving St. John's College, Cambridge, he became a Catholic and retained throughout life a devotion to St. John Fisher whose biography as well as that of St. Thomas More he was to write. From his ordination in 1856 until his death in 1899 he wrote and preached incessantly bringing to bear on the problems of his time a solid judgment and great integrity of character. Parallel to the influence of the priest converts was that of those who remained laymen, an important factor in the Victorian age.

Among the more durable effects of the nineteenth century movement of conversion was the increase of Catholic centres in the English countryside and the establishment of new religious houses. Those converts who came from the rather close-knit society of the mid-Victorian landed interest found a ready welcome from the hereditary Catholic element with whom their families had long been on terms of friendship. Such young convert squires as Ambrose de Lisle were readily accepted as sons-in-law by the old Catholics. It soothed the Protestant gentry at this epoch to reflect that, if religious contact had been lost, their erring children were preserved within the same social *milieu*. Again, although the converts of this class were in nearly all cases young men who had not entered into their inheritance, the estates were generally saved for them owing to the custom of entail. However angry the father he was rendered powerless by the inability of the life tenant to break the entail of landed property without the consent of the next heir. A few cases of disinheritance did occur : George Lane-Fox's loss of the Bramham estate was perhaps the most notable.

As the new estates fell into Catholic hands the old system of maintaining Catholicism in the rural areas was extended. Provision was made for the priest in the form of a total or partial endowment, a small church was built in the village and a private oratory in the squire's house was established. Throughout the Midlands new Catholic centres were developed on this model between the early 'fifties and 'eighties. In the country parts in the north, however, little progress was made ; for there were very few converts in that area with great landed possessions. Similarly in the west country the Church received little substantial increase by this means. The Midland predominance is apparent in the names of some of the houses thus rechristened, Bramshill, Newnham Paddox, Exton, Campden, Wroxton, Wytham and Kirtling. Among religious houses in the country Mount St. Bernard's and Belmont Abbey and the Capuchin friaries at Pantasaph and Crawley were founded on land recently returned to Catholic ownership. For the most part these monasteries and the more firmly established among the new mission centres dated back to the conversions of 1851–1855 or even earlier. The sons of several of the wealthiest converts of the later period remained Protestant. In these cases the system of entail worked in their favour and thus Catholicism could not benefit from Lord Ripon's possession of the magnificent Cistercian ruins of Fountains Abbey. Still the accession of these converts only served to emphasize the position held in late-Victorian life by the old Catholic squires.

As a factor in the general situation the close relationship between the richer families aided the religious revival and it is difficult to estimate the debt that they owed to the influence of the Duke of Norfolk and the wide Howard kinship. Politically both the older and the newer rich Catholic landowners were markedly conservative in politics. Both sections combined could muster at the end of the Manning period about forty peers, a definite proportion of the Upper House, very respectable in character, solid in quality, seldom erratic, rarely brilliant and politically distinctly inactive. As a body they stand out rather soberly against the Duke's strongly marked attractive character, while Monsignor Lord Petre added a touch of the bizarre.

Coming to the general body of the Catholic country gentry the absence of a proportionate share in political and administrative life appears even more striking. This was perhaps partly due to the unbroken character of their tradition, which nothing had seriously disturbed since the Revolution of 1688. Their emergence into practical political freedom had been gradual ; the use made of their liberty was intermittent. A certain proportion had bought commissions in the army and frequently had re-sold them. Few had risen to high military rank. In this connection the distinction of the Cliffords in the service of the Crown only served to emphasize the prevailing avoidance of public life. The county representation could alone give the greater squires a secure place in the parliamentary scheme ; but here they were sometimes hindered by religious prejudice and the vested interests of political families. In the boroughs they had frequently to contend with the hostile Nonconformist vote and for a long time could only succeed with a strong local influence, as Charles Langdale had held Knaresborough. But if even the rich gentry had so little general contact, the struggling squires had still less. In *Helbeck of Bannisdale* Mrs. Humphrey Ward overdrew her consciously sombre description ; but some Catholic families could live in a real isolation. Despite solidarity on religion there remained a wide gulf between the rich and the depressed rural Catholics.

It is worth noting *en passant* that the romantic spirit of the Scott tradition began at this time to affect the popular estimate of the old Catholic families. Their immemorial antiquity became an axiom in that Tennysonian world which took a solid pleasure in such a *Vere de Vere* inheritance as the coheirship of the moieties of Fitzwaryn and Umfraville. The position of heir male to the Plantagenet Earl of Wiltshire accorded in 1859 to Mr. Simon Scrope of Danby and the vast publicity which the Tichborne claimant brought[1] in 1870 to that family and to their romantic custom of the Tichborne dole firmly embedded this notion in the public mind. Baddesley Clinton of the Ferrers' became known also through the writings and the mild idealistic paintings of Lady Chatterton and Mrs. Dering. Ferrers and Scrope ; the names sounded almost too good to be true to a generation which particularly valued that form of truth. Still it is simpler to study the old Catholic squires in a concrete example and there can be no question that the predominant place occupied by the Welds in Catholic affairs in the late-Georgian period was paralleled in Victorian times by the great Vaughan generation. More religious than their neighbours they fully shared their outlook and their background. Much that was strong and yet attractive in that mentality is found reflected in the life of Herbert, Cardinal Vaughan, who succeeded Manning as Archbishop of Westminster.

Herbert Vaughan was born at Courtfield in Herefordshire in 1832. Since the seventeenth century his family had been one of the chief supports of Catholicism beyond the Severn. He was a grand-nephew of Cardinal Weld and, like that prelate, an eldest son. His mother, a convert of the pre-Oxford Movement period, very constant in prayer, led a life of heroic and serene devotion. The future cardinal was brought up principally by the Jesuits at Stonyhurst and Brugelette. He gained early and retained through life a particularly straightforward and simple devotional outlook. His tastes inclined him to a country life. He was tall and energetic, a good shot and fond of riding ; fishing he did not care for. His French schoolfellows called him *Milord Roast-beef*. He decided early to give up his inheritance and become a priest in Wales, and during his studies at the Accademia degli Ecclesiastici Nobili he became and remained a steadfast adherent of Dr. Manning. His ecclesiastical career opened at twenty-two with the vice-rectorship of St. Edmund's College and was continued first as founder and president of St. Joseph's College for missionaries at Mill Hill, then as Bishop of Salford from 1872 till 1892 and finally, for the last ten years of

---

[1] The cases, which lasted from 1871 to 1874, revealed a strong sympathy for the claimant among the Protestant working class, who regarded him as the enemy of Romish privilege.

his life, in the see of Westminster. He had an immense vitality as his journeys to South America for his missions, his work in Manchester and his building of Westminster Cathedral fully prove. His mind was vigorous, neither complex, not original but clear. He had an ardent chivalrous devotion to the Holy See and an impatience with hesitancy and reservations of judgment. His outlook in early manhood is indicated by one phrase. " The disloyal Catholic intellect," he wrote in 1865, " is growing with a luxuriance and the strength of a weed." In his actions and expressions he was at times impetuous, but experience of the world came to him with the years. With the Oxford Movement he had little contact and Newman he never really understood. A very deep devotion to duty, conceived along the lines of his spiritual work, to some extent bounded his interests. His tenacity of character was well shown in the negotiations which led up to the Bull *Romanos Pontifices* of 1880 in which the relations of the episcopate and the regular clergy were defined. He had an intense conscientiousness marked in his concern for the loss of children to the old faith, and with this went an entire absence of interest in anything concerned with literature and the arts, except in so far as they bore upon religion. A similar standpoint was at the basis of his attitude on political questions. His Conservatism was traditional rather than personal and his concentration was retained for the work connected with the disappointing Education Act of 1897 and for the difficult passage of the Act of 1902. A certain stateliness of bearing, well described by the phrase *maiestuoso*, was suited well to the cardinalate, but had sometimes a double effect on his personal contacts. He remained essentially remote from the unreligious sides of English life. He had never actually worked as a parish priest and in his dealings with the clergy tended to expect the high standard of detachment which he maintained in the austerity of his own life. The Anglican reactions to the Bull *Apostolicæ Curæ* declaring Anglican Orders to be invalid, the actions of Abbé Portal, the difficulties with Barnardo's Homes, and the condemnation of St. George Mivart the biologist for his articles on Eternal Punishment threw a sadness over the Cardinal's years at Westminster. He was far from the straightforward laborious existence at Salford and perhaps never felt completely at ease away from the downright atmosphere of northern Catholicism. Utterly secure in the application of his principles, he was sometimes uncertain of the exact effect of his method of statement and approach. It was not in his power to circumvent. Cardinal Vaughan in fact summed up in himself the strength of the centuries of persecution. He had a deep devotion to the Blessed Sacrament, an outlook wholly spiritual, the strong fidelity of the old squirearchy. Nevertheless the fact that he lacked Cardinal Manning's understanding of social problems had lasting consequences. The world of the young Trade Unions lay beyond his sympathies.

CATHOLICS AND LETTERS

BEFORE LEAVING the period of Manning and Vaughan it is essential to attempt a tentative estimate of the influence exerted on Catholicism in England by three figures on whom the attention of those outside the Church has been fixed so intently, Lord Acton, Fr. Tyrrell and Baron von Hügel. The second was a convert from Protestantism who died as a priest under sentence of excommunication, the other two were laymen hereditarily Catholic who lived and died in communion with the Holy See. Both laymen were educated abroad and the tone of their minds was coloured by German thought; both were brought up in a Liberal aristocratic tradition and, although not wealthy, were freed throughout life from pressing financial care. Both had a highly individual attitude towards Anglicanism, von Hügel being polarized as by a magnet to all forms of Christian thought and life, while Acton took the keenest interest in such High Anglican appointments as appeared to him to have significance for the intellectual world. It is probably true to say that to Catholics in England the manner of their concern seemed to have something of the zest of the foreigner.

Acton had a serious taste for Liberal politics and had some of Gladstone's qualities; his interests lay in history, conceived as developing to a state of perfection considered as free by which he implied laicized, liberal and parliamentary; his recreation in reasoned conversation and in the perusal of the solid respectable reviews, primarily foreign. Döllinger had been the mentor of his youth and his stepfather the polite Lord Granville, the Foreign Secretary, had provided an admirable link with conventional political society. At the time of the Vatican Council Acton had shown himself a vehement Inopportunist, sometimes dogmatic in his utterances. His influence with Gladstone, a rooted hostility to Manning and his difficulties with the episcopate over the *Rambler* and the *Home and Foreign Review*, short-lived organs of the Catholic Left, appeared as the prelude to a breach with Rome which never came. A faith, perhaps all the more profound for being rather unardent in its temper, passed through these vicissitudes and Cardinal Vaughan's friendly *rapprochement* eventually closed what had been under Manning a long estrangement. The last portion of his life, when he held the Chair of Modern History at Cambridge, was markedly serene. Nevertheless Acton's great reputation for erudition did not, perhaps, affect the Catholic body very deeply, since his reactions seldom synchronized with those of his coreligionists. Gasquet raised a tombstone to him ; but the *Cambridge Modern History* is his true sepulchre.

Baron Friedrich von Hügel was a very different character. The son of the Austrian Minister to the Court of Tuscany, he was profoundly affected by the Scottish Presbyterian stock of his mother's family. Göttingen University was the dominant influence in his mental growth and throughout a long life the problems of spirituality incessantly concerned him. He had great sympathy of mind, shyness, a vein of humility and abiding charm. His deafness was a factor in his intercourse ; he possessed considerable synthetic power, a cast of thought curiously almost monumentally Teutonic. This last characteristic was accompanied by a persistence in lines of thought which were unanchored in tradition. His personal religion was deep ; but his sympathies with the everyday expression of Catholic life was not instinctive. On the other hand he had a constant devotion to the Blessed Sacrament. It was in middle life that his *obiter dicta* were least in accord with general Catholic sentiment. But he was always happy in his Benedictine friendships and his family life was satisfying and delightful.

A generosity towards his friends, very marked in his relations with Fr. Tyrrell, went with a certain inexperience of their mental reactions and accounted for that deep but only partially understanding sympathy with those beset by intellectual troubles which brought him into contact with that Continental Modernism which was condemned by Pope Pius X in the Encyclical *Pascendi*. One factor dominates von Hügel's position. No Catholic in England ever had such power to win the sympathy of the religious circles outside the Church.

It is difficult to assess the prevalence of that vague, ill-defined point of view which was regarded by public opinion as adhering to George Tyrrell's self-conscious, highly personal interpretations of the Church's teaching, marked as they were by a certain rigidity of outlook and a system of strictly limited accommodation to the demands of the spirit of the age. Religious opinion outside the Church was over-sanguine in the hope that any Catholic in England sympathized with all the errors condemned in the *Pascendi*.

Fr. Tyrrell, as one would expect, appealed to the sometimes tired second generation of the Oxford Movement. He would hardly have expected to affect the squirearchy or the poor. After his ordination as a Jesuit Farm Street was his centre. The young men who admired the political Liberalism of Acton and his positive assertions in the domain of history, who believed in the balanced scale of values of the *History of Freedom*, were clearly susceptible to this influence. The wide academic distinction of his family served as a background for Tyrrell's swiftly moving intelligence and his penetrating nerve-wracked irony. He seemed impatiently fastidious as to the intellectual integrity of others and it is not surprising that he did not develop that ascendancy which *Nova et Vetera* led many to expect. Even in the period of his greatest influence he tended to be an intellectual inspiration to many who in spiritual questions sought other guidance. He had indeed a deep spirituality but it was perhaps hardly within a Catholic mould. His later actions, after his excommunication, destroyed his influence with his coreligionists. In general circles his development, anxieties and troubles were watched with eager sympathy. Possibly his miseries arose from the submission of an instinctively protestant mind to a Rome which it never really comprehended.

With the deaths of Cardinal Newman in 1890 and Cardinal Manning in 1892 a change came over the situation. Many contacts with the literary, scientific and intellectual worlds were snapped when Manning's brougham drove away for the last time from the Athenæum. Thus Acton had been one of the Cardinal's least pleasant preoccupations, but there was manifestly no association between the Vaughan régime and the literary activities of the 'nineties. After 1892 the lines of connection of the see of Westminster with the general English life were primarily administrative and philanthropic, concerned with war and peace, the relations between England and the Vatican and national questions.

In dealing with the Catholic life at the turn of the century it is therefore simpler to consider first such writers as were directly linked with the Church's hierarchy. In the first place three writers who had a certain prestige had come forth from the great ecclesiastical colleges, Canon Barry, Lafacdio Hearne and Frederick Rolfe. Canon Barry was a great figure, a man of diverse talent, author of

The New Antigone, golden voiced, appreciated. Not so Rolfe ; for only a posthumous fame has associated this ex-Church student with that well-established Catholic body into which he was not born and into whose ranks he never merged. A haunter of presbyteries Baron Corvo or Fr. Austin or Fr. Rolfe, to give him the designations which he chose successively, coupled a profound bitterness towards Catholic official persons and institutions with a permanent yet dilettante attachment to Catholicism. His brilliant tortured writing, overstrained and lapsing into bathos reflects this and he is seen always on the defensive and after his own manner fastidious and often sincere. He cleaved through the unmoving and undisturbed waters of Catholic life with the determined and clean-cut action of a shark. In that placid sea he could hardly fail to discover Hugh Benson.

Robert Hugh Benson, the convert son of the Archbishop of Canterbury, was fortunate in his life, death and period and possessed a very considerable influence on his generation. Converted when at Mirfield he subsequently became a priest and wrote with eager speed novels which were alive with Catholic atmosphere ; hence his unfortunate contact with Rolfe whose *Hadrian VII* he so much admired. But Benson was best known as a preacher, a sensitive man, slight and nervous and with much personal charm. He had a constant desire for sanctity partly foiled through lack of calm. His life was feverish in *tempo* ; he was deeply interested in people and had an accurate power of observation within his chosen limits. In his books very valuable data is provided for the social historian and he brings back with minute fidelity the observances of the Edwardian period, the well-born figures with their deer-stalkers, their conversational counters and the pathetic motor-cars. He had only eleven years of active Catholic life from 1903 until 1914.

Benson's own favourite among his books was *Richard Raynal* and at the turn of the century other writers followed in the same tradition of a leisured pleasant description of the mystic way. This was the Catholic fruit of the established tradition of quiet tranquil writing. Monsignor Bickerstaffe-Drew achieved a measure of success with the straightforward narrative of *San Celestino*, as did Montgomery Carmichael with his elaborate, precious, delicate, mannered portrait *John William Walshe*. Behind them rose Freidrich von Hügel static as a monolith and inevitably and unconsciously disturbing the swallows of that last Italian summer.

Besides this there was an encouraging quantity of definitely Catholic work which had something of the character of apologetic. Miss J. M. Stone's solid historical biographies were, perhaps, the soundest representatives of one species. Mrs. Wilfrid Ward's *One Poor Scruple* was published in 1899 and has since proved a social document of value, sympathetic in treatment and grim in its effect. James Britten the botanist had founded the Catholic Truth Society in 1884 and was toiling forward heavily and energetically. A delightful unconventional character was manifest through all his works whether he was writing on *Why I Left the Church of England* or on *European Ferns*. In close support was Lister Drummond. This was the hey-day of Fr. Philip Fletcher and Fr. Vassall. All was well within the bastions.

These writers and preachers represent those who were in close and in the case of Rolfe antagonistic contact with the mind of the Church and her organization, influencing a largely Catholic public. Benson alone had a wide circle of followers outside the Church, but his influence was inevitably confined to those who were interested in religious problems as he stated them.

It is possible to consider the question of Catholic contacts from another angle, that of the effect produced by those writers whose influence extended, strongly or faintly according to the measure of their success, across other religious and general groupings. The impact of Catholicism on English letters and the wide reading public can be said to have developed markedly between 1880 and 1905. Newman, who was perhaps the greatest single Catholic influence in England, had brought out his *Apologia* in 1864 and its first effect had by now died away. Meanwhile a vast reading public had grown up self-contained and insular and possessed of a deep unity of corporate outlook. It was inevitable that religions other than the Anglican and the Nonconformist should appear unbelievably remote. The advent of Catholicism as a popular subject can be traced to Thackeray's *Esmond* and to Scott whose romances lent to the simplicities of the old faith an aweful and mysterious character. But the baby of Catholicism-for-the-reading-public had been born in the unfriendly sleet of *Helbeck of Bannisdale*.

Here at last there was no undue mystery and a modern setting. In this objective, humourless and " scientific " work Mrs. Humphrey Ward's readers were introduced to a Jesuit of intellectual tastes who owed less to Mr. Howard, the mild old priest in Sir Walter Besant's

Dorothy Forster, than to the engaging and immortal Fr. Holt. This source is interesting, for the secrecy, efficiency and profoundly un-English character of the architectural detail of Esmond's Castle-wood, so serviceable to that distinguished member of the Society of Jesus, suggests the most impressive elements of a Whig tradition. From Fr. Holt to Fr. Brown, who is considered to be the right side of incredibility, is a vast journey. But this distance seems to indicate the unity of subject which links the passage from Pater to Corvo.

In the late-nineteenth century a curiously adventitious character attached to the contacts made between the literary representatives of the northern culture and the Catholic Church as they conceived it. This was markedly the case in regard to the group associated with *The Yellow Book* whose impulse towards Catholicism can be derived from Pater. This writer has a line of approach which is seen in its most complete expression in the study of *Sebastian van Storck* ; it involves a sympathy with the cultural background of Renaissance Catholicism, a sympathy perceptive, quick, all-embracing and rather tired. He had a sense of religion colouring all things, but never an incentive to action and not dominant in the moral sphere. In so far as Pater's studies carry conviction they are concerned with men whose Catholicism was moving to a stop : sensitive, appre-ciative, remote from the commandments.

In such a stress on accidentals it is difficult to rediscover the original Christian values. This is very notable in the case of those whose attitude towards religious phenomena derived from Pater. Thus Dowson has little of the careful ease of *Cynara* in his religious verse and that approach which in Pater was so calm, so infused with the spirit of Victorian Hellenism and so unfortunately well-bred suffered under an unfastidious mind. This in part accounts for those last vulgarities which mar the devotional work of Oscar Wilde. The verse of Lionel Johnson stands out in refreshing contrast ; but much as he owed to Pater they had no contact upon religious issues. A convert to Catholicism Johnson held a pur-posive faith ridden by a painful sense of that moral conflict which lies at the core of *The Dark Angel*. It was, however, a consequence of the dim still sense-bound character of the Pateresque progeny that the one result which does not appear to have emerged from the conflict is victory. Aubrey Beardsley in a sense ends this period. The title of a poem written by Dowson for a friend who was like-wise a Catholic gives an impression of the atmosphere of the 'nineties in its religious setting : " Vesperal for Hubert Crackan-thorpe."

At this stage it is clearly inappropriate to attempt to discuss the influence of Gerard Manley Hopkins who entered the Society of Jesus in 1868 and died in 1889. He belonged to this period only chronologically and the extent of his self-expression even more than of his reticences divided him from his literary contemporaries. His sudden vivid talent was long commonly regarded as the aberration or the relaxation of an excellent religious.

Among the friends of Hopkins was Coventry Patmore, who was many years his senior and yet survived to be a formative influence on Francis Thompson. To his contemporaries he was a great figure filling Heron's Ghyll with a personality of somewhat mid-Tenny-sonian grandeur. His insistence on the marital felicities carried one stage further the approved domestic contentment of Victorian life. Patmore had a painful dislike for Manning ; a personal religious life deep and sincere ; impetuousness allied with great integrity ; a dominant devotion to Art. The metrical experiments and the compositions of his later years brought him a new influence and a gradual appreciation of his qualities as a poet which belongs to a more recent period.

More in tune with his contemporaries was that character of a Christian inspiration moving freely which marked the work of Francis Thompson, for the *Hound of Heaven* required a response of a certain quality, a feeling for religious values, a sense of God and of secure moral standards and of the common infirmities of purpose. His work is inevitably associated with that of Alice Meynell who, with her husband Wilfrid Meynell, did so much for him. Mrs. Meynell's influence on the world of letters during the years of her life at Palace Court had penetration and depth and a religious quality ultimately tranquil. She had a particular gift of intuitive sympathy and her poems exacted the power to approach a noble spiritual landscape.

Moving along roughly parallel lines was the little Catholic world of philosophical scholarship. The figure of John Henry, Cardinal Newman dominated this group with Wilfrid Ward as his Lockhart. Here, too, moral issues were permanent and a sense of obligation which the outlook of the Cardinal had laid upon them. In this case a certain consciousness of the mission *Ad Anglos* was always with them. By now the spirit of the 'nineties had been liquidated.

Earnestly and religiously, some with hope and some with reverential fear, the varying Catholic literary groups waited upon the full development of the twentieth century. Before leaving the earlier period its seems advisable to attempt to gather together some impression of general Catholic contacts with English life.

CATHOLICS AND ENGLISH LIFE

IT CAN HARDLY be disputed that the Oxford Movement seriously disturbed the relations of the Catholics with the general community. A rather faded respect and a sympathy touched with condescension had seemed the normal approach on the part of Protestants of position towards their Roman Catholic equals. All this had been changed when the conversions of the mid-nineteenth century brought the question of the Roman Church into the intimate family discussions of households where this subject had been viewed with an urbane indifference[1] for generations.

In the close Victorian family life each secession from the Church of England would affect an inter-locking clan of parents, uncles, aunts and cousins. At the same time it was just that circle which was most attached to the then dominant institutions of the family living and the younger son in Holy Orders in which the first secessions of the Oxford Movement took place. The change from the calm of 1830 to the upheavals of 1845–55 was equally unexpected and disagreeable. Barset had hardly a more cordial welcome for the Roman Church than Barchester.

The settled character of the age and its attachment to institutions were reflected in the manner in which Catholicism impinged on those country districts where an estate passed into the hands of converts. These manifestations were profoundly shocking to the rooted Anglican tradition. Disapproval was aroused inevitably by the new chapel with its heavy statuary against the background of a dim and insufficient Gothic, by the frequent presence of members of religious orders at the dinner-table and (in the houses where this was to be found) by the little shelf on the bureau in the drawing-room filled with the works of Fr. Faber. It was part of the difficulty of an essentially dynastic period that this quality even affected the manner of the presentation of Catholicism.

Again the hesitation which frequently preceded conversion was

[1] In his excellent description of the Portrait of the Century in *Early Victorian England*, vol. ii, pp. 468–70 sq, Mr. G. M. Young, however, points out that the measure of English sympathy for Pope Pius VII had given place to hostility towards the Catholic aspects of Charles X's policy in France.

often interpreted as concealment and supplied that touch of the secretive which had for so long been inseparable from the picture which the English had formed of Catholic methods. This is very well conveyed in Mr. Winston Churchill's *Life* of his father where the effect of Lady Portarlington's conversion on the Blenheim circle in the days of Lord Randolph's childhood is described.[1]

A somnolent lack of consideration for Popery now gave way to a touch of acerbity in Anglican polemic. Thus Archbishop Benson's phrase concerning the Italian mission was in the nature of a retort to the developments under Wiseman and Manning. Mr. Gladstone with unction and a heavy skill manœuvred for the weather-gauge in the controversy on the decrees of the Vatican Council and made good controversial use of his material. With these changes a new hostility to English Catholics developed in Tractarian circles. During the earlier part of the century English Roman Catholics had always been preferred by their fellow-countrymen to foreigners of that persuasion, but now a change took place. Mr. Gladstone's intervention had been in part responsible for the preservation of the Benedictine community at Monte Cassino and there dates from this time the legend of those numerous cultivated and sympathetic French, Belgian or even Italian Catholics who were assumed to be so much more wide and discerning in their approach to Anglicanism than their narrow-minded English coreligionists. This sympathy was first directed towards Döllinger and the more extreme Inopportunists, then to the foreign priests of Modernist sympathies and finally to a number of diverse but orthodox clergy. The more Roman wing of the Anglo-Catholics (for it was only this section which was actively affected) fluttered moth-like towards Rome. They were unprepared, attracted and dazzled. The promulgation of the Bull *Apostolicæ Curæ* concerning Anglican Orders and the results of the conferences at Malines were the fruits of their seeking. They were enthusiastic and generous and found in Lord Halifax a leader of chivalrous, magnetic, unselfish devotion. For the vast majority of English Churchmen Rome has cast no spell and all the most characteristic qualities of the Established Church seem bound up during the last four centuries with an honest and invincible repugnance.

Still, except during the period between 1845 and 1855, there was little interest evinced in Catholicism by public opinion and the

---

[1] *Life of Lord Randolph Churchill*, i. p. 12.

disturbance of non-Catholic circles by Pius IX's *Syllabus* of 1864 was confined to the liberal and intellectual world. The interest in the proclamation of Papal Infallibility died down quickly and the venerable pontiff's personal misfortunes excited a measure of sympathy. Above all the reign of Leo XIII from 1878 until 1903 emphasized the diplomatic prestige of the Holy See and its freedom from political conservatism, while stressing the Pope's deep concern for the solution of social problems.

With the slowing down of the rate of conversion among the wealthier classes there came a lessening of antipathy, since to the non-Catholic officialdom Catholicism is naturally most acceptable when it is most static. Then at about this period another side-line of attack developed which was an inevitable result of the increased Catholic numbers.

The right of the Holy See to act as the supreme tribunal in matrimonial causes had been constantly exercised ; but during the penal times cases of the declaration of nullity in regard to parties of English domicile were at any rate extremely rare. Recourse was occasionally had to civil divorce by private Act of Parliament as in the cases of the seventh and twelfth Dukes of Norfolk ; but the purpose of this measure was generally to permit the re-marriage of the non-Catholic partner. In 1880, however, the Sacred Roman Rota issued a decree of nullity in regard to the union of the Prince of Monaco and Lady Mary Douglas-Hamilton. This was the first English case to attain a wide publicity and it is probably accurate to date from this time the beginning of a spirit of aggravation on the part of general English opinion upon this subject. The intensive press publicity of the twentieth century increased the public irritation in regard to declarations of nullity obtained by persons who possessed a social-news value. The extreme care, considerable and calculated delays, the nominal costs and perfect impartiality of the tribunal have not availed to overcome the Protestant Englishman's insularity and his distrust of the value of affidavits backed by witnesses to character.

Still in this matter of character Catholicism in England possessed one great asset the personality of the fifteenth Duke of Norfolk. He was, with his brother, the last example of the type of the great English Catholic nobleman. Like the eighth Duke of Devonshire he was a national legend. He was, in fact, the last duke to possess that legendary quality with which English popular sentiment once loved to surround its aristocratic leaders and which has now been absorbed wholly by the royal family.   The Duke succeeded to the title in 1860 ; he came of age in 1868 and died in 1917.   It was a long ascendancy marked by completely English feeling and a sincere determined devotion to the Holy See.   His position was valued by the " Black " Roman aristocracy and at the Vatican he had great authority.   A profoundly upright character and a great sense of fitness aided him to make the fullest use of his abilities.   He was singularly happy in his filial attachment to Cardinal Newman, while his instinctive care for proportion rendered him never less than adequate in his relation with the other princes of the Church.   Abbot Gasquet had the type of learning which generations of Howards had grown to appreciate and Cardinal Vaughan he read delightfully like an open book.   The Duke was a small man with a black thick beard, serious eyes and an easy native humour.   In Lord Salisbury's third administration he held the Postmaster Generalship and he was attached to Conservative policies, hopes and remedies.   A wide charity went with a half-conscious sense of high ecclesiastical prerogative.   He built the great church of St. John's, Norwich and St. Philip's on the hill at Arundel ; he endowed missions and constantly relieved the Catholic poor.   Arundel is, perhaps, the perfect symbol of grandeur as the nineteenth century understood it, lightened by the memory of the Duke's charity and the spirit of Newman.

A sense of security was induced by the shadow of Arundel, for the Catholic body fully shared in that illusion of social permanence which had gained on English life as the Queen's reign lengthened. The golden contented jubilee of 1887 and the more consciously imperialist celebrations ten years later enclosed a period of calm. Arundel and Cardiff Castle, Carlton and Allerton brought a suggestion of the Gothic. Memories of a Tennysonian past lingered in the minstrels' galleries and combined well with the footmen and the silver tea-trays and the formal dinner parties of a leisured present.   There were already many Catholics in diplomacy, a considerable number in the services and none among the new type of defaulting financier.   There were some unexpected converts like Colonel G. F. R. Henderson, the military historian.

The great mass of the Catholics of the working class were now settled in the manufacturing towns and cities.   The development of the steel works at Dowlais and Ebbw Vale and the building up of the industrial townships between the moors of Cleveland and the sea were completed by 1890. In the diocese of Middlesbrough in particular the Catholic element was always vigorous. About this time there was a slight displacement of Catholic labour owing to the migration of boiler-makers from Jarrow to South Wales. The mass of the Catholic population toiling and not vocal remained like their rich coreligionists in a state of stability.

Nevertheless by the close of the century the sharp differentiation between the different sections of the Catholic community which marked the 'sixties and 'seventies had become less clear-cut. The professions had received a steadily increasing quota of Catholics; law and medicine attracted the sons of those clerical families which had entered the Church during the Oxford Movement; the industrial populations developed a definite commercial element and began to filter into clerical posts of responsibility in offices and banks; there began very slowly the accumulation of a Catholic element in the Civil Service. An influx from Ireland, not numerically large, but very constant, aided these changes. It was a very different condition from the earlier portion of the century when the few Catholic conveyancers were balanced by an occasional and respected physician like Sir Arnold Knight.

At the same time the Catholics had benefited by the general improvement in the condition of the workers which was slowly developing. The generation which was at this time between thirty and forty was in many ways exceptionally fine. The strong devotion to the religion of the Irish hearth was manifest. They benefited from the parish churches that their fathers lacked; their social life was vigorous, and there was a deep sense of solidarity. A vivid political interest in Home Rule united those of Irish origin and gave them a sympathy with the Liberals during the years between Gladstone's conversion on the Irish question in 1886, and the emergence of the parliamentary Labour Party to real political significance. In a sense the Catholic workers were more separated from the rest of the population than they have since become. The national prejudice against Popery was powerful throughout the Victorian age and the Catholics were further knit together by the self-sacrifice which was required of them and by their burdens. It was this generation which built so many of the schools. They would never refuse money for the " chapel." Housing conditions were now rather better and employment, though badly paid, was constant. As the families sat in the kitchen at the hot Sunday dinner, with the girls in print dresses and the boys talking of the new League Football and the first boxing successes of Jim Driscoll, they would always have the money ready for the collector coming Sunday after Sunday for the school building. This generation among the workers had a profound reverence for the Mass; broad constant humour; vitality; a virile faith.

THE EDWARDIAN BACKGROUND

FOR THE MASS of King Edward's Catholic subjects in England the change to the new reign meant little. A strong sentiment for Ireland, Mr. T. P. O'Connor at Liverpool and the rise of organized labour dominated the outlook of the industrial populations. The eleven years of Conservative plenty, from 1895 till 1906, and a heartache over the continued Irish wrongs combined to dull their interest in the reign. Labour proved an amalgamating force for the Catholics in the towns both for those of English and Irish ancestry. It was among the prosperous that the reign left its mark.

In the Edwardian period Catholicism in England gained a certain recognition and prestige which had been lacking under the somewhat rigid conventions of the Queen's reign stiffened by her permanent distaste for that religion. Although this distaste softened a little in the Queen's old age when her command of the role of constitutional sovereignty became so perfect, Edward VII was the first English ruler since the Stuarts who was not in some measure anti-Catholic. It was during this reign that the change in the coronation oath and the removal of the old offensive phrases were decided. The marriage of Alfonso XIII of Spain with the King's niece Princess Ena of Battenberg and the latter's reception into the Catholic Church was a symptom of the changed relationship. Fr. Bernard Vaughan was popular with royalty ; preached his celebrated sermons ; worked among the poor ; made converts. It was in some ways a hopeful period. The prestige of the peerage stood high and Catholic peers were numerous and dignified : there was the Duke of Norfolk. One detail shows the erosion which had taken place in circles hitherto profoundly Protestant ; Lord Nelson built a chapel at Trafalgar. Among the King's own circle were Catholics and some who would turn to the Church before they died like Mrs. Cornwallis-West and Sir John Cowans. There was Sir Ernest Cassel's strange Catholicism.

With the aged Marquess of Ripon as an elder statesman of the Liberal party and Lord Edmund Talbot to represent his coreligionists in the conservative policies, and the Irish members still at Westminster the dissolution of Parliament in 1906 perhaps marked the climax both of the political influence of the hereditary and convert Catholic landed conservatism and of a strong Catholic representation in the Lower House based upon the Nationalists from the constituencies in Ireland.

Still the new reign was in a sense very far removed from the life of the mass of King Edward's Catholic subjects ; the formal occasions, the picture-hats, the white gloves to the elbow for the evenings, the King's journeys to Homburg for the waters, Cassel and Beresford and Fisher. These years saw the last broughams and the London hansoms with their turn of speed and riders still elegant in the Row. These were the great days of the Round Pond and Kensington Gardens and a new amiability to children and prams in the sunshine and sailor suits. In Barrie the reign brought forth its romanticist ; the soft quiet romanticism of an easy period so well symbolized by Peter Pan. The Catholic Church received a form of tribute and the decade which closed with the production of Reinhardt's *Miracle* opened with Robert Hichens' *Garden of Allah*.

At the same time sentimentality reached the point of saturation in certain novels by Catholics at this time : Henry Harland's forgotten work *The Cardinal's Snuff Box* is an example. A soft romantic attitude to rank was nourished by an enthusiasm for the imperial and royal houses of Austria and Bavaria. There was still a reverence for all that appertained to the old monarchies. These subjects were distant and pleasurable as the already very numerous reading public sat in the wide arm-chairs with their spreading chintzes under the new electric-lamp standards with their silk shades and tassels, with the firelight playing on the safe English landscapes in their gilded frames and on the heavy curtains with their brave colours ; while outside the suburban trains steamed slowly on their infrequent services and no one yet envisaged the B.B.C.

Edwardian England, apart from that mass of the population affected by its vital conventions, possessed wide sections of opinion, liberal, detached from current standards, eminently humane, open-minded and tentative. These, however, only serve to indicate more clearly a certain rigidity of thought, as of the girders of the Empire, which characterized the general political and social standpoint. The period fits within a certain frame ; the close stratification of society ;

Goodwood and Cowes; the fascinated outlook of the middle classes. Few social documents provide more clearly a tabulated list of the Philistines' requirements than Kipling's poem *The Mary Gloster*. And the new seriousness of the young Galsworthy had such certitudes behind it. The whole attitude to the House of Lords was deeply significant : to the imagination it was as real as some stoneminded Gibraltar. From the quiet domestic interiors not only hero-worship but enmity took on a personal character. Only twenty years separated the enthusiasm for Rhodes' heroic stature from the monstrous shadow cast over English imagination by the Kaiser. This magnifying of the personal factor and of direct personal responsibility is the natural corollary of assured comfort. One sees refracted in the plate-glass windows of security only two figures, the policeman and the burglar.

To this standpoint there came two replies, the lives of the elder Catholic writers and the work of the young Chesterton and Belloc. Baron Friedrich von Hügel had now reached the zenith of his influence in non-Catholic England. It was the middle period of Abbots Gasquet and Butler ; the middle age of Mrs. Meynell and Wilfrid Meynell, the time of Monsignor Bernard Ward and the Wilfrid Wards, of Dr. Burton writing his history and Hugh Benson making Hare Street House and pouring out his novels, of Sir Norman Moore and Sir Bertram Windle.

It was during these years, too, that Belloc and Chesterton established themselves as leaders of popular Catholic thought, although the latter's conversion did not actually take place until after the War. In Chesterton there arose a Catholic thinker who was really of the English people, a " character," utterly independent, a writer with something of the touch of Dickens ; a genuine upsurge of English feeling and idealism with that passion for broad justice which always receives a sympathetic and uproariously orderly hearing in this country. The torrential felicity of phrase and the bounding paradox intimately reflected the Englishman in his humours ; and he was aided in his search for justice by a deep understanding of the ordinary man.

A different cast marked Belloc's work. A prose of great distinction was here the medium for reflections which presented various facets of the European tradition with clarity and determination. A vivid power of portraiture is displayed in his historical works and a remarkable penetrating intuition in regard to moments of history. Perhaps his most lastingly valuable contributions to this subject will prove to be those books which are most concentrated and least general. His essays were marked by a careful and sincere accuracy of thought and he had a curiously deep impression of English realities ; all the deeper for being, as in some passages of the *Cruise of the " Nona,"* so external. It is a great range of talent which could include the achievement of *Belinda*. With all the illuminations of a Gallic wit he owed, among English institutions, a definite debt to Balliol.

Throughout this period and in the following years a very different influence, rather as a personality than as a writer, for his output was voluntarily restricted, represented Catholicism at Oxford. Francis Urquhart was for a generation a Fellow and subsequently Dean of Balliol, a man of instinctive sympathies which moulded their recipients, with a talent for very generous friendship and a well-defined civilized opinion, lit everywhere by Catholic standards, spoken quietly and accompanied by his creased attractive smile. Again, in 1909 Maurice Baring had become a Catholic and a very delicate touch and a perfect rendering of atmosphere marked all his novels in which the late-Victorian and Edwardian world is mirrored with such sensitive fidelity. Perhaps no other English novelist has ever succeeded in conveying so completely the reaction of spirits affected by the impact of religion. *C* and *Cat's Cradle* thus communicated a deeper understanding of Catholicism. It was a period in which the Catholic upper and middle classes were drawing together. At the same time these years had witnessed a certain narrowing of those generous conceptions which had been Cardinal Manning's legacy. The Trade Unions were often regarded with some coldness while political activity was discouraged by the older clergy. The parish priests would often look askance at the young men who joined the Labour Party while the Catholic leadership displayed small interest in wage-rates or in housing. A phrase such as Edwardian has no meaning for those below a certain income-level. Still, between the death of Cardinal Manning in 1892 and the outbreak of the first German war, there was very little study given to the provisions of the Encyclical *Rerum Novarum*. The reign, which saw so many transitions, was transitional also in regard to Catholic life.

ADMINISTRATION

A CERTAIN CONTINUITY was lent to the religious life of this period by the personality of Francis, Cardinal Bourne who held the see of Westminster for thirty-one years from 1903 till 1935 and gradually came to exercise a paramount influence over Catholic affairs in England. He was the son of an English father, a civil servant, and of an Irish mother ; by birth a Londoner always attached to that city and profoundly English in his preferences. In his education at Ushaw and Old Hall he absorbed the old Catholic traditions, but the formative influence on his deeply priestly spirit was undoubtedly his training in Paris at St. Sulpice. The Sulpician recollection and devotion remained with him always and a sympathetic understanding of French Catholicism. From this period, too, there came in his interest in the training of priests which found its full scope in the foundation of the Southwark diocesan seminary at Wonersh and later in his attachment to St. Edmund's College on which he spent so much thought and attention. Parish work in Surrey and Sussex had preceded his rectorship at Wonersh and he had therefore considerable experience of a priest's life in the south of England when he was selected as coadjutor by Bishop Butt of Southwark in 1896 at the age of thirty-five. In the following year he succeeded to the control of the diocese and in 1903 was appointed on the death of Cardinal Vaughan as Archbishop of Westminster.

Until this time he had had little concern with questions of general policy and he now found himself confronted with the difficulties resulting from the application of the Education Act of 1902 and the attempts of successive Liberal governments to pass legislation hostile to the voluntary schools, after the cry of " Rome on the Rates " had been raised at the General Election in 1906. The preservation of the *status quo* was attributable in great measure to his leadership. The Eucharistic Congress in 1908 was not without its anxieties owing to the impossibility of carrying out the projected procession of the Blessed Sacrament through the streets. But the difficulties of the first years passed away leaving the Archbishop's position stronger and his general outlook poised and consolidated.

He had early developed singularly harmonious relations with successive English governments : his intervention in public affairs was always dignified and he had an understanding of the temperament of the civil service. In this matter he was also assisted by a natural sympathy with the currents of English political thought in the period between the Peace of Vereeniging and the European War. His admirable relations with Lord Baden Powell and his encouragement of Catholic scouting serve as a reminder of this appreciation of the pacific ideals of service within the Empire. He was raised to the cardinalate in 1911, the year after King George V's accession, and he was thus by sympathies and temperament well fitted to be the spiritual leader of English Catholics during the War. His understanding of the French, his patriotism and administrative efficiency were of real benefit to the cause of Catholicism in England and there is no doubt that he deserves credit for the increased prestige of the Church. The establishment of the Legation to the Vatican in 1915 and the whole course of the relations between the British and Papal governments owed much to him. On the other hand he had little sympathy with certain facets of organized Trade Unionism. His action during the General Strike of 1926 aroused much support, sometimes in unexpected quarters, but also caused a lessening of his popularity among those big Catholic town populations which were attached to the Labour interest. He was a great builder of churches and of schools.

The Cardinal had a profound sense of his spiritual responsibilities, a sense of the guardianship of the peoples entrusted him by Christ. His public speeches were balanced and devoid of rhetoric. He would speak freely to those who could penetrate his marmoreal shyness and had a sympathy with any one in real distress. He greatly venerated the English Martyrs and had a satisfaction in the restored shrine of Our Lady of Walsingham. A judgment rather conservative in its mould and in accord with sound traditional opinion marked his conduct of the Church's affairs. In such a character, with its strength and mastering sense of duty, it is almost inevitable that a desire for centralization should have been found and a tendency to concentrate authority. Monarchical institutions appealed to him. He had a very clear understanding of what matters lay directly within the province of a priest and on other questions was accustomed to consult a few tried men proved by long years of fidelity on whose judgments he could rely. Thus to take one instance it would seem that Sir John Gilbert, for eight years Chairman of the Education Committee of the London County Council, held such a position in the Cardinal's counsels on the subjects within his field.

Ecclesiastical Training, a book written in the later years, gives a real impression of the Cardinal's intimate concerns. Of middle height, with white hair above a pleasant, frank and rather heavy countenance, he had a dignity of bearing which never left him and he was perhaps seen at his best in some of those great ceremonies in the magnificent setting of Westminster Cathedral which he carried through so perfectly. A deep interest in the questions of spirituality and a constant practice of prayer gave him strength and a wonderfully equable temper beneath the burden of the charge of *Sacerdos Magnus*.

During his fifty years of priesthood Cardinal Bourne had survived past the first two generations of the restored hierarchy. At the time of his ordination in 1884 the old vicars apostolic and the priests raised to the new sees in Cardinal Wiseman's time were disappearing. They had represented an old faithful generation, dogged and honest. Ullathorne and Cornthwaite were soon to vanish, but there would remain for many years the antique figure of Bishop Vaughan of Plymouth, who had been a boy of fifteen at the passing of the Emancipation Act and ruled his diocese from 1855 till 1902.

Three bishops, besides Manning, had come to Catholicism through the Oxford Movement; Dr. Coffin of Southwark the Redemptorist, Bishop Brownlow of Clifton the archæologist, and the intrepid Bishop Wilkinson of Hexham and Newcastle, profoundly apostolic, deeply interested in shorthorns, a north-country Tory who has given to the Catholic tradition the finest of the nineteenth-century legends.

For the rest there was a singular consistency in that episcopal generation which included an amalgam of the old landed stocks, Clifford, Vaughan, Knight and Riddell with the strong northern yeoman element represented by such names as Roskell, Bilsborrow and Chadwick. It was a combination strengthened by a small proportion of Irish prelates like Bishops Lacy and O'Reilly, whose presence was so essential in this work of shepherding the great populations which had come after the famine to a strange land not over-friendly to Irish labour.

In territorial organization there was to be little alteration. Middlesbrough became a diocese[1] in recognition of the growth of

---

[1] The dates of erection of the new sees were Middlesbrough, 1879, Portsmouth, 1882, Brentwood, 1917 and Lancaster, 1924. In 1911 Liverpool and Birmingham became archbishoprics and divided the suffragan sees with Westminster.

a Catholic population in Cleveland and on Tees-side and there were developments in Wales[1] which enabled the religious life of the Principality to exist more independently of England. It was a period of slow increase and consolidation ; the organizations not rich but stable ; the dioceses accepted as permanent facts of a certain value in the general make-up of England. The building of large churches as in the Pugin era and in the decade following Newman's conversion had slowed down throughout the country. Parish churches such as St. John's, Bath, and St. Gregory's, Cheltenham, were legacies which this generation had received from its predecessor. In many cases the large fabrics inherited from the middle of the century were left unchanged while emphasis was laid on the multiplication of schools and Mass centres. At the same time new parishes were founded in the industrial suburbs which continued to spread out into the countryside throughout the period of comparative prosperity. No cathedral was built save Westminster. In this case Bentley was markedly successful with his interior : the domes and vaulting and the dark background. The honey-coloured columns of the canopy of the high altar had a lightness lacking in the clumsy onyx pillars which Cardinal Vaughan had wished to substitute ; while the Stations of the Cross by Eric Gill reflected a sincere feeling detached from period. There was a contrast, too, between Bentley's domestic interiors or the chill rough wall spaces of his clergy houses and the resolute Gothic and thick curtains of the northern presbyteries to which the solidity of the ancient faith had grown accustomed.

It is pleasant to remember that the most obvious quality of the episcopate of the last generation was a straightforwardness which they shared with the strong parish priests of their then new dioceses. At Birmingham there was a virile tradition radiating from Ullathorne and subsequently kept alive with his memory ; while perhaps the most remarkable prelate of the post-Manning epoch was Archbishop Whiteside. He came early to power and held it firmly, ruling the see of Liverpool from 1894 till 1921. His was a character of enduring strength, fearless and rigid. Every interest was concentrated upon his pastoral office. An intense sense of duty, tireless energy and a life of self-chosen poverty governed his outlook. He could on occasion be extremely hard ; he was probably more determined than

[1] In 1898 the diocese of Menevia was created and in 1916 the see of Newport became the archdiocese of Cardiff.

imaginative ; certainly self-sacrificing. In him a character common to many northern Catholics reached a development approaching sanctity. He was little affected by his contemporaries but much by his heredity. When considering the Edwardian south and its gay pretty trivialities the figure of Catholic Lancashire is arresting.

1910-1918

THE TITLE OF this chapter is in a sense inaccurate, since it is not intended so much as a survey of the work of these eight years as a brief description of some elements of Catholic life during the earlier years of the century. It is impossible to confine within reigns such matters as the development of the parishes and the religious orders. By 1910 the industrial system in the north and Midlands had reached that position of comparative stability which was to be violently affected by the European War. Shipbuilding and ship-repairing were in good condition, the mercantile tonnage was rapidly expanding and the increase in the British Navy in face of German competition meant good employment. It was on the whole a fortunate period for heavy industries. The great cities which had developed in the previous century now seemed old-established. Housing estates were in the future and the development was mainly of a suburban character, while the Catholic populations remained closely packed in the tenements and the side streets of the cities which they had in many cases inhabited for two generations. In the rows of cottages in mining areas and in the sporadic industrial settlements the same stability was to be found ; it was a period of comparative rest before the clearance schemes. A proportion of the retail trade in working-class neighbourhoods was found in the hands of Catholics who, growing up in the towns, had opened small groceries, bakeries and tobacconist shops, those small family businesses which would provide a moderate profit (when bad debts had been written off) before the coming of the multiple store. The people now entered into the inheritance of the churches and schools built by their parents and grandparents and embarked upon fresh plans for extension and reconstruction. The parishes were by now factors in the general framework of their city ; their dances and whist drives were known ; they were recognized centres of the social life. The Catholic elementary schools had also built up their position ; the red-brick walls of their newer buildings were landmarks ; their boys' football teams had often a first-class reputation. This last characteristic was fairly general in regard to Catholic schools and the boys would be accustomed to playing in the streets between the close of school and nightfall and were early hardened by falls on the stone pavement. Some good boxers, too, came out of the Catholic schools and parishes.

Altogether it was a strong-rooted Catholic life ; the churches crowded for the Lenten Mission ; the old men and women with their rosaries ; the sometimes too-ordered crowds of school children ; the collectors and the scrubbed and tousled altar boys. On the Sunday afternoons there were the Brothers of St. Vincent de Paul upon their rounds ; the tea on the hob and often the *News of the World* spread on the kitchen table ; the mothers with the *Catholic Fireside* and the eldest daughter getting the children ready for Benediction. It was perhaps at the parochial gatherings that the spirit of those days was best caught up ; the young men crowding at the back of the hall against the worn distemper ; the parish clergy on the platform and, in so many cases, that memory of an Irish past, *Oh ! Danny Boy*. It is in such a form that the Catholicism of 1910 comes back to us in its vigour and simplicity.

The colonies which had come from abroad and had settled in the last century in the ports and in some industrial areas had been assimilated, while apart from them was the floating population of the seamen's lodging-houses, the Goans and the men from the Cape Verde islands. In the parlours of the dockside towns, the French and Spanish captains took wine with courtesy. Far removed from these stable and respected elements the Catholic boys from the West Indies and the coastlands of Nigeria moved on the fringes of the religious life. From the schools in the dock areas the children would run home along the pavements dodging the clanging heavy tram-cars and sit silently in the kitchen while their fathers talked to the men of their own nation in the coast dialects. In greater seclusion there would go forward the Chinese Catholic life in Cleveland Square.

The disasters of this peaceful time, the explosion in the Senghenydd mine and the loss of the *Titanic*, seemed all the more devastating in the general atmosphere of calm. In prosperous Catholic circles the younger generation was now entering into the inheritance of Victorian prudence. With the low income tax and death duties still negligible they gathered in those nests of capital which their parents had accumulated.

In the last section of this book covering the period since 1910 it is impossible to do more than suggest an outline. A generalized study of present-day conditions has been attempted rather than a discussion of the value of the individual contributions made by persons still living. This is made easier because the reign of George V possessed a singularly consistent quality, gathering prestige as it moved forward and greatly strengthening the position of the Crown. The Court was not without its Catholic contacts, but these were less close than in the time of Edward VII. Still an equable dignity marked the relations with the Holy See maintained by the first English sovereign to re-establish permanent diplomatic contact with the Vatican. In the first years of the reign, however, the preoccupations of the Catholic community were of a domestic character far removed from court or government. They were interested in development and in conversions and in the affairs of their own body. As a contrast it is worth noting that the Catholic layman upon whom public interest was most concentrated at this time was Dr. Crippen.

In the world of religious ideas a hopefulness was apparent : in 1910 the Brighton vicars were received into the Church and with them a proportion of their two congregations ; in 1913 the Anglican community at Caldey under Dom Aelred Carlyle made their submission to the Holy See as did the nuns of St. Bride's Abbey, a sister foundation guided by Dame Scholastica Ewart. Although an offshoot of the original Anglican foundation continued at Pershore and Nashdom, the conversion of the Caldey monks was a source of great and perhaps undue encouragement to the Catholics in England. At the same time the Kikuyu dispute gave rise to the impression that a considerable mass-submission to Rome might be imminent. Fr. Bernard Vaughan and Monsignor Benson were still active as was that *doyen* of the convert preachers Fr. Maturin, who was to die in 1915 in the sinking of the *Lusitania*. The liturgical movement, which under one aspect is so closely associated with Caldey and its monastic successor Prinknash, was already developing as was the extension of the Gregorian plain chant enjoined by the *Motu Proprio* of Pope Pius X.

In addition to the work of the English Congregation the general Benedictine influence was increasing with Dom Cabrol the liturgiologist as Abbot of Farnborough and Abbot Vonier engaged on the reconstruction of Buckfast and Dom Chapman as prior of the German community at Erdington. With Abbot Butler, Dom

I

Chapman and Dom Cabrol, Benedictine erudition whose influence had been quiescent in the previous century impinged upon the English learned world. This by chance coincided with the emergence of the first generation of Catholics who were allowed to go freely to Oxford and Cambridge. In this connection it would be a mistake to over-emphasize the influence of the small Catholic groups in these universities, but they were certainly fortunate in their leaders. Although their work really belonged to a later period it seems appropriate to mention at this point the Professors of Italian in the universities of London and Cambridge, Edmund Gardner and Edward Bullough. Edmund Gardner brought a wide and tranquil erudition to bear on his Italian studies and showed throughout the influence of his serene magnanimity of spirit. Edward Bullough's official work at Cambridge lay in a similar sphere ; but he was also deeply concerned with every form of Catholic international co-operation and a president of *Pax Romana*. He was a convert, a Lancashireman with linguistic gifts, immense energy, great zeal, unselfish and God-seeking, a profound sense of the vocation of the laity and a devotion to Thomism. The organization of the Catholic students who were crowding into the modern universities owes much to him.

By this time the effect of the expulsion of the religious orders from France under the Combes Laws had been felt in England. Numerous communities had been established with their schools and one considerable monastery Quarr Abbey, a Benedictine house of refuge from Solesmes. Members of the expelled Carthusian communities had come to fill the great cloister at Parkminster in Sussex and the Jesuits were established at Ore Place in the same county. Yet, except in regard to teaching orders, the influence of these French religious was for the most part transient and the majority returned to France under the more settled conditions of the post-War period.

Religious communities devoted to the active life had spread throughout the nineteenth century and the Nazareth House nuns, with their orphanages for children, were as familiar throughout the country as the Sisters of Charity.[1] In 1899 the Hospital of St. John and St. Elizabeth had been removed from Great Ormonde Street to

[1] In addition the work of the Sisters of Charity of St. Vincent de Paul, the Sisters of Mercy and the Little Sisters of the Poor, to mention only some among the many congregations, was deeply appreciated and generously supported. The Sisters of the Good Shepherd had long devoted themselves to their work of reclamation and after-care, while maintaining that contemplative life which was the *raison d'être* of the Carmelites and Poor Clares.

its present site and had become a London landmark. One consequence of the provision of homes for the aged and the development of extensive rescue work for children was that the Catholic population with its separate arrangements for these charities remained to some extent an " island " community. This separateness was emphasized in another direction by the more severe application of the law in regard to marriage consequent upon the promulgation of the decree *Ne Temere* in 1909.

In regard to education the formation of the secular clergy was carried on in the ancient colleges to whose number Upholland (subsequently to be much enlarged) and Wonersh had been added.[1] In Bishop Giles, the rector of the English College in Rome, and especially in Monsignor Parkinson, the president of Oscott, remarkable figures were added to the Catholic legend. Perhaps the chief work of the Jesuits in the opening period of the century lay in the building up of their day schools. On the literary side Fr. John Gerard, S.J., had been the moving spirit of the elder generation[2] and had accepted from Fr. John Morris that deep interest in the English Martyrs and in the period of the Elizabethan and Jacobean persecution which he in turn transmitted to Fr. Pollen and Fr. Newdigate. The names of Fr. Bampton and Fr. Considine recall the influence of Jesuit preaching and spirituality in the pre-War Catholic world, while the young Fr. Plater was developing that application of the Church's teaching on social questions which was to lead to the establishment of the Workers' College at Oxford and the foundation of the Catholic Social Guild. The traditional Catholicism of Yorkshire was represented by Frs. John and Joseph Rickaby. Gervase Elwes and Mark Sykes and Charles Russell stood in their very different ways for the then rising generation.

In politics this was a time when there was no outstanding Catholic personality during the long Liberal administrations under Campbell-Bannerman and Asquith. Such political influence as then existed came from Ireland with John Redmond and the Nationalists. In other fields there were the buildings of Leonard Stokes, Sir Richard

[1] The English Colleges in Rome, Valladolid and Lisbon dated from penal times and the Beda College at Rome for the training of priests who began their studies late had recently been established.

[2] A consideration of the contribution of the Society to the study of English history during the sixteenth and seventeenth centuries would provide much interesting matter. Behind the fathers who have been mentioned lay the immense industry of Brother Foley.

Terry at Westminster Cathedral, the late maturity of Elgar. Then came the War.

The four years of the first German war did not have any great effect on the position of Catholicism in England. The Catholics suffered the same crippling loss as the other sections of the community ; their schools had a very high percentage of old boys on active service and Stonyhurst produced in Maurice Dease the first V.C. of the War. Sympathy for the patriotic effort was very strong. The attitude of Pope Benedict XV, so travestied in the Press of the Allied countries, met with an imperfect sympathy in some Catholic circles. The frame of mind indicated in the Lansdowne Letter was as remote from average Catholic opinion as it was from that held by the bulk of the nation during the war years. The chaplains at the Front won general sympathy and their losses were serious. There were on the whole few contributions to war literature among Catholics ; the most remarkable was perhaps the diary of the Master of Belhaven. One of the most painful phases of all this period was the acute lack of sympathy between the English Conservatives of the old faith and their coreligionists in Ireland.

1918-1935

IN REGARD TO the period which followed the conclusion of the war of 1914–1918 it is only possible at this date to give a brief impression of tendencies within the Catholic body. The number of conversions to Catholicism had greatly increased during the period of the War, especially among those in the fighting lines who became more conscious of the need for an anchorhold of faith. With the return of peace a mood of optimism settled upon the Catholics who fully shared in the general impression that English life was becoming more fluid against a bright horizon. It took some years before this optimism was dispersed entirely. In 1922 Mr. G. K. Chesterton was received into the Church.

At the same time the covey of converts of the first decade of the reign was already in motion ; infinite in variety, many-hued in plumage. The names of Compton Mackenzie, Algernon Cecil, Shane Leslie, Dr. E. W. Tristram, Alfred Noyes, Ronald Knox, Christopher Dawson and Edward Watkin belong to the generation which was at school or university at the turn of the century. The numerous converts who were born in the years between 1882 and 1889 perhaps reflect the first real freedom from the domination of the accepted Victorian truths.

In regard to national affairs Catholic life moved forward smoothly past the period of the General Strike and out into the governments of the late 'twenties. In politics there was no very considerable representation and no outstanding leader. Those Catholics who were most familiar to the public of that time belonged not to politics, but either to diplomacy like Sir Esmé Howard and Sir William Tyrrell or to the borderland of imperial policies and administration like Lord FitzAlan, Sir Hugh Clifford and Sir Gerald Strickland. In the 'twenties the most-known Catholic figures seem to have been Conservative in background and associated with the circles of privilege. On the other hand this was also the time of the dissemination of the idea of Distributism and of the Land Movement, and the development of the leadership of Eric Gill. In a very different sphere it was a time of ecclesiastical organization.[1]

The Labour governments aroused much enthusiasm among sections of the Catholic industrial population, but their strength among the leaders of the party was less considerable than would have been the case had all the young men of Catholic parentage, who entered politics, remained in touch with their religion. As far as the Catholics were concerned Sir James O'Grady was probably their best known coreligionist in English Labour politics and John Wheatley, whose career really belongs to Scotland, their chief representative in the left-wing councils. In the Conservative and National governments there was no figure of parallel influence and no cabinet minister. The premature death during the peace conference of Sir Mark Sykes, whose name survives in diplomatic history as the negotiator of the Sykes–Picot Agreement of 1916, had deprived his coreligionists of the one Catholic Conservative member who seemed destined to reach the front rank in his party. During these years Catholic affairs impinged directly on political life on the occasions of the passage of the Catholic Relief Act in 1926, a measure piloted by Mr. Francis Blundell, the development and carrying of Mr. John Scurr's Amendment to the Trevelyan Education Bill and the protracted dispute in regard to the elections and government of Malta. The last question had repercussions in everyday life and helped to reveal, as did the Prayer Book debates and the annulment of the ninth Duke of Marlborough's first marriage, the continuance of widespread distaste for Rome beneath the surface of the calm and courteous attitude of the elder generation of well-educated Englishmen. The next generation had other springs of action and were probably but little affected by the rather elderly dialectic which these happenings occasioned. For them the Catholic teaching on the use of marriage was the principal irritant. This and kindred questions, which enter so deeply into private lives, seem perhaps to be tending to erect a barrier between the Catholics and a great body of general opinion such as did not exist in earlier generations. There was always a wall between us, but

---

[1] This was consequent upon the appointments of Archbishops Mostyn and Williams to the sees of Cardiff and Birmingham in 1921 and 1929 which provided these dioceses with effective leadership. The elevation of Dr. Downey to the see of Liverpool in 1928 had also a special importance, above the other episcopal appointments of this time, since it ushered in that era of Catholic life in the north of England which will always be associated with the building of Liverpool Cathedral.

now it is crowned with broken glass. It is improbable that dissensions on such large questions as " mariolatry " and papal infallibility would have the same effect of social disintegration as a divergent outlook on the most personal of all questions.

Similarly the prevalence of divorce and the strain which the Catholic life involves in an increasingly alien social ethic tend to exert a pressure upon the more loosely knit elements in the body. It is probably accurate to state that throughout the greater part of Europe complete indifference to religion is both easier to attain and more irremediable than was the case in former generations. Even in England the element of wastage is perceptibly increased and in some fashionable circles there is apparent a frame of mind of almost nominal Catholicism which is unwilling to move even slightly against the stream and does not seek, but certainly does not shrink from the Divorce Court. The acceptance of any standard of values resting on convention is obviously destructive of the former bases of the Christian life. Like those who become devoted to purely humanitarian ideals without relevance to a Christian foundation and those who are oppressed by the ethical values of Catholicism, the families who completely subordinate their religious interests are naturally carried slowly outside the Catholic Church. On the other hand a quality of greater determination, sometimes aggressive in its manifestations, is becoming characteristic of the manner in which Catholicism is held by the large majority of its adherents. The life and its implications have penetrated deep and the Thomist philosophy is giving a background to a section of the Catholic body whose forefathers seldom troubled themselves about such general questions.

It is to this period between 1922 and 1926 that the Malines Conversations belong. These celebrated exchanges of opinion held under the presidency of Cardinal Mercier at Malines were attended by Lord Halifax and Anglican divines and by French and Belgian clergy ; they were carried on with the cognizance of the Archbishop of Canterbury and the Holy See ; they were terminated on the death of the Cardinal. One meeting was held after Cardinal Mercier's death but only for the purpose of winding up the affair.

The Conversations only concern this study in so far as they affected English opinion and the fortunes of Catholicism in England. It is possible to hazard a few impressions. The attitude of the Holy See seems throughout balanced and consistent and Archbishop Davidson acted with a generosity which was the more notable in view of his prudent temper of mind and the rooted Protestant feeling in England. The whole affair emphasized Lord Halifax's chivalry. It appears, however, that Cardinal Mercier had an inadequate perception of the background of Catholicism in this country.

The attitude of the English Catholics on this subject has suffered much misrepresentation. They were not lacking in sympathy but were awake to the realities of the situation. They realized that Lord Halifax's supporters were a small minority of the English Christians who were outside the Catholic Church. All forms of antipathy to Rome and to Catholic doctrines were familiar to them as was the average Englishman's candid and impatient indifference. If proof was needed of the inappropriateness of Lord Halifax's ideas it was only necessary to wait for the storm over the question of Prayer Book Revision. It is difficult to imagine that an Abbé Portal or any other enterprising Frenchman will ever be able to explain the English to one another. Much more valuable than these attempts at hasty doctrinal equation was the growing appreciation for work of scholarship, the singularly happy relations between Dean Armitage Robinson and the Downside community and the Anglican appreciation of Abbot Butler. Ultimately the chief asset of the Catholics in England may prove to be integrity of thought.

The Catholic population, estimated at between two and three millions, is now spread fairly evenly throughout the urbanized areas of English life. This new development as a result of which Catholics are found in all sections of the professional and business worlds has brought a cohesion which was formerly lacking in the southern counties. The large secondary schools controlled by the Jesuits, the diocesan clergy, the modern congregations and the various orders of teaching brothers have contributed to this result and are gradually building up a central core of Catholic life, which is almost free from that erosion of indifference which affects wealthier circles.

The effects of the development of the great Benedictine schools to their present numbers also only became apparent in the decade since the War. They now began to impinge on the public consciousness in which Stonyhurst had been firmly embedded by the memories of the Tichborne Claimant. These and other schools of similar standing produced a considerable effect on the Catholic body and provided a background for the expanding fortunes such as the Arnold system had given to Anglican prosperity. The school buildings at Downside, the magnificent abbey church, consecrated in 1935, with the

Comper glass and the Gasquet tomb ; the abbey church at Ampleforth, Gilling and the Gilbert Scott school houses became factors
in the general English social landscape, taking their place beside
that great mass of Stonyhurst which had been completed two
generations earlier. Well defined and sharply differentiated types
of character emerged from these large schools and could be judged
by the standards of a Catholic public-school opinion. The Jesuit
tradition is strong and constant and education has greatly benefited
from the vigour and charity of northern Benedictinism. These
years were marked by the strong development of Douai. The
more expensive schools combine a religious background with some
of the characteristics of the nineteenth-century public-school system.
With the advantages of that system they have not in all cases
avoided its defects.

It was a consequence of the degree to which the Catholics had
penetrated London life that the Church should have increased
throughout that stretch of dormitory town and urbanized countryside which grew up between the southern outskirts of London and
the Channel coast. In no part of England has the proportion of
churches mounted so rapidly ; the Catholic variants of that
Edwardian creation the comfortable preparatory school clustered
upon the southern hillsides ; occupants of weekend and summer
cottages raised discreet clamour for Sunday Mass ; the tide of
salaried Catholics pressed out farther and farther into the country.
In 1933 the Downside Benedictines bought one of the most remarkable of the late-Victorian Sussex mansions, Paddockhurst near
Worth, and set to work to tame to religious uses its opulence of
stone balls and entrances, heraldic drawing-rooms and clock-towers.
It is, perhaps, a small detail to mention but there is something
significant in the character of this victory of St. Benedict over a
symbol of Midas.

Like Corby in Northamptonshire, the Kent coalfields represent an
area recently opened up for an industrial development which has
brought with it a new section of Catholic life. At the same time the
problem of scattered Catholics in rural areas has been more fully
investigated in Kent and Sussex than in any other part of the south
and Midlands, although undoubtedly the presence of a large Catholic
population in South London has led to the development of scattered
colonies in the southern counties such as could not be found in
Wiltshire or Gloucestershire.

Except in certain parts of the north of England a serious difficulty is usually felt in maintaining the religious life of the small parishes in the country which have come down from the first half of the nineteenth century and the penal times. The incidence of death duties and the consequent sale of estates has fallen particularly heavily upon the Catholic landlords who more often belonged to the less wealthy section of their class. In many instances the houses from which the mission was maintained are sold or let or empty. In most places that solidly Catholic character of the tenantry, which was a commonplace a century ago, is hardly even a memory ; no section of the community has diminished so rapidly as the tenant farmers of the old faith. Land settlement may assist to build again the Catholic life of the countryside, but in so far as it was bound up with a feudal principle it is not easy to imagine a revival. In one area, however, there has been definite progress ; that portion of Somerset which is within reach of the influence of Downside Abbey. Around other religious houses groups of the faithful have gathered, but in Somerset there is something approaching a revival of that indigenous Catholicism of the soil which has survived in certain districts of the north of England and in oases in the south.

The convert stream which has helped to strengthen the other sections of the community has done little for the country districts. In the nineteenth century a number of landlords were converted but very few independent agricultural labourers : conversions were more often made among the farming stocks after their migration to the towns. With the exception of the villages, which in the south of England are seldom touched by Catholicism outside of the home counties, the increase of the Church by conversion is spread fairly evenly over the cities, industrial and suburban areas and country towns and is found at all economic levels. The rate varies between eleven and twelve thousand each year, and a few notes will indicate their effect on the general body.

Speaking generally the least interesting and satisfactory is that section which enters the Catholic Church with the view to marrying members of that faith. When these changes of allegiance are directly occasioned by a love affair it is not surprising that the new ideas sometimes fail to take root and an atmosphere of lassitude develops. Conversions subsequent to marriage are among the strongest and most solid additions, since they have been tested and attracted by an intimate knowledge of Catholic standards. Similarly there are many instances when an attraction towards the religion develops simultaneously with a friendship which may end in marriage. The conversions of boys and girls who are coming to the end of their school days tend to be firm and enduring, perhaps because of their sincerity and the effort which they must make to obtain permission from their parents to embark on a course of action which is generally unpalatable to them. On the other hand this enduring quality is not always found in the cases of those who are received during their undergraduate period at Oxford. *Then* it is often pleasant to go against one's parents and to adopt lines of action which will support the impression of an Oxford, as opposed to an university career. It is not that the changes are ever really lacking in a measure of sincerity at the time, but they are made against a background of imaginary values. This sometimes holds good of the conversions of young men of leisured and cultivated taste. Their transient adherence to the Catholic Church sinks gradually and tranquilly out of sight.

On the other hand the vast majority of those who become Catholics after the age of twenty-five remain steadfast and interested and in many cases vehement in their new-found religion. They bring to the religion some of that quality of consistent but not un-critical enthusiasm which is so marked a characteristic of those educated French circles in which a feeling for Catholicism has re-awakened. It is remarkable how considerable a proportion of the writers of this faith are converts and how very great has been their influence over their new coreligionists. This is particularly true in the case of the rising Catholic generation in the south of England leaving the public and secondary schools. In the north country the situation is different; interest in new books is perhaps less widespread; there are centuries of Catholicism behind them and a consistency, sometimes unimaginative, in their granite faith.

The important matter of elementary education and grant and rate-aided schools is still the subject of negotiation and falls outside the scope and date of this survey. The question of those elements in the industrial areas which tend to drift away from Catholic influences has a quantitative significance in the south and Midlands. It is frequently a disintegration of allegiance lasting over two or some-times three generations. Such loss is to some extent inevitable in the case of any minority which is not racially and socially distinct from the community of which it forms a part. It is increased by the growing displacement of the industrial populations consequent upon the shrinkage of markets. Concentration of industries in the Thames valley has caused a trek towards London with the resulting tendencies for the young unmarried men to drift away from their former associations once they have come to a strange city. In earlier generations an open hostility might make them conscious of their religion which is better fitted to withstand certain forms of persecution than that profound and tolerant indifference to personal religious practice which has become a marked feature of the national character.

These movements in search of work and the consequent break-up of the connection with the parish unit have a definite share in the loss of religious contacts. The strength of Catholic massed populations in East and South London depend to a considerable extent on the parishes and their organized life. In this connection it is as well to mention the characteristic activities in which the regular Catholic life finds its expression, the Society of St. Vincent de Paul, the Knights of St. Columba, the Catenians. A network of parishes and parochial and diocesan organizations builds up the strength of the Catholic Church throughout the country. The idea of pilgrimages is linked with it, journeys in bands to Lourdes or Walsingham or Holywell, a Catholic line of travel for those who would otherwise hardly find themselves so far afield. Buckfast Abbey, which was consecrated in 1933 and is certainly known to more Englishmen than any other monastery in the country, is found within the same orbit. A very considerable religious Press concentrates interest on events within the Catholic Church, and provides a full account of the pronouncements of Ecclesiastical Authority.

In a general view it may be said that there is a good proportion of communicants and a sound attendance at Sunday Mass among the Catholics in England. Nevertheless there does seem very great need for a revitalizing of the religious spirit and a wholly new approach to and desire for sanctity, which would result in the destruction of content.

There is a spirit of co-operation between the clergy and that band of laymen who take a definite part in the public activities of their community. Anti-clericalism in the Continental sense of the word is practically unknown and its place is taken by an impatience with the clergy manifest in some circles. Akin to this impatience is a form of quite polite indifference to all the external phenomena associated with the Catholic life in England. Various factors combine to account for this standpoint which is consistent with fairly regular and lethargic attendance at a late Mass and marked energy in all secular concerns. These and other forms of indifference and impatience are largely confined to the wealthier and more sophisticated sections of the Catholic body. It is not clear that means have yet been found to deal adequately with this particular problem.

Politics play little part in the Catholic community as such, except in the circle of the Distributists. There is little racial distinction ; the German and Austrian stocks, although numerically inconsiderable, have proved a very valuable addition and a singularly stable element. A great proportion of the industrial population still reflects the debt to the Irish infusion and forms with the Catholic areas of Lancashire the popular stronghold of the faith. The old landed families, although diminished in number, still survive together with some fifty peers of unequal value. Descendants of the Oxford Movement families tend to lead a fairly definite but quiet Catholic life ; the vigour of their grandfathers' affirmation is now balanced by that of the converts of this generation.

This book is an incomplete but honest attempt to describe a consistently developing religious situation. Catholicism carries within itself the seed and power of renovation and it is a fortunate hope that a new St. Charles Borromeo or St. Francis of Sales may illumine the Christian standards. The distance which separates the Church from the standpoint of the surrounding world is increasing, while its members are more and more bound up in their daily lives with those who are entirely freed from all theological conceptions. Catholicism is permanently in stress and it is inevitable that those who believe in the divinity of Christ should look to the Saviour on the waters.

CARDINAL HINSLEY

CARDINAL HINSLEY, WHO was nominated to the see of Westminster in 1935, had a fellow feeling for all Englishmen, and especially for Yorkshiremen. He believed in the straightforwardness of those with whom he had to deal; he was a little on his guard with foreigners. His years in Africa had reinforced that implicit belief in the justice of all British administration which he had held from early manhood. He sought for and expected to find his own straightforwardness among the leaders in British public life. He was not at ease with the complex and he loved simplicity. Among the political leaders of his time at Westminster the Cardinal's personal attachment centred upon Neville Chamberlain. He was attracted by Chamberlain's simplicity and selflessness. No event in internal British politics roused his indignation so sharply as the circumstances, as he conceived them, of the Prime Minister's fall in May, 1940. His admiration for Churchill was strong but not excessive, Baldwin he never liked.

The quality that appealed most to the Cardinal was reckless and self-sacrificing moral goodness, and it was this that led to his always deepening affection for the Bishop of Chichester. It was part of Arthur Hinsley's attractiveness that he responded immediately to charity in others. He had an affinity with his Protestant fellow-countrymen in their religious mood; he, too, thirsted after justice. He had another quality which is very rare in any ecclesiastical world. He never thought in denominational terms. The chapel-goers in his own Yorkshire responded to his broadcasts. The Cardinal was a great hater of oppression; he believed in that justice for which Wilberforce and Gladstone fought; their thoughts had been his own since he had been a Yorkshire lad at Ushaw.

This in part explains his difficulty in regard to Ireland. He had visited that country once, going ashore for a few hours at Queenstown in 1906 on his way out to India as chaplain in a troopship. He had something of the Gladstonian approach to Irish questions. " I have been," said the Cardinal in the summer of 1941, " a Home Ruler all my life." The Cardinal was persuaded with every fibre of his being that the cause of western civilization was bound up with the maintenance of Britain and the Empire. He had that English Catholic devotion to the Throne and to the persons of a Royal Family which showed but faint interest in him. He had a deeply loyal esteem for the Christian family life of his sovereigns, an esteem which his own ancestors had shown for George III. This will indicate the Cardinal's attitude towards a controversial issue in his early years at Westminster. He admired George V and the Duke of York, he did not care for the Duke of Windsor.

Cardinal Hinsley believed strongly in the maintenance in England of those Christian moral virtues which had found so universal a public acceptance when he was young. He was convinced that England was still a profoundly Christian country and he wished to play his part in the maintenance of every Christian value. This was his conception of the *Sword of the Spirit* movement which he launched. It is perhaps too early to judge this work in its true proportions. It seems, however, fair to say that the general idea of co-operation with Anglicans and Free Churchmen was welcomed by the Catholic laity in the south of England, but that it found no support among the northern Catholics. In the shape proposed the *Sword of the Spirit* did not win the favour of the clergy. Under another aspect it was too closely interwoven with a particular political situation, the heroic unanimity of 1940.

The Cardinal captivated those who came to him; he had both zest and ease in personal intercourse. He was completely unselfconscious and in some ways the least cardinalitial of men. His position of leadership was always present to his mind but not his rank. His mastering sense of duty led him to carry out the public side of his work very exactly. Still it was a pleasing trait in him that he never liked the ecclesiastical pomp to which his figure and bearing were so well suited. His æsthetic taste was vague and had not crystallized. He never cared for Westminster Cathedral and preferred the chapel in his garden at Hare Street on account of its simplicity.

In his last years he was perhaps happiest at Hare Street, the house which Hugh Benson had left to Cardinal Bourne and his successors. This was the place of Cardinal Hinsley's repose if such a term can be used of a man so constantly active. His middle life and his 'sixties had been periods of great activity. He had enjoyed the English College and had liked moving about Africa. Certain parts of his life at Mombasa he had found tedious; the desk work; the appreciations; the reports. He would sit in his eastward-facing study attempting to unravel some tangled situation with the soft damp air seeping through the teak window frames and the Indian Ocean below him as blue as the sea off Sicily. He always needed human contact; it was the students who had made the English College for him. By the time he settled in his home at Hare Street he was in his seventy-fifth year and very tired. Then he was happiest when he could sit and learn and listen, the silver cigarette box beside him as he smoked continually.

The Cardinal was a good listener. He admired heroism and endurance. He brought Fr. Roderick O'Sullivan down to Hare Street after his work in sustaining the children in the open boats following on the torpedoing of the *City of Benares*. The Cardinal was devoted to children all his life, to African children and English children; he was always very good with them. He liked missionary nuns and also nuns who taught children, especially the poor. He had less interest in nuns who gave themselves to the education of the middle classes. He was concerned primarily with the poor, to assist and educate them. He had a sense that life was short and that it must be filled with apostolic work; he was constantly praying. As soon as a visitor left he would put on his cloak and go out and walk up and down the trim paths of his garden saying the rosary. It was in keeping with his outlook that he should have opposed the building of very large churches. He always disliked the expenditure on what he called " bricks and mortar." In this connection he criticized the building plans of the Franciscans in the Holy Land. In his view every effort should be directed solely to spreading the knowledge of Christ.

He was intensely proud of his country and of the record of England in the fight against slavery. He was most determined to preserve both religious and political freedom. Convinced of British integrity he had an almost personal detestation for Hitler, Mussolini and Stalin. He hated all tyranny. The Cardinal was convinced that the return of Tanganyika Territory to Germany would result in the strangling of all the missions and he was deeply sympathetic with the Abyssinians in the war of 1935. This was in part a consequence of his appreciation of British Africa. By contrast, although he had lived in Italy for ten years and came to know the language well, he never understood the Italian character or ways of thought. In Rome the man whom he admired was his own patron the Dutch Cardinal van Rossum. A blunt approach was needed to win Arthur Hinsley's sympathies.

The Cardinal had throughout life that intense devotion to the Papacy which marked the old English Catholic tradition among the people. His personal feeling for Pius XI, from whom he had received such great encouragement, was one of a deeply affectionate loyalty. The fact that he gave such little thought to rank had, however, two consequences. He had only a diluted sympathy for other members of the Sacred College, unless they earned his friendship by some other title, and he was not drawn to the *majesty* of the Holy See. This last factor made possible the sermon that he preached at Golders Green during the Abyssinian War. During the second German conflict he was prepared to speak as the Cardinal of England.

He was by nature impulsive, devoted and humble. He could be both stern and generous. He had a sense of the need for haste and to the end of his life he would reply immediately to his correspondents. He was unsparing of time and energy ; he was a singularly spontaneous letter writer. Looking upon those pages in his thin determined script one can see how clearly they reflect the Cardinal's mood. He was intensely personal in all his relationships ; no man was further from the automaton. It may be held that this personal quality, which was invaluable as rector of the English College and had its merits for certain aspects of his work in Africa, was a disadvantage in the administration late in life of a large archdiocese.

Coming to Westminster in his seventieth year it was impossible for Archbishop Hinsley to acquire that intimate knowledge of his priests and of their needs which Cardinal Bourne had gained in his long episcopate. He was strange to the temper of the archdiocese and he was, perhaps, never really at home in the core of the diocesan life, St. Edmund's College. His mind went back to the *Venerabile* and he considered the standard of his Roman students the ideal. His candour and that open commonsense humility prevented him occasionally from seeing how heavily his rebuke could fall. He believed very readily all those who came to him. Like many north-countrymen sympathy was stronger in him than imagination.

His relation with his bishops was singularly harmonious having none of those cross-currents which marked his predecessor's dealings with the hierarchy. He always possessed the deep respect of the whole episcopate. Very few bishops would adopt his own line towards the Church of England and the Free Churches, but all paid tribute to the national position which the Cardinal had attained in 1940. In matters of domestic and educational policy he relied very much on the judgment of Archbishop Williams of Birmingham, and there was no member of the bench with whom he had a more sympathetic relation than his former diocesan Archbishop Amigo. In his last years his friendship with Archbishop Godfrey grew very close. Throughout his time in Westminster he had the devoted help of his niece Miss Hinsley ; his secretary Mgr. Elwes was like a son to him. From the summer of 1940 onwards he was very seldom away from Hare Street, and Val Elwes and the Cardinal's niece were always with him. He had the power to inspire affection in those closest to him, in his students at the *Venerabile*, and in Dom Engelbert the Benedictine monk who was his secretary for six years in Africa.

The inner circle among those who had been students in Rome under him gave to the Cardinal a most attractive loyalty. They were the fruit of the work of his maturity ; they were his " band of brothers." Reflecting his candour they regarded the " boss " with a not uncritical but loving enthusiasm. They were working in all parts of England, united by this bond. Speaking of the Cardinal they would often explain to their own bishops that there was no one like him. The most intimate link in all this discipleship was with Fr. Heenan ; the Cardinal had a deep and paternal affection for Mgr. Smith. Both men have written of him. His chief consolation lay in the *Venerabilini*.

The Cardinal was a great worker and as honest as the day. He was interested in everything connected with Yorkshire, beginning with cricket. Conditions of work and rates of wages concerned him ; he was determined on obtaining a free and fair prospect for the men and women of England in whom he believed so deeply. He had no patience with Pacifism. His mind was essentially practical and on certain aspects of East African life he had acquired a specialist's knowledge. In consequence when he was made Archbishop of Westminster the Colonial Office was the first of the government departments to welcome him.

With the exception of the African interlude, when he was first visitor and apostolic delegate in the British Colonies between 1927 and 1934, Archbishop Hinsley's life had been divided between

England and Rome. Coming from a Yorkshire Catholic stock, who had long been tenants of the Stapletons of Carlton on the levels south of Selby, he shared the same background as Bishop Ullathorne. He went as a boy to Ushaw and returned on the staff there. Later he was curate in the West Riding and a headmaster in Bradford. As in so many ecclesiastical careers he had had his setback, the quarrel in 1903 with old Bishop Gordon. After leaving the Leeds diocese there followed rather more than twelve years in the south at Amberley, Sutton Place and finally Sydenham. In 1916 he was proposed to the hierarchy by the Bishop of Southwark as a candidate for the vacant rectorship of the English College at Rome, where he had made his studies on leaving Ushaw.

Here at the age of fifty-one scope was at last given to him ; he came into his own. The period as rector of the *Venerabile* was quite certainly the happiest of his whole life. It seems just to add that, with the exception of his last years as leader of the English Catholics, it was also the most valuable. He was then at the height of his vigour with the strong frame and robust health which broke under his subsequent journeys. His task of organization was stimulating, uncomplex and heavy. He came to the work as he found it ; neither at the English College nor later at Westminster did he give much thought to his predecessor.

The English College in his time was an island of strict training. The whole life was carried forward by Monsignor Hinsley's profoundly spiritual and urgent enthusiasm. The atmosphere was one of deep devotion to the English Martyrs and strenuous loyalty to the Holy See. Quite early the rector evinced his dislike for the *Duce*. Relations with the then Cardinal Archbishop of Westminster were cold. Francis Bourne with his balanced and rather scholarly Sulpician preferences was not likely to understand or be understood by the priest who was destined to succeed him.

Monsignor Hinsley had a great feeling for Christian Rome, but none for the antiquities. It was current affairs and day to day problems that held his mind. He would refer sometimes to *Gli Promessi Sposi* ; he had a clear memory for Dickens since he does not seem to have read him in later life ; but all his keenness was retained for contemporary matters. He liked where possible to accept a political thesis or standpoint completely. In the second category it is only necessary to recall his outlook on General Franco and Poland. In the literary field no book moved him like *Church and State in Fascist Italy*, which was published eighteen months before his death. " Binchy's masterpiece," he used to call it. The Cardinal had a great feeling for the depicting of good men. He admired A. J. Cronin's book *The Keys of the Kingdom*.

The Cardinal had a very warm natural kindliness ; he was a delightful neighbour. There was an heroic quality in his patience in suffering. An Ignatian element is discernible in his approach to the bearing of pain. He had a deep devotion to the Society of Jesus, a devotion strengthened by his friendship for Fr. Joseph Welsby during his Roman years. In London this was succeeded by a similar close relationship with Fr. Joseph Keating, then editor of the *Month*. Fr. Keating's death in 1938 was a positive loss for the Cardinal who was deprived of his solid and dispassionate guidance. Henceforward the Cardinal had no intimate contemporary who was not enclosed within his pyramidal hierarchy. Like many aging men he had a certain lack of sympathy for the old ; his affection went out to his young pupils.

A tendency to impetuous action marked the Cardinal's tenure of his three main charges. He was not interested in the history or traditions of the Westminster archdiocese for his mind was bent on the needs of the present, the needs of 1935–9. His hopes as to what could be achieved were disproportionate. It may be maintained that his temperament required a plain and testing issue. Certainly with the outbreak of war every problem came into focus. Earlier the Cardinal had given himself to the reorganization of the diocesan schools and to Catholic Action. This last question appealed to him partly because he felt that he was carrying out the orders of Pius XI and partly on account of his wish that the laity should have a responsible share in developing the work of the Church in the parishes.

The laity were always at ease with Cardinal Hinsley and it was among them that he made most of the true friends of his last years. Thus his appreciation of the *Tablet* and the admiration which he gave to Douglas Woodruff's knowledge and judgment led on to his enthusiasm for Professor Binchy. He admired Christopher Dawson and, in another field, Arnold Toynbee. When he launched the *Sword of the Spirit* movement he was brought in contact with a fresh grouping ; Barbara Ward was the most vital figure. The Cardinal had a great feeling for Chesterton, who died soon after he came to Westminster. Hilaire Belloc was just an acquaintance.

In the final period of the Cardinal's life he was perhaps happiest in 1940 invigorated by the conviction of the superb justice of his country's cause. His broadcasts will long remain in the memory, that grating masculine voice as he spoke of the peril to Christian values. He felt the conflagration close upon him *flammantia mœnia mundi*. In 1942 he was disquieted. The heart weakness and the pain were now increasing. He rejoiced in the German defeat at Stalingrad.

Cardinal Hinsley died at his house at Hare Street in Hertfordshire in the early hours of 17 March, 1943. He had laboured all the day long. His prayer in his last illness was constant. With his native humility his faults came up to accuse him. He was one of those rare beings who are quite free from either pride or vanity. He was absolutely single-minded. He did his duty and believed in men's sincerity. His life was ruled by the desire to bring his countrymen closer to Christ his master.

POSTSCRIPT, 1948

DURING THE LAST twelve years nearly all the various tendencies which were present within the Catholic community in England in the mid-thirties appear to have strengthened. Thus the number of conversions has not diminished and there seems reason to suppose that various factors will result in a gradual increase. The contribution made by converts is very striking when compared to that of hereditary Catholics. Omitting the older generation and confining the enquiry to the fields of politics and letters the Catholics by descent have produced little that can compare with the work of Graham Greene, Evelyn Waugh, David Jones, Christopher Hollis and Lord Pakenham.

On another side the note of crusading apologetics is almost confined to those, like Arnold Lunn and Roy Campbell, who have joined the Catholic Church in adult life. In the presentation of Catholic life and ideas the *Tablet* under the editorship and control of Douglas Woodruff has reached a solid influence to which none of its nineteenth century forebears could attain. It has indeed a truly representational significance. It both leads and is supported by the mass of those practising Catholics who come through the quiet mill of the Jesuit and Benedictine public schools. Further, it meets the need of the majority opinion among those converts who have experienced a similar kind of education. It is a persisting background not only for Catholics but also for those who see Catholicism as a preservative element in the western scale of traditional values.

The work of Douglas Woodruff underlines the essential conservatism of the more prosperous strata in that instinctively Tory body which the Whigs emancipated. Attached to this broadly conservative standpoint there is the greater part of the Catholics in the managerial class, who with each decade are separating themselves more clearly from that Irish Nationalism-in-England which had so often been their fathers' creed. The influence of the Catholic secondary schools grows steadily. Dr. Vance as headmaster of the Cardinal Vaughan School and Fr. Paul Nevill as headmaster

270

f Ampleforth have a place in the field of education which was not ccorded to their predecessors. Catholics whose annual income is bove the £600 level seem increasingly united in outlook.

Certain intrinsic factors have combined to emphasize this olidarity of opinion. The outbreak of the Spanish civil war aroused vivid sympathy for General Franco among the Catholic upper and niddle classes. In 1936 this standpoint was crystallized ; it was ne view held by the great majority of the clergy and by all the nembers of the then hierarchy with the exception of the Bishop f Pella. At the same time all Catholics, who considered foreign fairs, had a sharp awareness of Russian imperialism.

For these reasons it seems accurate to suggest that the corporate uality in the outlook of the vocal Catholics tended to strengthen. he old priests who had been great figures in the first part of the ntury were dying, Archbishop Goodier, Abbot Vonier, Fr. hurston, Fr. Vincent McNabb, Fr. John Talbot. As a survivor om the younger section of that generation Fr. Martindale alone mained. Two priests, Mgr. Ronald Knox and Fr. D'Arcy, had rough their writings and personality an unparalleled influence on e literate part of the Catholic community. From one angle it is erefore not incorrect to regard these years as marked by a omogeneous effect on the development of Catholicism in England. In this connection the contrast between the influence of Mgr. nox and Fr. D'Arcy and that of Fr. Bede Jarrett, who held a key osition in similar circles in the years between the end of the first erman war and his early death in 1933, is most instructive. A otation from Gervase Mathew's appreciation will make this clear. He (Fr. Bede Jarrett) was intensely sensitive, embarrassingly shy nong strangers, romanticist. The sensitiveness was soon to be mpletely under his control, the shyness vanished slowly, the manticism was to be continually tempered by experience. He as only thirty-five when he was first elected Dominican Provincial the autumn of 1916, and he was to be three times re-elected. one of his successes were won easily. He planned and then he rried out his plans through years of indomitable patience. Yet ring an arduous administration he had written eight of his books, had preached ceaselessly, he had made, and kept, as many friends any man of his time. His life of crowded action was only possible cause he was primarily a contemplative. Intensely English, ensely Dominican, even his consequent limitations had seemed

to mark his role. His sense of reality had always led him to worl
through existing institutions rather than create new ones. I
seemed his life work to reconcile Catholicism and the English mind
a new synthesis of Catholic and English traditions—an uncomplete
synthesis." Here was a welcoming and a stretching out in sym
pathy towards divergent lines of English thought. Later thi
attitude would be replaced by an increasing tendency to close th
ranks. It was a note of Fr. Bede Jarrett's period that his approac
was essentially non-political, although his instincts and pre
possessions were all conservative. In the mid-thirties a politica
approach, using that word in its broadest sense, was conceived c
as a matter of duty. It is not fanciful to attribute this to the Spanis
war.

The solidarity just described was not seriously affected by th
minority, Dominican in inspiration, which shared the views c
Maritain and Bernanos on the struggle in Spain. Most Catholic
interested in this question gathered on the conservative right win
and found their ablest spokesman in Douglas Jerrold. This genera
position was emphasized by the views of the bishops. There is
sense in which this matter of the Spanish war was a landmark fc
that section of the English Catholic body which was conscious of th
Continent.

A question in the same order is that of the effect produced by th
Churchillian epoch. The Catholic community entered on the secon
German war with that whole-hearted and emphatic patriotism whic
is in part a consequence of their position as a minority. Durin
this struggle no continental churchman became a figure of heroisr
to the English mind as Cardinal Mercier had done. The Catholi
upon whom public attention focused were naval or connecte
with the Navy, Admiral Sir Henry Harwood, the victor of the batt
of the River Plate, Captain Fegen of the *Jervis Bay*, Wing-Command
Esmonde who led the attack upon the *Scharnhorst* and *Gneisena*
Cardinal Hinsley's contribution has already been assessed.

With Winston Churchill's premiership there came a change fro
the unsympathetic decades in which Asquith, whose cool sha
distaste for Catholicism was rooted in his Nonconformist origin
was followed by Macdonald and Bonar Law with their Presbyteri
or post-Presbyterian ideologies. Churchill on the other hand h
a Whig's tolerance for Catholicism which was combined with
approach to the machinery of the Establishment that was casu

when compared to the care lavished on Anglican detail by the first Earl Baldwin and the first Earl of Halifax. Again through his Catholic cousins, the ninth Duke of Marlborough and Sir Shane Leslie, he had a contact in his private circle which the middle class premiers so often lacked. Thus among Churchill's close friends the first Lord Lloyd of Dolobran had a real knowledge of the Catholic Church. There was much in Catholicism that appealed to George Lloyd's vivid and romantic courage, but these sympathies were firmly held in check by the quality of his imperialist patriotism as well as by a special brand of anti-papal sentiment.

One considerable figure of that time had been educated in the old religion, the eleventh Marquess of Lothian who died in 1942 as ambassador in Washington. His interest in this question had faded out beneath Lord Milner's spell; his later life did not suggest his Catholic post-Tractarian upbringing. Lord Lothian had been secretary to Lloyd George, but Catholics among the Liberals were growing rare. Lord Perth is the solitary distinguished example.

The children of the men who had voted Liberal at the turn of the century were now divided, a section going to swell the Conservative Catholic vote, while the great mass gave some support, occasionally keen and more often tepid, to Trade Union Labour.

Looking over the general position it may be held that the second German war, like the first, had no considerable consequence for the internal Catholic position in England. Still the run of years since 1935 had brought to an end some characteristic features of the old-fashioned Catholic life. Thus Herbert Weld, the African naturalist and Ethiopic scholar, Fr. Charles Newdigate and his brother Bernard and in a measure also Abbot Chapman belonged to a world whose contact with the universities developed in maturity. They were part of a tradition of private scholarship that owed much to Gasquet's mentor, Edmund Bishop; it has now completely passed away.

Again this was the final period of the old bishops who had been trained in the nineteenth century. In the southern half of England these prelates carried over something of that family spirit which had marked the close-bound Irish groupings in Bermondsey or Poplar and the small domesticated country parishes of the later part of Queen Victoria's reign. No man has left a firmer imprint on the parochial and diocesan life of the Catholic community than Archbishop Amigo. He has a knowledge of all his people that is exact

and lit by a piercing and astringent sympathy ; his sense of dut
came from an earlier day. No member of the episcopate has been
more truly loved in Ireland. Archbishop Mostyn of Cardiff, who
died in the first months of the war, was on the other hand in characte
and by inheritance the last of the bishops of the squirearchy, th
last of those whom Cardinal Vaughan would understand with
intimacy. He had shrewd and oaken competence ; the ease of an
established simplicity ; an element of what can best be called th
Cardinal von Galen touch.

As against such prelates of the pastoral and administrativ
tradition the episcopate which Archbishop Hinsley found contained
two men who were national figures, the Archbishop of Liverpoo
and Bishop Brown of Pella. Archbishop Williams of Birmingham
was less known outside the Catholic body, a man of practical spiri
and undaunted courage with a strength of will matured in constan
pain. It was in keeping with the family atmosphere that th
episcopal bench should have contained bishops of a delightfu
homeliness and simplicity of character like Laurence Youens o
Northampton and Francis Vaughan of Menevia, the most attractiv
and most innocent of the Courtfield stock. Bishop McNult
revealed to those who knew him the same unpretending and direc
integrity. The imprint of St. Edmund's House, Cambridge, neve
left him. In the eastern Midlands he was the precursor in the worl
of co-operation with the Church of England. Even the younges
of these men had grown up in a time when the Catholic communit
was smaller, the working classes tied to the wrongs of Ireland, th
whole more manageable.

Meanwhile changes were taking place both among the body o
the clergy and as a result of the cohesiveness and solidarity that wa
coming to the great mass of the working class. In the first place
the fine old Irish rectors were disappearing. On the other hand
for over thirty years the standard of secular education in the
seminaries had been steadily assimilated to that of the schools in
which the professional men and civil servants had their training
In this matter Cardinal Bourne's influence was bearing fruit. The
gathering in of vocations to the priesthood from the parishes in
the south of England combined with the educational emphasis jus
described to lead the clergy to approach more closely in habit
of thought and standard of life to the very large and loosely
conceived English professional body. This change has led to

the breaking down of one barrier but has also helped to erect another.

In the " white collar " parishes the impatience with the clergy, which was noted in 1935, seems now to be growing sharper. The desire to participate in the work of the parish is becoming stronger among the laity in the dormitory towns and they show a desire that the priests who share their interests and tastes should also share with them in consultation. It appears that this tendency is in general confined to the south of England ; it is found among the keenest of the laymen ; there are reflections in the world of the new universities ; this standpoint is reflected in the *Catholic Herald*. The next matter is of a different character.

The steep and general decline in Sunday observance, which has marked the present century, has not been without its effect upon the Catholic body lodged within the English matrix. In the carefully preserved separateness of the Englishman's home this effect has been less marked ; it is the young working men who board in hostels and lodging houses upon whom the general negligence bears most hardly. At the same time the widespread *toleration* of Catholicism has had unforeseen consequences. In those sections of English life where privacy is most easily obtainable the Catholic church-going has not seriously weakened, but in the great industrial *milieu* the ties of religion are much relaxed. Throughout the second half of the nineteenth century there were large masses of Catholics who were always ready to defend the interests of their faith, Manning's great phalanxes. They and their priests were united by the cold distaste shown to both by Protestant local government. But now that in the lists in the lord mayors' parlours the Catholic priest has his place in the hierarchy of official influence alongside the Anglican incumbent and the Free Church minister, one of the links with the poor is broken.

Regarded from a tactical point of view, it was a just instinct which led Bishop Henshaw of Salford and the other prelates of the minority to oppose Cardinal Hinsley and demand a struggle against the Education Act of 1936. The working class Catholic will always fight. It is compromise that kills his failing interest.

It would require a sociological study to describe with accuracy the reactions of this mass grouping to the views often held by richer Catholics. It may be said that the body of the Catholic working class is negligently trade unionist, profoundly local in its interests and in fine insular. It seems there is in fact a lack of conviction in regard to politicians which is accompanied by an ineradicable distrust of all Conservatives. The sense of class solidarity is instinctive, strong and generous. A practical scepticism as to the interest of any outside body in the nature and conditions of employment is possibly the key note. It follows that the great problem before the Catholic Church in England is that of re-penetrating effectively its working class upon whom its hold is loosening. In a world now so wholly industrialized the boys and girls of the great cities and the linked factory towns go out on leaving school to those employments where the cleric (and the priest) is an alien and disregarded figure. There is no longer present that happy unity of expert knowledge which draws together the small farmer and his workers and the farmer's boy turned priest.

Other factors have played their part. The development of the new housing estates has led to the break-up of the old units. It is a gain that so many of those long rows of houses, built back to back, have disappeared. Those courts and alleys with their crowded families are now condemned. Still a sense of community has been lost in the process of the dispersal. For seventy years there had flourished what can best be described as a religious public opinion of the street. This had ruled, sometimes too negligently but rarely harshly, in that net of inexpensive housing around the church and school where economic circumstances had placed the Catholic working class. It had dominated those short closes and places running down to the railway lines of industrial cities where the children scrambled on the low grey pavement. In the bedrooms mild sunlight would strike the coloured oleographs of the Sacred Heart ; the engines whistled and the smoke from the factory chimneys moved over slowly above the walls of sidings and the mean house fronts ; the soot was flaking from the worn rose brick.

Yet this was never more than the setting and the work was carried forward in those expert trades which were often hereditary as in the case of the shipyards and old engineering firms. For those who follow this type of work the sense of tradition, so strong in the Welsh mining valleys, may prove a lever for the reconquest of religious values which were once so vital and are now weakening. The world of the big shipyards and great engineering plant has long possessed the power to weld men in community. Shared work, the family tie and love alone seem real. Outside there lies the sphere of recreation. To this belong the film and football queues, the fish and chip shops, the church bazaars, the priest turning in to the tobacconist. There still remains a vital religious experience that strikes each family, the Last Sacrament brought to their own home.

The break at school-leaving is very sudden. When the boys take their notes to the foreman and go through the big gates for the first time, they begin a life which is spiritually intensely lonely. The Catechism that has been pumped into them soon seems like a kid's dream that belongs to childhood. At fifteen and sixteen they know themselves to be workers. The sermons heard as they thrust against the grimy pillars by the font for the last Mass do not retain them. By seventeen the effort of weekly attendance is given over and their juniors have taken their places at the back of the church.

In the north this is often a phase and boys go to church again when they find a Catholic girl. In the south this occurs less frequently and the men often go to swell the big post-Catholic population. This again requires sub-division. One section passes away from all contact ; another section will give their own children some Catholic schooling. It is largely a matter of whether they stay in the same locality. Those who resume Catholic practice through courtship and those who drift farther away are alike in need of a re-conversion if Christian values are to become real to them. Such a change can in nearly all cases only be brought about by their fellow workers.

Yet certainly there are compensations. The corporate and individual effect of privilege, which has vitiated so much Catholic life, is quite unknown to them. Neither formalism nor exclusiveness as applied to religion have meaning for the working class mind. It is only that the following of Christ has not been made actual and real.

Mobility of labour constitutes a further problem. Thus those who are apprenticed to the new trades and go to the centres of light industry find themselves in an environment which makes the acceptance of serious Christian belief much more difficult. In the old industries, tied to the soil and conditioned by harbour facilities and the presence of coal and iron ore, the young Catholic is often surrounded by a hearty, bawdy and generous indifference. On the other hand in aircraft works and in modern light industry in general the attitude to institutional religion is more clearly pointed and hostile. The new techniques of themselves give their possessors assurance in a materialist and strictly contemporary outlook.

Nevertheless each broad generalization must be qualified and, though there is no light industry area where the old faith is strong among the workers, there is still a mass of partly traditional and partly keen adherence in most of the regions of the old industrialism. A very strong Catholicism permeates the mining and shipbuilding areas in County Durham and on Tyneside. To a less extent this also obtains in the industrial area around Middlesbrough, in certain parts of Lancashire and in a section of the Potteries.

It is clear that in the industrial situation the priest is dependent upon the layman for the effectiveness of his work. This requires in the priest an apostolic spirit and energy and humility. This last quality, conceived in a realistic sense, is more easily come by after some years of experience than as a new-gilt seminarian of twenty-four. Work of an outstanding character presupposes a dedicated and self-spending lifetime which leaves no opportunity for the maintenance of middle class standards of possession. In fact the priest and layman bent upon the re-Christianization of the working class must both free themselves from the tyranny of a standard of living. This work needs a simple and unselfconscious sense of equality with all men and a desire for a good life for them and freedom. It is in the essence of the Evangelical appeal that man will not hear too readily, that there is in fact the constant presence of costing struggle. In the movement of *Jocisme* founded in Belgium by Canon Cardijn and known as the Y.C.W. in England there seems to lie the solution of this crucial problem. Yet for success there is needed in priest and layman an intense desire to spread the knowledge of God. The working classes in the Catholic tradition will deepen their strength in the exact measure that they can see the Church as the harbour of the poor and as always most concerned with the needs of those whose lives have least security. A unity of spirit is essential for both priest and layman. All great religious awakenings turn upon a clear realization of the person of Christ, His freedom and poverty.

BIBLIOGRAPHICAL NOTE

A NOTE is appended giving details of some primary printed sources which throw light on the development of the Catholic tradition as exemplified in post-Reformation English life. In this brief list only such sources are described as help to build up an impression of the actual detail of the daily life and habits of thought of the Catholic community. Thus avowedly narrative histories, like those of Nicholas Sander or Tierney-Dodd, are not mentioned, since even when they incorporate documents little light is thrown on the normal round of Catholicism in England.

I. *The Register of Sir Thomas Butler*, Cambrian Journal IV, Henry Machyn's *Diary* and the Churchwardens' Accounts of Ludlow (Camden Society) combine to give a most interesting impression of the incidence of the sixteenth-century religious changes in parochial life.

II. The account of Philip Howard, Earl of Arundel printed in Volume XXI of the Catholic Records Society's publications is drawn from various sources and gives a description of the life of the community in the years before the Armada, while the Tresham Correspondence printed by the Historical Manuscripts Commission in the Calendar of Clarke Thornhill MSS. provides the most vivid impression of late Elizabethan Catholic life.

III. The series of papers dealing with the Blundells of Crosby give a singularly complete idea of the background of a family of recusant squires in the seventeenth century. They include *Crosby Records* (Chetham Society) and *A Cavalier's Note Book* (1880). The Letters of William Blundell of Crosby 1620–1698 were admirably edited in *Cavalier*, a study published by M. Blundell in 1933.

IV. *The Life of Thomas Howard, Earl of Arundel*, by M. F. S. Harvey (1921) contains some interesting and hitherto unprinted material from the Norfolk MSS. at Arundel, while the letters in the Calendar of Coke MSS. and the narrative of the *Conversion of Sir Tobie Mathew* throw light on Jacobean Court Catholicism. The *Tixall Letters*, edited by Arthur Clifford in 1815, have a certain interest for the life of rich Cavalier Catholics of a rather later period. The *Diary* of John Rouse, the *Autobiography* of Thomas Raymond and the *Diary* of Walter Yonge, all edited by the Camden Society, give a curious view of the way in which Catholics were regarded in Puritan circles in the years before the Civil Wars. It is instructive to read them at the same time as the Blundell letters. The brief *Note Book of John Southcote* (C.R.S., i.) contains memoranda jotted down by a priest on the English mission during the years 1623–1637.

V. *Bedingfield Papers*, printed in the Catholic Records Society, Miscellanea VI, contain Marwood's *Diary* and other sources of information for the end of the seventeenth and the early eighteenth century. *Blundell's Diary*, privately printed in 1895, covers the same period. The *Tyldesley Diary*, ed. J. Gillow, gives details of Lancashire Catholicism in 1712–1714 and an impression of the grey depressed life of some of the old families under the early Hanoverians is suggested by the extracts from the Everingham MSS. printed by Mr. R. C. Wilton in the *Dublin Review*.

VI. The *Jerningham Letters*, edited by Egerton Castle, give an unequalled impression of the point of view and social habits of the wealthier Catholic circles in the generation preceding Emancipation. The working of the educational system between 1790–1800 is indicated in the *Haydock Papers*, edited by Joseph Gillow in 1888. The line of contact between the clergy and laity in the second half of the eighteenth century and the years before Emancipation is made clear in the correspondence printed in the *Life and Times of Bishop Challoner* by Canon Burton and in the detailed history published by Bishop Ward. The Cisalpine standpoint can be gathered from the historical works of the Rev. Joseph Berington (1746–1827).

From the mass of printed correspondence dating from the period since 1800 it is only possible to refer to a few works which appear particularly characteristic.

The Life of the R. R. John Milner, D.D. By Frederick Charles Husenbeth, D.D. (1862). This gives a very clear impression both of the subject and of Provost Husenbeth and throws a delightful light on Catholicism in the pre-Wiseman period.

The Life of the Rev. Aloysius Gentili, *D.D.* Edited by the Very Rev. Father Pagani (1851). This is, perhaps, the best description of the spirit of the Italian missionaries and is valuable on account of the letters which it contains and the fact that it was compiled by one of the first fathers. The works dealing with Fr. Dominic Barberi have been referred to in the text.

Life and Letters of John Lingard 1771–1851. By Martin Haile and Edwin Bonney. The letters from the Ushaw MSS. give a primary value to this refreshing and candid book.

The Life and Letters of Cardinal Wiseman (two volumes). By

Wilfrid Ward. The extensive correspondence printed in these volumes suggests very vividly Wiseman's enthusiasm and generous talent and give an especial value to this non-contemporary biography.

In this connection Cardinal Manning has suffered in comparison with his predecessor on account of the manner in which Purcell presented his immense correspondence and from the unctuous commentary in which he sunk it.

The Life of John Henry Cardinal Newman. Based on his private journals and correspondence. By Wilfrid Ward. This is a classic biography containing many of Newman's letters which are equally attractive and revealing.

The Life and Times of Bishop Ullathorne. By Dom Cuthbert Butler. This objective and balanced account has a special value when considered in connection with the fragment of the Bishop's *Autobiography* and the *Letters of Archbishop Ullathorne* edited by the nuns of Stone in 1892.

The Life of Cardinal Vaughan. By J. G. Snead-Cox. This official biography of the third Archbishop of Westminster is a remarkable mine of information for the period 1872–1903. A very clear impression can be built up despite the inevitably studied dignity of presentation.

The Life and Letters of Janet Erskine Stuart. By Maud Monahan. The many letters printed in this well-constructed biography give an invaluable impression of Catholic thought in England in the period between 1879 and 1911. They indicate very clearly the spirit of the Society of the Sacred Heart. The *Life of Cornelia Connelly* is of parallel interest for the Society of the Holy Child Jesus and gives in admirable detail Mother Connelly's deeply religious and spirited correspondence.

Charles Dominic Plater, *S.J.* By C. C. Martindale, S.J. This account of Fr. Charles Plater is a measured, careful and deeply sympathetic biography and a primary source for an important aspect of Catholicism in England between 1907 and 1920. It has all Fr. Martindale's candour.

J

Nihil obstat *Reginaldus Phillips*, S.T.L.
Censor deputatus

Imprimatur   *E. Morrogh Bernard*
Vic. Gen.

Westmonasterii, die 12a Januarii, 1948.

INDEX

A

Abergavenny,
  Edward, third Lord, 25
  George, twelfth Lord, 102
Abingdon, Anna Countess of, 134
  Montagu, seventh Earl of, 211
Abington, William, 69, 85
Acton Burnell, 149
Acton, Charles Cardinal, 170, 193
  Sir Richard, 170
  John Emerich, first Lord, 224–6
Ailesbury, Thomas, second Earl of, 116, 120
Albemarle, William, seventh Earl of, 212
Allen, William, Cardinal, 36, 39, 46, 48
Allerton Park, 235
Allibone, Sir Richard, 114
Amberley, 267
Ambleteuse, 119
Amigo, Archbishop, 266, 273–4
Ampleforth Abbey, 257, 271
Andrewes, Bishop, 58, 90
Anglesey, Christopher, first Earl of, 76
Anne, Queen, 101, 118–9, 124–130
Anne (Boleyn), Queen, 8–9, 20, 29
Anne (of Denmark), Queen, 64
Apreece, Robert, 88
Arblay, Madame d', 171
Argyll, Anne, Duchess of, 211
Arlington, Henry, Earl of, 100
Arne, Thomas Augustine, 165, 168
Arrowsmith, Edmund, 82
Arundel, 170
  Castle, 167, 235
  Anne, Countess of, 53–4, 60
  Henry, twelfth Earl of, 21, 36–8, 53
  Philip, thirteenth Earl of, 53–4
  St. Philip's Church, 235
  Thomas, fourteenth Earl of, 64, 75
Arundell, Humphrey, 17
  Sir John, 44
Arundell of Wardour, 22, 143
  Anne Lucy, Lady, 201
  Blanche, Lady, 88
  Henry, third Lord, 105–7, 108, 114
  Henry, eighth Lord, 134, 160
  James, tenth Lord, 181, 182
Ashby, Ralph, S.J., 69
Aske, Robert, 16
Asquith, see Oxford and Asquith
Aston of Tixall, 94
  Sir Arthur, 88
  Sir Walter, 75
Audley End, 64
Aughrim, 120

Austen, Jane, 171
Axholme, 14
Axwell, 142
Aylmer, Bishop, 43

B

Babington, Anthony, 49, 66
Bacon, Sir Nicholas, 27, 33
Bacton, 58
Baddesley Clinton, 51, 221
Baker, Augustine, O.S.B., 78, 85, 94
Baldwin, Earl, 262, 273
Baltimore, George, first Lord, 75
  Cecil, second Lord, 92
Bampton, Joseph, S.J., 251
Banbury, Elizabeth, Countess of, 75
Barberi, Dominic, C.P., 204, 216
Bard, see Bellomont
Baring, Maurice, 241
Barlings, Abbot of, 15
Barlow, Ambrose, O.S.B., 87
Barnard, James, 139
Barrets of Milton, 148
Barry, James, 165
  William, Canon, 226
Basing House, 85, 89
Bath, 147, 170, 245
Bayly, Thomas, 90
Beardsley, Aubrey, 229
Beaufort, Henry, first Duke of, 102, 123
Beaumont College, 217
Beaumont, Sir John, 84
  Miles, eighth Lord, 189
Bedingfield, Sir Henry, 44
  Sir Henry, third Bart., 127
  Charlotte, Lady, 169
Bedloe, William, 106
Belasyse, see Fauconberg
  John, first Lord, 88, 105–6, 108, 114
Bellasis, Edward, 211
Belloc, Hilaire, 240–1, 268
Bellomont, Henry, Viscount, 90–1
Belmont Abbey, 219
Belson, Thomas, 61
Bennet, see Arlington
Benson, Archbishop, 227
  Robert Hugh, 227
Berington of Moat, 155
  Bishop Charles, 156, 159, 160
  Joseph, 160
Berkshire, Charles, second Earl of, 92
Bermondsey, 147, 202
Bertie, see Abingdon
Berwick, James, Duke of, 116
Besant, Sir Walter, 228

283